The Thread of Dao

Thank you to the many teachers, scholars, priests, monks, and practitioners who have shared insights into Daoism and Classical Chinese in online communities. Were it not for your thoughtful input, correspondence, and fellowship, I would not have put this book out into the world.

Thank you also to Daniel P. Reid, Red Pine, Hu Xuezhi, Michael Rinaldini, Dr. Michael Saso, Solala Towler, and Wu Zhongxian for welcoming and encouraging my efforts in the fields of publishing and Daoist studies. You have provided me with a standard of excellence to reach for, and the confidence to continue in this pursuit.

The Thread of Dao:

Unraveling Early Daoist Oral Traditions
in Guan Zi's
Purifying the Heart-Mind (Bai Xin),
Art of the Heart-Mind (Xin Shu), and
Internal Cultivation (Nei Ye)
Second Edition

Translations, annotations, and commentary by
Dan G. Reid

Center Ring Publishing
Copyright © 2018, 2019 Dan G. Reid
Last updated March, 2022
Montreal, QC, Canada
dan.g.reid@gmail.com

Cover art: Patching the Robe, 补衲图, by Liang Kai (1140-1210)

All rights reserved. No part of this book may be reproduced in any form or by any means, electronic or mechanical, including photocopying, recording, or by any information storage and retrieval system, without permission in writing from the author.

The Thread of Dao: Unraveling Early Daoist Oral Traditions in Guan Zi's *Purifying the Heart-Mind (Bai Xin)*, *Art of the Heart-Mind (Xin Shu)*, and *Internal Cultivation (Nei Ye)*, Second Edition
Paperback book
ISBN13: ISBN13: 978-0-9949781-5-8

Disclaimer

The intention of this publication is for guidance and suggestion relevant to the subject matter presented. Readers should use their own discretion and consult their doctors before engaging in any of the physical or mental exercises contained therein. The author and publisher shall have neither liability nor responsibility to any person or entity with respect to any loss or damage caused, or alleged to be caused, directly or indirectly by reading or following the instructions in this book

CONTENTS

1	The Development of Proto-Daoism in Ancient China	1
2	Guan Zi, Jixia Academy, and Chu Kingdom	12
3	Compiling the *Guan Zi*, circa 26 BC	22
4	Proto-Daoism in the *Guan Zi*	24

Internal Cultivation in the *Guan Zi*

5	*Bai Xin* (Purifying the Heart-Mind)	29
6	*Xin Shu Shang, Xin Shu Xia* (Art of the Heart-Mind)	32
7	*Nei Ye* (Internal Cultivation)	39
8	*Guan Zi*'s Influence on the *Guigu Zi* (Ghost Valley Master)	45

From the *Guigu Zi*'s Seven Techniques of Yin Talisman

9	Broadening the Spirit in Accordance with the Five Dragons	46
10	Cultivating Will in Accordance with the Spirit-Tortoise	50
11	Consolidating Intention in Accordance with the Soaring Snake	52
12	Will, Intention, and Thought	54
13	The Zen of *Guan Zi*	59
14	Oneness in Buddhism and the *Guan Zi*	60
15	Translating the *Bai Xin*, *Xin Shu*, and *Nei Ye*	66

The Proto-Daoist Texts of the *Guan Zi*
Translations, annotations, and commentary by Dan G. Reid

16	*Purifying the Heart-Mind (Bai Xin)*	69
17	*Art of the Heart-Mind: upper volume (Xin Shu Shang)*	132
18	Ancient commentary included in the *Xin Shu Shang*	156
19	*Art of the Heart-Mind: lower volume (Xin Shu Xia)*	170
20	*Internal Cultivation (Nei Ye)*	203
21	A Meditation, Inspired by the Material in *The Thread of Dao*	282
22	Bibliography	297
23	Index	300
24	About the Author	307

今境內之民皆言治，藏商，管之法者家有之

"Today, the people of the state all discuss good governance, and everyone has a copy of the works on law by Shang Yang and Guan Zi in his house."

- Hanfei Zi (circa 250 BC)

Introduction

THE DEVELOPMENT OF PROTO-DAOISM IN ANCIENT CHINA

At the heart of Lao Zi's *Dao De Jing*, the most celebrated writing in Chinese history, is an ancient oral tradition that pulsated throughout Chinese culture. This river of knowledge carried advanced mystical understandings of nature and spiritual alchemy that transformed every system of the ancient world, from medicine, to politics, to the inner worlds of human beings. Though infusing every branch of human life, the wisdom of China's ancient peoples continuously returns to one source-principle: Dao.

The earliest evidence of this ancient wisdom tradition is found in the work of Chinese shamans – wise men and women with a deep connection to the cosmic principles of the universe, the same principles underlying King Wen's elucidation of the *Yi Jing's* (*I Ching's*) divinatory hexagrams, and the enigmatic poetry of Lao Zi's *Dao De Jing*.

Written history, artifacts, and even the etymology of written Chinese characters, show the prominence enjoyed by these shamans in ancient China, arising primarily from their talents in ritual and divination. The practice of divination was considered paramount to the success of endeavours and in determining the favour of "the spirits" (shen ming) when emperors and high government officials had to make their most important decisions. Such practices appear in Confucius' teachings and stories – said to be preservations of early Zhou culture – and are evidenced in the Confucian Classic of Rites (Li Ji) with mentions of divining by tortoise shell and divining stalks (龜策).

Great weight was given to reading "signs" that indicated the favour or disapproval of Heaven and foretold the outcomes of various decisions and events. If one had the favour of Heaven, they would be protected by "the spirits" and allowed to succeed. If not, their paths would be blocked, seemingly good events would turn bad, and if by relentless effort the goal was reached, it would still result in unforeseen negative consequences.

Introduction

According to the ancient shamans, one element would determine whether a human being could obtain the favour of gods and spirits: *virtue*.

The Book of History, in providing discourses from early kings on how the powerful might obtain "the will of Heaven," makes abundantly clear that only virtue will endear the gods and spirits. Nepotism, power, and sacrificial offerings are said to be of no avail if they are not accompanied by deep and sincere virtue.

Naturally, great sages were sought out by imperial hopefuls looking to find, or otherwise contort, a clear answer to the question: "What is virtue?"

Confucius (551-479 BC) described and promoted virtuous conduct, refining its definition with descriptions and anecdotes of benevolence, righteousness, filial piety, etiquette, and loyalty. For Confucius, these virtues depended heavily on acting appropriately. While benevolence was considered of highest importance, one could also distinguish Confucian morality by its common thread of duty throughout. If one could fulfill their duties in acting appropriately towards others, taking one's role within various power dynamics into account, they could approach the level of the noble "junzi." It should be understood, however, that acting appropriately was superior to obedience for Confucius. Righteousness, for example, was not simply a matter of prescribed actions, but entailed consideration of larger consequences, while loyalty was not simply obedience, but a matter of putting others needs before one's own.

In Confucius' profound writing on the guidelines and importance of music, we can see that he viewed social harmony much as he did musical harmony. When events and behaviours are timed correctly, harmonized in accordance with a central key, and adhere to the ceremony of interaction, society may function in concert to create flourishing symphonies of life. To quote from Confucius' *Yeu Ji*, or *Book of Music*,[1] "The knowledge of music leads to the subtle springs that underlie the rules of ceremony. He who has apprehended both ceremonies and music may be pronounced to be a possessor of virtue.

---

[1] Confucius was known to play the guqin, an ancient stringed instrument played on the lap, with a sound resembling the sitar. Ancient Chinese music incorporated a variety of percussive and melodic instruments, including a pitch-pipe mouth-organ (sheng), flutes, harmonized bells, and stringed instruments.

Virtue means realization (in one's self)."[2]

While Confucius established a zeitgeist of self-cultivation throughout Ancient China, his inner endeavours were not without their own foundations, and Confucius was not without his own heroes of sagely wisdom. The *Shang Shu* volume of the *Book of History* (*Shu Jing*) contains accounts of the the ancient kings and battles that ushered in the founding of the Zhou Dynasty (c. 1046-256 BC) by King Wen and King Wu. Documented conversations from this time illustrate the underlying foundational ideals of Confucius' philosophy, as Confucian philosophy is known as an attempt to revive the ethics and culture of the early, or "Western," Zhou Dynasty (c. 1046-771 BC).

The Zhou Dynasty began when King Wu overthrew the earlier Shang Dynasty (1600-1046 BC), completing the campaign begun by his father, King Wen. King Wen is known as the author of the original explanations of the *Yi Jing* (*I Ching*) hexagrams, later added to by another one of his sons, the Duke of Zhou, who expanded briefly on the hexagrams' individual lines. The *Yi Jing* is considered the first book ever written in China, and was revered by Confucians and Daoists, alike, for its cryptic wisdom and efficacy in divination.

Though King Wen and Wu are held up as the ideal examples of rectitude, and responsible for the cultural stability and refinement that lead to the flourishing philosophical schools of the Spring and Autumn (771-476 BC) and Warring States (475-221) periods, *The Book of History* suggests that King Wen and Wu in fact received a wealth of knowledge from the preceding Shang Dynasty by a wise advisor to King Zhou, the last king of the Shang Dynasty. This advisor's name was Ji Zi.

Ji Zi was a relative of King Zhou (King 紂Zhou of the Shang Dynasty, not to be confused with the Duke of 周Zhou or the 周Zhou Dynasty), known during his lifetime as Emperor Xin. The earliest written record of Ji Zi appears in the "Ming Yi" chapter of China's oldest extant book – the *Yi Jing*. In this chapter, the Duke of Zhou puts Ji Zi forth as an illustration of light and intelligence being smothered or suppressed. The image of this chapter is that of Earth over Fire. Earth smothers fire, just as tyrants like King Zhou block

---

[2] *The Sacred Books of the East: The texts of Confucianism.* Translated by James Legge. Vol. 4. Clarendon Press, 1885. p. 95

wisdom and guidance from shining through and bringing a nation out of darkness.

Accounts of Ji Zi appear in many ancient texts, including Confucius' *Analects*, the *Yue Ji* (*Book of Music*), *Zhuang Zi* (*Chuang Tzu*, within the earlier "Inner Chapters"), *Hanfei Zi*, *Huainan Zi*, *Mo Zi*, amongst others. However, it is the *Book of History* that describes the moment when Ji Zi passed his ancient knowledge onto King Wu, allowing it to survive the falling Shang Dynasty and live on in the new Zhou Dynasty.

In the chapter entitled "Patterns of the Flood 洪範" (found in the Zhou Shu volume), Ji Zi explains to King Wu that the father of the ancient King Yu (2200-2100 BC), Gun (鯀 "Giant Fish"), committed an affront to Heaven by damming up the flood waters, bringing chaos and turmoil to his people and himself. King Yu reversed this catastrophe by creating water channels which allowed water to flow throughout the land, arriving where it was needed, rather than attempting to simply block it up at the source. According to Ji Zi, King Yu was able to determine the correct solution because Heaven bestowed upon him the "洪範, 九疇, 彝倫攸敘 patterns of the flood, with its nine categories, the principles of which are expressed throughout all relations… beginning with the five elemental phases."[3]

The Zhou Shu volume, in which this chapter appears, is believed by scholars to have been written earlier than the vast majority of the other chapters in the *Book of History*; however, it is still dated only to the 4th or 3rd century BC. Thus, it is difficult to say whether "the patterns of the flood"[4] were passed down through Ji Zi and King Wu, or appeared in this chapter as a result of their emergence during the "100 Schools of Thought" that developed between the 6th and 3rd centuries BC.

One indication that "the patters of the flood" may have existed earlier on is that they included the categories and principles of the five elemental phases. The theory of five elemental phases seems to have emerged with the Yin-Yang School, and so is attributed to Zuo

---

[3] The "nine divisions" indicates that the "patterns of the flood" referred to the Luo Shu diagram, a series of dot patterns used in Feng Shui, divination, and Chinese numerology. Another early mention of the Luo Shu appears in *Zhuang Zi* (Outer Chapters), "Revolutions of Heaven."

[4] Translated by James Legge as "The Great Plan."

Yan (305-240 BC). Zuo Yan's use of these concepts, however, appears nearly 100 years after the Zhou Shu is now believed to have been written. This would suggest that teachings on the principles of the five elemental phases were already in circulation before Zuo Yan wrote of them, though perhaps being taught in a less literary and expounded upon form. Thus, the original time of their emergence should be open to debate. If the five elemental phases were written about before Zuo Yan, and their intellectual origins cannot be traced, it may be that knowledge of them had been quietly passed down to worthy students for several centuries.

The story of Ji Zi offers a key turning point in the development of Daoism, and lends credence to the theory that Lao Zi's *Dao De Jing* was in fact the tip of a cultural iceberg, one laying in the same type of quiet obscurity so often celebrated in Lao Zi's depiction of the Sage's interactions with society. Ji Zi's delineation of the Heavenly principles regulating Humanity may have set the foundation for many of China's 100 Schools of Thought, and preserved a thread of teachings on behaviour, divination, and moral ideals which became essential to later Daoist practices.

What this account of Ji Zi may most vitally reveal, is that Daoism developed as an extension of Ji Zi's assertion that King Yu's father committed an affront to Heaven by damming up the floods. This damming of the floods brought chaos and turmoil to his people, while King Yu succeeded in every way by allowing the water to flow according to the principles and patterns of nature. In the *Dao De Jing*, Lao Zi explains that by effortlessness (wu wei), and following nature (zi ran), things fall into their proper alignment. Nature ("Heaven") does no harm, while the forces of life nurture all things if unobstructed. When these operations are obstructed, generally as a result of desire and force, the prevailing alignment becomes aberrant, and disorder begins.

Seeing that Gun's great crime was attempting to force and block the flow of water, and that "the will of Heaven" and favour of the spirits are bestowed only upon those with virtue, it then follows that King Yu's virtue was evident in his effortlessness, and ability to allow nature to follow its own natural patterns. This wisdom allowed King Yu to quell any desires to use force against the powerful currents flowing between Earth and Heaven, and through this virtue and wisdom, bring life-giving waters to the people, thereby averting disaster, and cultivating prosperity throughout his provinces.

The principles of effortlessness (wu wei) and naturalness (zi ran) are also shown in the *Dao De Jing* (traditionally dated c. 500 BC) to be of pervasive applicability, reaching throughout the universe and within every living thing. Though Lao Zi speaks on the imperative of cultivating effortlessness, however, he also speaks of shaping and fashioning vessels to be outwardly harmonious, while inwardly empty. Just as King Yu did not sit idly by and allow the floods to overtake his provinces, Lao Zi does not suggest allowing emotions and desires to overtake oneself internally. Instead, they both speak of bringing harmony to what can be shaped, and fashioning the inexhaustible capacity of emptiness. Within emptiness, the flow of these currents and forces will contribute to, rather than disrupt, the growth and prosperity of the surrounding whole.

The principles of wu wei (effortlessness, more literally "without doing") and zi ran (naturalness, more literally "as itself") are found not only in the cosmic and inner realms of existence, but also in the physical realm of the human body, as evidenced by practical applications of acupuncture theory. Acupuncture works by opening and unblocking the flows of energy and blood circulating throughout the body. Daoist meditation techniques that "empty the heart-mind," similarly, open these same energy channels and allow qi (chi) to move vital essences throughout the body's systems. By allowing the energy channels and blood vessels to relax and open, circulation increases and the body's systems can be harmonized and revitalized. This might also be achieved with medications, though rarely do such medications not bring unwanted, often dangerous, side effects. Daoists, on the other hand, have devised ways to open the body's pathways without disrupting the natural alignments necessary for long-term health and vitality. Whether using medicinal herbs, needles, massage and joint manipulation (tuina), cupping, or moxibustion, the layout of the body is essentially being energetically irrigated according to the connections and principles of the five elemental phases – a sort of Feng Shui of the body, which ensures that correct internal alignments will not be imbalanced by the treatment in the long run.

The wisdom of Chinese medical theory and Feng Shui could be said to have descended from the wisdom of King Yu, benefitting from the long veneration of his idea to work with, and not against, the harmonious flow of nature – to allow circulation and avoid the dangers of excessive build-up.

Lao Zi's *Dao De Jing* reads somewhat as an homage to King Yu's "flood control" strategy, which can be felt running through the text's untold gems of wisdom waiting in the depths of Lao Zi's words. Note the importance given to accepting direction from the harmonious flow of nature in chapters two through nine,[5] below:

<u>Chapter Two</u>

When the whole world knows the pleasing to be pleasing
This ends in despising
When all know the good to be good
In the end there is "not good"

Thus, existence and non-existence are born together
Difficulty and ease result in each other
Long and short are compared to each other
Above and below are opposites of each other
Noise and tone are harmonized by each other
Front and back accompany each other
Therefore, sages handle affairs with non-action

They practice wordless instruction
And the myriad things all take their places
Without responding

Given life, but not possessed
Acted for, but not expected of
Perfection is cultivated, and not dwelled upon
Surely, what is not dwelled upon
Does not leave

---

[5] All translations of the *Dao De Jing* found in *The Thread of Dao* are borrowed from: Reid, Dan G., translator. *The Heshang Gong Commentary on Lao Zi's Dao De Jing*. Montreal: Center Ring Publications, 2015.

Introduction

[Trying to accumulate a positive persona through artificial means will only result in ruin. "Too much of a good thing" is precarious.]

Chapter Three

Do not exalt the worthy
And the people will not fight
Do not praise goods which are difficult to obtain
And the people will not steal
Do not display what is desirable
And their hearts will not be in chaos

Therefore, the Sage's government
Empties the heart and enriches the stomach
Softens the will and strengthens the bones
People then remain uncontrived and without desires
While the scheming do not dare to act
Act by not acting
And everything will fall into place

[Excessive desires only ruin people's happiness; therefore, the Sage reduces these desires and opens people up to appreciating what is truly valuable in life – social harmony and inner peace.]

Chapter Four

Dao is a container
Though used (filled) again and again
It is never full
Profound! As though the ancestor of all things

Rounding the points
Untying the knots
Softening the glare
Unifying the dust

Tranquil! As though having a life of its own
I do not know whose child it is

It appears to have preceded the primordial ruler

[Like King Yu's irrigation channels, the Dao spreads life giving energy throughout and so is never full.]

Chapter Five

Heaven and Earth are not (willfully) benevolent
The myriad things are treated no differently
Than grass for dogs
Sages are not (willfully) benevolent
The hundred clans are treated no differently
Than grass for dogs

The gate of Heaven and Earth
Is it not like a bagpipe?
Empty yet not finished
It moves, and again more is pushed forth

To speak countless words is worthless
This is not as good as guarding balance within

[Speaking countless unnecessary words, fabricating reality and accumulating artificial ideas, will not provide the understanding acquired by allowing situations to flow in their natural direction, thereby revealing themselves]

Chapter Six

The valley with a spirit does not die
This is called the Fathomlessness of the Female
The gate to the Fathomlessness of the Female
Is called The Root of Heaven and Earth
Soft and gentle
This is her way of existence
To engage her is not laborious

Introduction

[Valleys are often river channels. Lying low, water flows through these channels as it makes its way through a mountain range.]

Chapter Seven

Heaven has longevity, Earth has continuity
Heaven and Earth have the power of longevity and continuity
because they do not live for themselves
This is how they can live for so long

Therefore, sages leave themselves behind
And they end up in front
They do not cater to themselves
Yet they persist

Is it not because they are without selfishness and wickedness
That they are able to fulfill themselves?

[Because sages remain empty (of ego) and take the low position, like a valley or water channel, life flows through them with a loving ease.]

Chapter Eight

The highest excellence is like water
The excellence of water benefits all things
And does not fight against them
It dwells in the places that people detest
How close it is to Dao!

Such excellence in dwelling can be found in the Earth
Such excellence in the heart can be found in its depths
Such excellence in giving can be found in benevolence
Such excellence in speech can be found in sincerity
Such excellence in alignment can be found in order
Such excellence in professionalism can be found in competence
Such excellence in action can be found in appropriate timing
Simply because it does not fight

(Water) has no enemy

[When people are empty (of ego) and take the low position, like the valley or water channel, the above benefits are found in them, all of which, according to Daoists, require an unobstructed flowing with nature.]

<u>Chapter Nine</u> (as it appears in the earliest known copy of the *Dao De Jing*, found at Guodian)

To accumulate until full
Is not as good as coming to a stop
When rushing waters gather
Nothing can be long protected
When gold and jade fill the halls
Nothing can preserve them
When fortune and wealth bring arrogance
They bring the misfortune of their own loss
Having achieved the goal, withdraw yourself
This is the way of Heaven

[Consider that hoarding wealth, rather than circulating it back into the economy, suffocates the economy that this wealth relies upon. Hoarding power, rather than allowing rights and credit where they are due, will result in resentments and thus a reduced level of influence. Allowing wealth and power to flow outwardly in a natural course secures their perpetuity.]

As these chapters show, the sayings of Lao Zi benefitted greatly from the long-standing veneration of King Yu's wisdom, while the *Dao De Jing* functioned somewhat like a juncture point in King Yu's water channels, accumulating and spreading this wisdom throughout ancient China, and beyond.

Introduction

Guan Zi, Jixia Academy, and Chu Kingdom

Some one-hundred years before Lao Zi or Confucius were born, the reputation of a wise advisor named Guan Zhong, aka Guan Zi, swept through the states of the Zhou Empire.

Guan Zhong (720-645 BC) was the Prime Minister of Qi State under the leadership of Duke Huan who ruled Qi from 685-643 BC. By following Guan Zhong's advice, Duke Huan amplified the power and prosperity of Qi, earning himself recognition as Hegemon – the most powerful leader amongst all the states of the Empire.

Guan Zhong's wisdom and achievements are mentioned in the vast majority of early Chinese texts, including the Confucian *Analects*, *Xun Zi*, and *Meng Zi*, the Daoist *Zhuang Zi*, and *Huainan Zi*, and also in *Mo Zi*. His reputation as a multi-disciplinary genius is reflected in the *Huainan Zi*, for example, when one of its authors exclaims,

> If chaos is fomenting, and the people chase profit all day and night; if they are angry and shallow, and laws and righteousness go against each other, while their actions and benefits are in opposition: even ten Guan Zhong's couldn't rectify this situation!

Along with his reputation for implementing successful and lasting reforms was his reputation for breaking with common principles of conduct, and choosing his own path, as described in *Analects*:

> Zi Gong said, "Guan Zhong, I apprehend, was wanting in virtue. When the duke Huan caused his brother Jiu [Huan's brother, Zhong's friend and student] to be killed, Guan Zhong was not able to die with him. Moreover, he became prime minister to Huan." The Master [Confucius] said, "Guan Zhong acted as prime minister to the duke Huan, made him leader of all the princes, and united and rectified the whole kingdom. Down to the present day, the people enjoy the gifts which he conferred. But for Guan Zhong, we should now be wearing our hair unbound, and the lappets of our coats buttoning on the left side.[6] Will you re-

---

[6] This reference suggests the Guan Zhong introduced more refinements into the culture of Confucius' time, but may also suggest that Guan Zhong saved Qi from being taken over by Chu State. Chu had earlier claimed independence from the

quire from him the small fidelity of common men and common women, who would commit suicide in a stream or ditch, no one knowing anything about them?"

Guan Zhong was the tutor of Gongzi Jiu,[7] as Jiu was the younger brother of an earlier duke of Qi – Duke Xiang. Jiu was also the older brother of Prince Xiaobai, later known as Duke Huan. In the power struggle for Qi, Xiaobai killed Jiu and eventually decided to take Guan Zhong as his Prime Minister, rather than killing him for being one of Jiu's accomplices.[8]

Given Guan Zhong's far-reaching reputation, unattributed documents reflecting his strategies, policies, and wisdom were apparently appended to his name in recognition of his influence. Consequently, the works found in the *Guan Zi* are now generally believed to have been written by scholars of the Jixia Academy in former Qi State, during the 4th century BC.[9] It should also be noted that these writings were not compiled into the complete *Guan Zi* encyclopedia of 86 books until about 10 BC. Though Guan Zhong's lasting influence on the culture and society that followed him is without question, distilling his contribution from the convergence of ideologies that went into such writings may no longer be possible.

The *Guan Zi* is generally considered a Legalist text – a school of thought that became more closely associated with Qin State after the fall of the Zhou Dynasty in 256 BC. Legalism had already gained much attention by 360 BC, however, after Duke Xiao of Qin followed the advice of his minister Shang Yang and implemented the strict Legalist policies of Qin in 363 BC. These policies afforded Qin the power and might to take on, and soon thereafter replace, the Zhou Dynasty.

While Legalists argued that strict enforcement of laws would ensure

---

Zhou Empire, and its culture favoured the left side over the right side, while Chu men often did not put their hair into a topknot.
[7] Gongzi meaning "son of a Duke."
[8] Wikipedia contributors, "Guan Zhong," *Wikipedia, The Free Encyclopedia*, https://en.wikipedia.org/w/index.php?title=Guan_Zhong&oldid=857887189 (accessed November 27, 2018).
[9] Rickett, Alynn, translator. *Guanzi: Political, Economic, and Philosophical Essays from Early China, Volume II*. New Jersey: Princeton University Press, 1998

order, the proto-Daoist texts within the *Guan Zi* emerge as a counterbalance to this position, pointing to deeper sources of social cooperation and harmony, cultivated by fostering *inner* peace and *inner* harmony – the "true nature" of human beings. The *Guan Zi*'s repudiation of over-reliance on laws was also in contrast to a combination of Daoism and Legalism found in *The Four Canons of the Yellow Emperor (Huang Di Si Jing)*. The *Four Canons*, perhaps written somewhat earlier than the *Guan Zi*, closer to 400 BC, resemble Lao Zi's philosophy that rulers must be frugal, modest, and humble. It advocates not over-taxing the citizens, nor killing captives, or forcing corvee labour. It also speaks of yin and yang, and touches on the natural interplay of these forces in nature. It does not, however, speak at any length on the subject of internal cultivation, beyond the general principle that a ruler should dwell in the absence of desire. Further, it advocates the invariable and merciless application of punishments. Overall, *Four Canons* is closer to Legalism than the *Guan Zi*.

Though the *Four Canons* may pre-date the *Guan Zi* as an example of Daoist philosophy, the *Bai Xin, Xin Shu,* and *Nei Ye* not only adhere more closely to Lao Zi's philosophy, but also to the idioms, form, and style in which his proposals and prescriptions appear in the *Dao De Jing*. Such similarities, detailed throughout *Thread of Dao*, show that these texts, rather than the *Four Canons*, are the likely precursors of the *Dao De Jing*, if any exist.

The *Bai Xin, Xin Shu,* and *Nei Ye*, along with all Warring States era Daoist texts, appear to have come from the culture of Chu State, located in the south of China, though they may have ultimately come to fruition at Jixia Academy.

Jixia Academy, located in Qi State[10] (north of Chu, on the eastern coast), hosted scholars from many different states, and is said to have been instituted by Guan Zhong's ruler, Duke Huan of Qi. The academy was later revitalized by King Xuan, ruler of Qi from 319-301 BC.[11] It is likely that Chu scholars were most active in Qi around 330

---

[10] Other scholars from Qi State include Sun Zi (approx. 544-496 BC), author of the *Art of War*, and Confucian scholars Meng Zi (Mencius, 372-289 BC) and Xun Zi (313-238 BC).
[11] Sima Qian. *Records of the Grand Historian*. c. 100 BC.

BC[12] thanks to stable relations between Qi and Chu, a result of the rising power of Qin in the West, and so it may have been during this time that the *Bai Xin, Xin Shu,* and *Nei Ye* found their way into the scholarly lectures and conversations at Jixia Academy.

Warring States Period, China circa 400 BC

13

Considerable power shifts driven by Qin's expansion east and south would have encouraged Chu scholars to travel north-east to Qi around 330 BC. King Huiwen of Qin began exerting military pressure

---

[12] Some modern scholars believe that Jixia Academy was actually started by King Xuan. Though this may be the case, it is likely that Qi was already frequented by scholars seeking out Guan Zhong's secrets to success, and that this trend gave rise to the full development of Jixia Academy. Thus, Jixia Academy may very well have been an institution before it had a proper name.

[13] From "Wikimedia Commons, the free media repository." Edited by D.G. Reid to add Chengzhou in place of present day Luoyang, and new title.

eastwards on Chu around 337 BC. Chu then absorbed Yue, to its east, in 334 BC. Qin later absorbed Ba and Shu to the west of Chu in 316 BC. These ongoing invasions may have given Chu scholars further incentive to travel east and north, towards Qi, after 337 BC, though it wasn't until 278 BC that Qin successfully attacked the capital of Chu, forcing them to relocate it.

In 313 BC, King Huiwen of Qin enticed King Huai of Chu to cut ties with Qi, so as to repair ties between Chu and Qin after a failed allied attack of several states against Qin. This cooling of the previous relations between Chu and Qi may have strained the camaraderie at Jixia Academy and driven notable Chu scholars out of Qi around 313 BC, suggesting that proto-Daoist writings coming out of Jixia Academy likely pre-dated this perfunctory alliance between Qin and Chu.

In 299 BC, when the prolific Daoist philosopher and storyteller Zhuang Zi (aka Zhuang Zhou; Chuang Tzu) was 30 years old (died at 45), and Meng Zi (aka Mencius) was 73 years old (died at 83), King Qingxiang of Chu, son of King Huai, came to power. King Qingxian's childhood tutor newly rose to fame in 1993 when it was discovered that he was buried with the earliest known excerpts of the *Dao De Jing* in Guodian village, nine kilometers from the former Chu Capital, Ying. The above timeline could put King Qingxian's tutor[14] at Jixia Academy around 330 BC, while relations were relatively calm between Qi and Chu.

Adding to support for this timeline of authorship is the rising counter-current in the *Guan Zi* texts to the (proto-)Legalism of Shang Yang. Shang Yang's ideas likely found their way into Jixia Academy around the time of their official implementation by Duke Xiao of Qin in 363 BC, continuing to hold influence following Shang Yang's execution by Xiao's successor, King Huiwen of Qin, in 338 BC.[15] If the Legalism in *Four Canons of the Yellow Emperor* (circa 400 BC) pre-dated the implementation of Shang Yang's policies (363 BC), it may be that Shang Yang's ideologies were simply a radical form of the prevailing philosophical climate, a climate that the authors of the *Guan Zi*

---

[14] It is possible that this tutor also instructed the father of King Qingxian, King Huai of Chu, who adhered to Zhou rites to the point of fault, costing him dearly when dealing with King Zhaoxiang of Qin who did not adhere to these rites.

[15] Though King Huiwen executed Shang Yang, likely as retribution for Shang not commuting punishment against the former earlier in life, King Huiwen maintained Shang Yang's policies.

hoped to transform. Their words foresaw the consequences of too much rigidity and, thus, shared methods for cultivating inner peace and enlightenment in an effort to mitigate tyranny, violence, and the inevitable chaos that follows them. It, therefore, seems likely that the proto-Daoist *Guan Zi* texts were first written down sometime after or during Shang Yang's lifetime, when Legalist ideas began to pull philosophers further and further into inflexibility.

As to the spring from which Daoist wisdom, fostering inner peace and flexibility, arose – these teachings may have quietly flourished within the chambers of the Zhou capital in Zhou State[16] (north of Chu, surrounded by Han State), where Lao Zi is said to have lived around 500 BC. This, however, is not to discount the common understanding that Daoism began in Chu Kingdom.

If we are to go by the traditional dating, and legendary authorship, of the *Dao De Jing* and *Guan Zi*, Lao Zi seems to have been inspired by the *Bai Xin, Xin Shu,* and *Nei Ye*, which would have been available to him as the Zhou imperial librarian. This is to assume, of course, that he was not personally instructed in the "art of the heart-mind" while working amongst the empire's best in the Zhou capital. Given Qi State's loyalty to the Zhou Empire, any traditions on the subtleties of leadership and internal cultivation that Guan Zhong benefitted from would have been accessible to important scholarly officials in the Zhou capital.

Chu, which went from being a rogue Zhou state to an independent kingdom in 704 BC, began to implement Zhou customs in its political and martial activities with the inspired reforms of King Zhuang of Chu, who ruled Chu Kingdom from 613-591 BC. It is worthy of note that King Zhuang began his rule 30 years after the end of Duke Huan's rule in Qi, during which time Guan Zi served as Prime Minister of Qi, and approximately 100 years before Lao Zi's employment in the Zhou imperial library.

If proto-Daoism spread from Zhou to Chu, owing to King Zhuang's reforms, these esoteric teachings would have slowly come to light on finding a welcome environment in Chu's combination of shamanic and scholarly culture. It may otherwise be that the moral

---

[16] Not to be confused with Zhao State in the north.

teachings of Zhou were gradually interpreted by Chu's shamanic elders and transformed into the Daoist teachings later attributed to Lao Zi.

King Zhuang of Chu (ruled 613-591 BC) was a particularly boisterous and ruthless leader until meeting with the unsolicited counsel of Zhou minister Wang Sun Man, who admonished him that virtue and not bronze (a resource Chu had in abundance and used for weaponry) provides a king with true power.[17] This inspired King Zhuang to observe the Zhou rites, and make Chu a leading example of Zhou culture in matters of state and war.[18] King Zhuang brought Chu from being viewed as a state ruled by 'barbarians' to later being lauded by Confucius (551-479 BC) as a true example of high culture, and proof that prosperity will follow an adherence to Zhou's evolved political guidelines. As a result of his social and cultural reforms, and the power that they afforded him, King Zhuang was named Hegemon of the Zhou Dynasty, reaching the same level of power held decades earlier by Duke Huan of Qi.[19]

King Zhuang ensured that those holding positions of power in his kingdom were familiar with Zhou rites and ancient classics such as the *Book of Songs*. This influenced even Chu warriors to become proficient in Zhou rites and moral standards. One example of King Zhuang's instructions to his troops comes from the story of Chu's victory over the Jin army, after which King Zhuang would not allow his troops to pile the bodies of the Jin soldiers as a victory celebration, but insisted that they bury the bodies in the same manner as their own troops. Following this burial, King Zhuang paid his respects by worshipping the God of the Yellow River.[20] This respect for one's adversary is distinctly prescribed in Lao Zi's chapter 31:

> Beautiful weapons are instruments of ill omen

---

[17] Various scholars in *The Rise and Fall of the State of Chu*, part four. Directed by Zhang Xiaomin. China. 2016: CCTV-9 Documentary. Contributing scholars include: Prof. Xu Wenwu, Yangtze University; Liu Yutang, Vice President of Hubei Academy of Social Sciences; Prof. Chen Yantang, China Academy of Social Sciences; Zhang Hongjie, Phd., Fudan University; Gu Jiuxing, Central China Normal University

[18] Ibid.

[19] Between Duke Huan of Qi and King Zhuang of Chu, Duke Wen of Jin (ruled 636-628) was the recognized Hegemon.

[20] Ibid.

All creatures should despise them
Therefore, those who have Dao do not stay with them
The superior man (junzi) prefers to stay on the left
But those who use weapons prefer the right
Weapons are not instruments of good omen
They are not instruments of the junzi
If an attacker cannot be stopped, and weapons are used
To be calm and unemotional is considered most important
If victory is then won, do not be pleased
For to be pleased with this would be to celebrate murder
Anyone who celebrates murder
Is not capable of obtaining the will of the world!

For auspicious matters they [junzi] stay on the left
For ominous matters, they [junzi] stay on the right
When the low ranking officer is on the left
And the high ranking officer is on the right
This is said to observe the rites of mourning
When many people are killed
This is cause for sympathy and mourning
Victory in war
Is also cause for the mourning rites to be observed

Lao Zi is believed to have lived in Chengzhou during his service in the imperial library, the same place where King Zhuang was admonished by Wang Sun Man; however, it was 100 years after King Zhuang's rule that Lao Zi, aka Li Er, is said to have worked in the Zhou library, and instructed Confucius on Zhou rites. Nonetheless, we can see in King Zhuang's adoption of Zhou culture and the parallels between his behaviour and Lao Zi's teachings, that Lao Zi was also influenced by the moral ideals of Zhou. For example, King Zhou punished his own son for breaching the somewhat trivial proprietary law of not dismounting his horse before entering the court gates, holding even his own family members as equals under the law (see *Dao De Jing*, chapter five, on all people being equal under Heaven); he also consistently showed mercy once his authority had been adequately established (see *Dao De Jing*, chapter 30, on achieving one's aim without flaunting power).

Introduction

Though Lao Zi is believed to have worked in Zhou State, scholars ascribe Daoist thought mainly to the Chu region. This discrepancy might be mitigated by the belief that Lao Zi's birthplace was in what is now Guoyang county, Anhui Province, in the north-eastern corner of the former Chu Kingdom. We can also see, for example in DDJ31 above, that the author of the *Dao De Jing* subscribed to Chu's elevation of the left side over the right side, in contrast to the Zhou preference for the right over the left. [21] Furthermore, after King Zhuang made Chu a stronghold of Zhou culture and scholarship, it follows that Daoist interpretations and expansions of this culture were likely to arise, especially alongside the potent shamanism and nature worship that Chu was formerly looked down upon for by the other Zhou states. Chu had a reputation for being culturally anarchistic, rejecting the authority and norms of the Zhou Empire, and absorbing from the various cultures that Chu Kingdom enveloped. It appears to have been this syncretism, infused with a pervading influence of Zhou culture, which gave rise to the Daoist school of thought, and provided a fresh approach to the Zhou teachings of Confucius, and, perhaps more significantly, a fresh approach to the rigid Legalist policies of the rising Qin powers. Had Qin Legalists taken heed of the Daoists' guidance, Qin Dynasty (221-206) may have survived longer than the 15 years it took for a rebellion to rise up and usher in the Han Dynasty. As Lao Zi states in chapter 76 of the *Dao De Jing*:

> As with all things
> When plants and trees begin to grow
> They are flexible and pliant
> Yet, when dying
> They become dry and rotten
> Thus, hardness and inflexibility are the approach of death
> While softness and pliancy are the approach of life

Though getting cut short, the Qin Dynasty nearly managed to stop the transmission of China's ancient wisdom when in 213 BC, the first emperor of the Qin Dynasty, Qin Shi Huang, ordered the burning of any books which might be used to prove his leadership unjust,

---

[21] Ibid.

and buried alive 460 Confucian scholars. Were it not for the 1978 AD discovery of a complete *Dao De Jing* (including all 81 chapters), found in a tomb that had been sealed in 168 BC, the earliest known copy of Lao Zi's text to survive from this period would date from approximately 1 AD, in Yan Zun's commentary, and even this only contains the De (Virtue) volume, and not the Dao (Way) volume. In 1993, an earlier copy containing only fragments of roughly a third of the chapters was discovered in the tomb of King Qingxian's tutor, at Guodian, dated around 300 BC. Thus, it appears, Qin Shi Huang's purging of texts was so thorough that only two copies of the *Dao De Jing* from that time period, both buried in tombs, survive to this day.[22]

Thankfully, the *Guan Zi* texts survived, possibly because of their technical practicality and association with Guan Zhong. This association could have made the texts valuable to Legalists, and spared them the fate of other philosophical texts.

Following the end of Qin Dynasty, brought about by a rebellion allied with Chu loyalists, the ensuing Han Dynasty absorbed the Daoist culture of Chu Kingdom, along with the spoils of concluding "the Chu-Han Contention." Ascendents of Liu Bang, the founder of Han Dynasty and leader of the rebel forces against Qin, even contributed greatly to the preservation and continuation of Daoist knowledge; for example, Liu An who compiled the *Huainan Zi*, and Liu Xiang, editor of the *Guan Zi*.

Liu Bang, later known as Emperor Gao of Han, had a son named Liu Heng,[23] later known as Emperor Wen of Han.[24] Emperor Wen's

---

[22] For evidence as to why theories that the Dao De Jing was compiled after the Qin Dynasty cannot be considered conclusive, please see the "translator's introduction" in *The Heshang Gong Commentary on Lao Zi's Dao De Jing*, translated by Dan G. Reid

[23] Early copies of the Dao De Jing can be dated according to an Emperor's "name taboo" which demanded texts not use the character of an Emperor's given name, in this case - Heng 恆 ("enduring, eternal"). Heng 恆 was, thus, changed to chang 常 (enduring, eternal) throughout the Dao De Jing, including the first line of chapter one: "The Dao that can be named is not the eternal Dao." Early copies of the Dao De Jing, such as those found in the Mawangdui tombs, that did not change heng 恆 to chang 常, were thereby known to have pre-dated Emperor Wen's rule.

[24] Emperor Wen is the same to whom, according to legend, Heshang Gong is said to have given his commentary on the Dao De Jing. Other datable factors in Heshang Gong's commentary, however, suggest that it was written closer to 200 AD. Nonetheless, it seems unlikely that another scholar of the Dao De Jing would not have tutored the Liu family and expounded on Lao Zi's philosophy.

wife, later known as Empress Dowager Dou, followed the teachings of Lao Zi and influenced both Emperor Wen and their son, later known as Emperor Jing (Liu Qi), in their light-handed, frugal, and benevolent governance. The rule of Wen and Jing is considered one of the golden ages of Chinese history, and evidence of the validity and efficacy of Lao Zi's political teachings.

Following Emperor Jing in the Han Dynasty succession was Emperor Wu, born Liu Che. Liu Che was also the nephew of Liu An, editor of the Daoist compilation, the *Huainan Zi*. Liu An presented Liu Che his "newly completed" *Huainan Zi* in 139 BC when Liu Che was 17 years old, two years before he began his 54 year rule as Emperor Wu. Emperor Wu's rule from 141-87 BC was the longest reign of any Chinese Emperor up until the 17th century.

Compiling the *Guan Zi*, circa 26 BC

The *Guan Zi* was compiled by Liu Xiang, beginning in 26 BC, and completed and submitted to the Emperor by his son, Liu Xin, around 6 BC. Though it was not compiled until this time, an existent corpus attributed to Guan Zi (Guan Zhong) was widely known to scholars by at least the time of Hanfei Zi, who wrote around 250 BC:

> 今境內之民皆言治, 藏商, 管之法者家有之
> Today, the people of the state all discuss good governance, and everyone has a copy of the works on law by Shang (Yang) and Guan (Zhong) in his house.[25]

Evidence of such texts also appears in the *Huainan Zi* (139 BC) when it states in chapter 12:

> Thus, a great person's actions cannot be restricted to a straightening line. He stops when he has reached the end. This is what is meant in the *Guan Zi*: "An owl's flight path holds a straightening line."[26]

---

[25] Han Fei Tzu. *Basic Writings*, trans. Burton Watson (New York: Columbus University Press, 1964), 110. Quote edited by Dan G. Reid.
[26] From chapter 12 of Liu An's *Huainan Zi* (139 BC). Translated by Dan G. Reid.

To compile an official encyclopedia of Guan Zhong's teachings, Liu Xiang gathered 564 book bundles, including 389 from the imperial library, and the rest from various government officials,[27] to be collated with the help of several scholars. Over a period of two decades, they "eliminated 484 duplicate bundles to make the standard text of 86 books."[28]

There is no mention as to how many duplicates were found of the *Bai Xin, Xin Shu,* or *Nei Ye,* but with 6.5 times more duplicate bundles than what eventually made up the *Guan Zi,* it seems likely that these texts also had duplicates. It should be noted that Liu Xin had initially categorized the *Guan Zi* as part of the Daoist school of thought,[29] surely due in large part to the weight and content of the *Xin Shu, Bai Xin,* and *Nei Ye,* which scholars generally agree to be among the earliest texts included in the compilation. Though the *Guan Zi* was not categorized as a Legalist text until the Sui Dynasty (581-618 AD),[30] it is generally categorized as such to this day.

Liu Xiang (77-6 BC) was a Confucian scholar and distant relative of Liu Bang (256-195 BC), founder of the Han Dynasty. He was, thus, also a relative of Liu Bang's grandson, Liu An (179-122 BC), who edited the *Huainan Zi,* an early compilation of Daoist thought, around 139 BC.

Liu Xin – Liu Xiang's son who finalized the *Guan Zi* soon after his father's death – was a Confucian scholar, founder of the "Old Texts" Confucian school, and the imperial librarian under Xin Dynasty Emperor Wang Mang. Wang Mang leveraged his position and family connections in the Han Dynasty to briefly replace the Han Dynasty with the Xin Dynasty (9-23 AD), dividing the Han Dynasty into the "Western Han (206-9 BC)" and "Eastern Han (25-220 AD)" periods. Liu Xin may have had a considerable influence on

---

An exact quote of what appears here in the *Huainan Zi* does not exist in the received version of the *Guan Zi,* though likely existed in a lost document attributed to Guan Zhong.

[27] P. Van Der Loon. "On the Transmission of Kuan-tzŭ." *T'oung Pao,* Second Series, 41, no. 4/5 (1952): 357-93. http://www.jstor.org/stable/4527337.

[28] 564 – 484 = 80, so presumably one of these numbers was mistaken, or some of the bundles were divided into more than one book.

[29] P. Van Der Loon. "On the Transmission of Kuan-tzŭ." *T'oung Pao,* Second Series, 41, no. 4/5 (1952): 357-93. http://www.jstor.org/stable/4527337.

[30] Zhengyuan Fu. *China's Legalists.* (New York: M.E. Sharpe, 1996), 14

Wang Mang, who sought to restore much of the ancient Zhou Dynasty systems and Confucian rites. While at the outset, Wang Mang's ideals seemed to be in line with Daoist counsel – eliminating government excesses, sanctioning social equality, and abolishing slavery – his approach to handling affairs proved gratuitously meddlesome, restrictive, and lacking flexibility, ultimately leading to discontent, chaos, and defeat.

Proto-Daoism in the *Guan Zi*

As touched upon earlier, the proto–Daiost texts in the *Guan Zi* often read as a repudiation of the surging Legalist philosophy that ushered in the Qin Dynasty. Legalism is characterized by a reliance on staunch adherence to laws, rewards, and punishments. It also values virtues such as righteousness and benevolence, but does not trust in them as Confucius and his followers did. Though Legalism appreciates a leader's duty to display virtuous qualities in order to influence those below them, it holds reliable demonstrations of rewards and punishments as the primary determinant in human behaviour, provided these rewards and punishments match the likes and dislikes of their recipients. While this strategy has predictable short–term effects, the proto–Daoist philosophers point out its inability to bring about true transformation of the population's inner virtue, a limitation that would in fact make the people more deceitful and beguiling, leading to further disorder, and distortions of their true nature. The *Bai Xin*, lines 144-150, describes the situation as follows:

> Affairs have suitable and unsuitable (solutions). For example, it is suitable to use an ivory bodkin to untie (knots). What cannot be untied is then untied.
>
> As for those who excel at improving situations, when the nation's people cannot figure out how to "untie" (a situation), they apply their skill but do not hold onto the situation without letting go. This would be unskillful, for it submerges the situation in laws and punishment. Such ability is not skillful. Attain trustworthiness (xin 信) and then stop.

Humanity's true nature, the proto–Daoists explain, is the easiest and most trustworthy state of being that rulers can bring about, if the ruler first cultivates this simplicity, economy of desires, and sincerity of personality in himself. Allowing people to return to this natural simplicity would ensure abundance in resources and communal harmony; while the power of the ruler's virtue, and that of his people, would eventually win the hearts of those in other states, ensuring strong alliances and pervasive loyalty.

Relying on virtue rather than law may resemble Confucius' approach to political order, however, a defining difference between Confucianism and Daoism is that Confucius advocated adherence to rules of conduct much in the way that Legalists demanded adherence to laws. These forced adjustments, in the view of Daoists, were external and too easily fabricated, despite Confucius' emphasis that virtue must come from within. Thus, the Daoists called for leaving off any externally imposed restrictions, and a realization, or re-awakening, of one's true heart. Reaching to this true heart, all else will follow, just as water allowed to sit undisturbed will eventually purify, of itself.

The authors of the *Guan Zi* also try to impart that law is much greater than the rules and precepts decided by lawmakers. They explain that there are natural laws in the universe which govern the success or failure of all things, regardless of what the human powers that be may demand. For example, in *Bai Xin* (*Purifying the Heart-Mind*), lines 102-118, we find:

> ... for human beings.
> There is something that governs them.
> Much like rolling drums of thunder
> Cannot incite themselves.
> There is something always inciting them.
> What is this constant thing? It is present at all times.
> Looking for it with the eyes, it will not be seen;
> Listening for it with the ears, it will not be heard.
> Scattered throughout, it fills all under Heaven.
> Though not seen on the surface,
> It is collected in the harmonious shape of the face;
> It is known in the muscles and the skin.

> Dutifully, it comes and goes,
> Yet no one knows its timing.
> So small, it is (within) the square (of Earth);
> So expansive, it (exceeds) the circle (of Heaven).
> Expanding and expanding, no one can reach its gate.

The *Bai Xin* goes on to explain the futility of ruling only with laws, and simply trying to gain control of a population by heaping more and more laws upon them. As lines 144-151 of the *Bai Xin* illustrate, this is like trying to untie a knot by continuously pulling at a string rather than employing a bodkin (an analogy for a sage). *Bai Xin,* lines 34-37, even argue that people would be better off if "the correct man" simply stopped telling people how to act so that they could find the true righteousness and filial piety naturally residing within themselves. Further, having found these qualities within, people would stop competing with each other over who displays these traits the most.

To connect with the highest law – the Way (Dao) – Daoist teachers counseled finding peace and order within oneself so as to first attain this peaceful vantage point before trying to guide the world towards it. In sharing this point of view, the Daoists employed guidance which likely came from a formerly obscure tradition of internal cultivation.

Always looking to the source to see how things come about, Daoists learned how to cultivate one's kingdom by understanding how to cultivate oneself, and they understood how to cultivate oneself by looking at the source of every human being: Heaven and Earth. With a body as stable as the Earth, and a mind as vast as the Heavens, Daoists sought transcendence of the seeming limitations of existence. Through Heaven and Earth they also found manifestations of Dao in the laws by which all things proceed. Daoists therefore modeled their behaviour on Heaven and Earth in order to achieve ultimate longevity, and advised kings to preserve their kingdoms by these same principles. In lines 18-20 of the *Xin Shu Xia* (*Art of the Heart-Mind, lower volume*), we find:

> Therefore, sages resemble Heaven during such times. They are without thought of self when sitting above all.
> They resemble Earth during such times. They are without thought of self when supporting all.

As for thought of self, it puts the world in chaos.

In the *Xin Shu Xia*, we also find a contradiction of one of the Legalists' greatest faiths: the ultimate power of rewards and punishments. Lines 92-99 retort:

> The ancient enlightened kings' love for all under Heaven
> Allowed the world to depend on them.
> The violent kings' hatred of all under Heaven
> Caused the world to abandon them.
> Thus, rewards are not enough to demonstrate love,
> And punishments are not enough to demonstrate fierceness
> For this love will end with the rewards,
> And this fierceness will end with the punishments.

Thus, it appears that the proto-Daoist *Guan Zi* texts, though found in what is generally considered a Legalist compilation, were in large part written in response to Legalist ideologies. The writers' attempts to warn Legalists of the imbalances that result from such stringent adherence to their doctrines turned prophetic when the Qin Dynasty, bolstered by the Legalist policies of Shang Yang earlier on, swept all of China by 221 BC, and then fell in 206 BC, only 15 years after unifying the "warring states."

Political guidance in the *Guan Zi* is far closer to that of Confucius and Lao Zi than that of Shang Yang. The writers of the *Guan Zi* advise considering the welfare of the people as most important, and instilling righteousness, benevolence, frugality, and simplicity in them, rather than simply manipulating them with rewards and punishments, laws, and even poverty as Shang Yang does.

While the *Bai Xin*, *Xin Shu*, and *Nei Ye* are its only texts on Daoist internal cultivation, a great deal of the writings on government in *Guan Zi* seem to heed Lao Zi's teachings in the *Dao De Jing*, though they may have been transcribed at an earlier date than this canonical classic. If we are to faithfully ascribe these writings to Guan Zi and Lao Zi, Guan Zi (720-645 BC) would have written his texts some 100 years before Lao Zi wrote the *Dao De Jing*. Perhaps, as suggested earlier, the historical thread of these teachings goes back even further to the shamans and sages of the Shang (1600-1046 BC) or Xia (2070-1600 BC) Dynasties.

Because of Qin Shi Huang's order to burn all philosophical books in 213 BC, it is difficult to say with any certainty when the Daoist approach to government first appeared in writing. The influence of Zhou rites and culture on King Zhuang of Chu shows that such ideals for government, and virtuous rule, were in place long before Confucius' time, even if fidelity to these ideals was not constant throughout the Zhou Dynasty. Confucius, who helped to revitalize these ideals, was likely a product of the zeitgeist of his time, realizing the precipitous nature of an empire losing its principles while its states had begun declaring themselves kingdoms.

Though the virtuous rule touted in the *Guan Zi* is considered Confucian in many respects, Confucius was a teacher of Zhou culture, and the philosophy and rites of Zhou are what Li Er (aka Li Dan, Lao Zi) is said to have taught while working in the Zhou imperial library. Seeing this blend of Confucianism and Daoism in the *Guan Zi*, then, one has to question if this approach to government is not simply a product of studying Zhou culture, a subject which comprised the education of the nobility for hundreds of years prior to Confucius. That Confucius did not even leave his home state of Lu until he was in his 50s, and yet still knew so much about Zhou culture, shows that the influence of Zhou-centered education was widespread, and likely well documented until "the burning of the books" during the Qin Dynasty.

The *Guan Zi* and *Dao De Jing*, however, put forth political wisdom that is wholly unique to Daoism: by bringing order and peace to oneself through non-effort, minimizing desires, and utilizing the course of nature, one will then understand how to bring order and peace to a nation. Included alongside this political guidance are instructions for bringing peace and order to oneself, internally, often employing metaphors of pacifying the nation which serve to blur and unite the differences between internal cultivation and external government. Though this strategic process begins by finding inner peace, it is nonetheless difficult to say for certain if this approach to meditation inspired the corresponding approach to government, or if the corresponding approach to government enlightened sages as to its facility in cultivating the inner domain.

Much of the inter-textual analysis in *Thread of Dao* focuses on the complementary relationship between the *Dao De Jing* and proto-Daoist *Guan Zi* texts, as they expound in subtler and more overt ways on the same principles of government and internal cultivation.[31] It appears, at times, that the *Dao De Jing* pre-supposed a familiarity with the concepts and principles in the *Guan Zi*, and was written to clarify the relationship between government and internal cultivation. At other times, it appears that the *Dao De Jing* describes, more esoterically, elements of government that the *Guan Zi* texts present more clearly as elements of internal cultivation. This, again, makes it difficult to determine which application of these principles came first – the skillful application of Dao and De in government, or the longevity and spiritual cultivation that colours every thread of Daoist philosophy.

Internal Cultivation in the *Guan Zi*

Bai Xin (Purifying the Heart-Mind)

Often collectively referred to as "the art-of the heart-mind (xin shu) texts," the *Bai Xin, Xin Shu Shang, Xin Shu Xia,* and *Nei Ye* are the earliest available examples of Daoist methods for internal cultivation. Given its emphasis on more external matters of leadership, the *Bai Xin* may be the earliest of these four texts. Of the proto-Daoist *Guan Zi* texts, the *Bai Xin* is also closest to the language in some of the more definitive chapters of the *Dao De Jing* (DDJ), especially DDJ chapters one, two, five, and nine, offering important insights into how Lao Zi's inner meanings would have been processed by those already introduced to the oral traditions from which they arose.

Aside from clarifying early internal practices, the *Bai Xin* also provides early support for later Daoist beliefs in the spirit world – beliefs which "philosophical Daoists" have often claimed to be without any

---

[31] Credit should be given Harold Roth for bringing the *Nei Ye*, its presentation of early Daoist cultivation practices, and potential pre-dating of the Dao De Jing, to the attention of most Western Daoist enthusiasts. Please see:
Roth, Harold, translator. *Original Tao: Inward Training (Nei-yeh) and the Foundations of Taoist Mysticism.* New York: Columbia University Press, 1999.

connection to early Daoist writings. The view that spirits can influence the physical world, however, is unmistakably present in lines 41-44 of the *Bai Xin*:

> The success of an army follows good fortune, and the approach of virtue depends on the individual. This is why it is said that omens and apparitions (gui) (arrive to defend) the righteousness of others. (Thus) an army must never lack righteousness.

And in line 143:

> To those who are righteous towards others, the spirits (shen, deities, gods) bring good fortune.

If the *Bai Xin* pre-dates the *Xin Shu Xia* and *Nei Ye*, it is also the first to prescribe a physical bearing for meditation, an emphasis given more weight in the *Xin Shu Xia* when it speaks of aligning the body. *Bai Xin*, lines 201-207, read:

> Turning to the left, right, front, and back, running full circle, return to the place (at the center).
> Holding to a ceremonious outward appearance (執儀服象),
> respectfully welcome that which approaches (敬迎來者).
> Those today who seek its approach require this method to (invite) Dao.
> Without soaring (into the sky), without spilling over, the destined life-force (ming) will be extended.
> Harmonize by returning to the center, where both body and pure nature (xing) are preserved.
> Be unified and without (doubt or) division.[32] This is called "knowing Dao."
> Wishing to be enveloped by it, you must unify to the furthest extent, and solidify that which is protected within.

---

[32] "Undivided," more commonly meant "無貳爾心 without doubt (undivided) in your heart," but its literal meaning is emphasized within the context of these lines of the *Bai Xin*.

"Holding to a ceremonious outward appearance (執儀服象), respectfully welcome that which approaches (敬迎來者)," means to take the appearance of someone welcoming a respected guest, and to demonstrate refined conduct. Doing so, the posture would be upright yet relaxed and dignified. As the comment on this section in *The Thread of Dao* states:

> ...this posture should be calm and dignified, but not prideful and stiff, putting the ego aside and being open to the guest. In both meditation and welcoming guests, the mind should also be bright, open, and attentive (internally and singularly attentive for the case of Daoist meditation). Guests are not welcomed ceremoniously with dull and lethargic minds, nor inattentive minds.

The line preceding this also suggests a stable and centered posture, not leaning or asymmetrical: "Left, right, front, and back, (running) full circle, they return to the place (at the center)" (line 201).

In addition to this early description of physical positioning, this section offers what may be the earliest description of mindfulness, or "inner observation (nei guan)" in Daoist literature. Lines 196-200 instruct:

> By rejecting what is close and chasing after what is far, how can one but squander their power?
> Thus it is said: "Desiring to take care of myself, I must first know my true inner state.
> By observing the universe, I investigate my own body."
> As such, comprehending this image, one thereby understands the tendencies of their true inner state.
> Knowing the tendencies of their true inner state, they will know how to nourish life.

Notably, the focus of this excerpt is a quote ("thus it is said...") from an earlier source, one which was either an early version of Lao Zi's chapter 47,[33] or likely to have influenced it, such as an ancient saying from the oral tradition.

---

[33] DDJ47 does not appear in the earliest known chapters of the *Dao De Jing*, found at Guodian. A translation of DDJ47 can be read in the comments following *Bai Xin* lines 196-200, below.

Also significant to the *Bai Xin*'s composition is its early mention of cultivating and preserving "destined life-force (ming)" and "pure nature (xing)." The cultivation of xing and ming plays a central role in later Daoist internal practices, and was mentioned early on in Zhuang Zi's (circa 350 BC) parables and fictional discourses. Whereas Zhuang Zi mentions xing and ming as important factors in the development of a Sage, the *Bai Xin* offers more direct and practical instructions for their cultivation. Given that Zhuang Zi never provides much in the way of defining xing and ming, or methods focused on their cultivation, it would appear that these topics were already understood by his contemporary audience, and so did not need reiterating. Earlier philosophical text, lost tragically to the Qin Dynasty book burnings of 213 BC, may have shown the introduction of xing and ming cultivation into the cultural sphere at the time. Thankfully the proto-Daoist *Guan Zi* texts are still able to provide a clear example of these early cultivation practices, and thus help to trace their influences to writings from this era.

Xin Shu Shang and *Xin Shu Xia*
(Art of the Heart-Mind, upper and lower volumes)

The ***Xin Shu Shang*** illustrates the symmetry between methods of ruling the kingdom, and methods of cultivating the self. This connection is considered, by Daoist initiates, an esoteric undertone of the *Dao De Jing* as emphasized in Heshang Gong's commentary around 200 AD. Scholars have long argued that such connections are largely imagination and fancy. The *Xin Shu Shang*, however, clarifies that this metaphor had been a part of the proto-Daoist tradition since at least the time of Zhuang Zi. The opening lines of the *Xin Shu Shang* read:

> In the body,
> The heart-mind holds the throne of the ruler.
> The nine apertures hold offices
> Of various public servants.
> When the heart-mind remains with Dao,
> The nine apertures act reasonably;
> When desires and euphoric feelings are plentiful,
> The eyes don't see appearances

And the ears don't hear sounds.
Thus it is said: When those above lose the Way,
Those below neglect their duties.[34]

This connection is again made clear in lines 41-42:

When scattered, it is as though a rebellion rises up within you.
When calm and still, order naturally arrives.
Force cannot widely establish such order.
Wisdom cannot formulate all strategies.

As stated in my comments on the *Xin Shu Shang*'s opening lines:

What the *Xin Shu Shang* immediately reveals about the *Dao De Jing*, is that the Sage is not only a wise counsel to the nation's presiding authority, but is also within, guiding the ruler – the heart-mind – towards sovereignty over "all under Heaven" and "the myriad things" – ie., the senses, emotions, desires, stress, impulses, and anything else which must be stabilized in order to preserve inner unity. When these things are disordered, confusion reigns, and the sovereignty of the heart-mind is imperiled. The Sage is to the ruler what the spirit's illumination is upon the heart-mind. She brings clarity, perception, and peace to the ruler. To invite the Sage, the ruler must first become stable and orderly, kind and genuine. Then the Sage will find it safe to convene with him, seeing that the ruler is capable of giving up tyrannical power and instead following Dao. The art of the heart-mind is not simply a way to find peace, but a way to bring forth the spiritual intelligence – the Sage.

This connection appears again in lines 41-42:

When scattered, it is as though a rebellion rises up within you.
When calm and still, order naturally arrives.
Force cannot widely establish such order.
Wisdom cannot formulate all strategies.

---

[34] *Xin Shu Shang*, lines 1-11

Introduction

The Yellow Emperor's Classic on Internal Medicine, Plain Questions (Huang Di Nei Jing, Su Wen) contains, perhaps later,[35] expansions of the administrative metaphor found in the *Xin Shu Shang*. For example, in chapter eight of this text we find a more detailed illustration of the *Xin Shu Shang*'s opening lines:

> Qi Bo replied...
> The heart holds the office of the ruler;
> It brings forth spiritual intelligence.[36]
> The lungs hold the office of the grand tutor;
> They bring forth order and moderation.
> The liver holds the office of the general;
> It brings forth ambitions and planning.
> The gallbladder holds the office of the rectifier;
> It brings forth decisiveness.
> The pericardium (enclosure of the heart) holds the office of minister and envoy;
> It brings forth joy and pleasure.
> The spleen and stomach hold the office in charge of grain storage;
> They bring forth the five tastes (flavours).
> The large intestine holds the office of transportation and distribution;
> It brings forth change and transformation.
> The small intestine holds the office in charge of receiving bounty;
> It brings forth things which have been transformed and processed.
> The kidneys hold the office in charge of increasing power;
> They bring forth ability and expertise.
> The triple burner holds the office of regulating channels;
> It brings forth pathways for water.
> The urinary bladder holds the office of regional administrator;
> Bodily fluids are stored in it, and when their qi has been transformed, they are brought forth.

---

[35] Scholars generally date the *Nei Jing Su Wen* to as early as 200 BC, though it's traditional attribution to the Yellow Emperor would date it circa 2600 BC.

[36] See lines 1-2 of the *Xin Shu Shang*, and my above comment on the Sage as a representation of spiritual intelligence.

All of these twelve offices must not lose their connection to each other.
Thus, when the ruler is enlightened, the subordinates are peaceful.
Cultivating life in this way, longevity ensues
And until the end of the era, there will be no danger.
Thereby all under heaven will greatly flourish.
If the ruler is not enlightened, the subordinates are endangered.
They seal up the paths of communication, and the body is greatly injured.
Cultivating life in this way brings disaster.
Ruling the world in such a way endangers the ancestral heritage.
Be careful of this! Be careful of this![37]

As the heart-mind, which also houses the spirit, brings peace to the body's subordinate organs and functions, the art, or method, of the heart-mind is not only for the benefit of the mind, but also to generate the complete harmony of the physical and spiritual self. It is a method of ruling the body through the spirit. By dissolving internal forces that can destabilize the spirit, for example the energy of anger and its ability to wrest decision making power from the spirit, practices in the *Xin Shu* aid in re-establishing homeostasis and thereby preventing myriads of illnesses. Given that Classical Chinese Medicine rightfully held prevention as superior to all other forms of treatment, the art of the heart-mind was duly revered as a profound and enriching technique of self-healing and preventative health-care.

It should be noted that the modern equivalent term for *xin shu* (心術) is *xin fa* (心法). The shared meaning between *shu* and *fa* is method, or technique, while *shu* also means skill and art, and *fa* also means law, principle, and dharma. *Fa* appears in the titles of a few other books in the Guan Zi, for example "Principles of War" (Bing Fa) and "Principles of Law" (Fa Fa).

The ancient commentary included in the *Guan Zi* as part of the *Xin Shu Shang* offers a number of clarifications of Daoist concepts, such

---

[37] From *Huang Di Nei Jing, Su Wen*, chapter eight. Translated by Dan G. Reid

as the relationship between Dao and De, and the interchangeable use of Virtue (De, 德) and attainment (de, 得).

> Virtue is the abode of Dao.
> When things attain (Virtue), they live.
> Being alive, they can know the office of Dao's essence.
> Thus, Virtue (De) also means "attainment (de)."
> As for this attainment, it is called "attaining the causality."
> The effortlessness of this (causality) is called "Dao."
> The abode of Dao is called "Virtue."
> Thus, between Dao and Virtue, there is no space.
> For this reason, it is said "they are not separate."
> (XSS 113-121)

That such an early commentary on the *Xin Shu Shang* exists shows its popularity at the time. Commentaries are most often written when a text has reached a considerable audience and thereby generated enough discussion that someone more familiar with the subject eventually seeks to address this audience, especially when that audience has spread beyond the reach of those immersed in the traditions from which the teachings arose. For example, detailed commentaries on the *Dao De Jing* did not appear for nearly 500 years after it was written, and commentaries on the *Huang Di Nei Jing* did not appear for nearly 1000 years after it was written,[38] despite the interest and questions that these texts were sure to have inspired.

The *Xin Shu Shang*'s renown may also be evident in the writing of Confucian scholar Xun Zi (313-238 BC), who shows a great deal of influence from Daoist thought, though he is also critical of Lao Zi.[39] In his chapter "Removing Obstacles," (c. 250 BC), Xun Zi echoes the opening lines of the *Xin Shu Shang*, referring to the mind as the

---

[38] These are conservative estimates, dating the *Dao De Jing* to circa 250 BC (first commentary, by Heshang Gong, circa 200 AD), and the *Huang Di Nei Jing* to circa 200 BC (first full annotated version of the *Su Wen*, by Wang Bing, completed 762 AD). We could otherwise say the first commentary on the *Huang Di Nei Jing* was written around 200 AD, citing the *Huang Di Ba Shi Yi Nan Jing (Classic of the Yellow Emperor's 81 Quandaries)*, though this short text is more an expansion on select points of confusion, rather than a complete commentary. Regardless, the *Nan Jing* did not appear for another 400 years after the *Su Wen* was completed.

[39] See *Xun Zi*, chapter 17, "Discourse on Heaven."

ruler of the body ("and the host of spiritual intelligence"). He then continues in a fashion that further reflects the teachings of inner unification found throughout the proto-Daoist *Guan Zi* texts:

> The mind is the ruler of the body, and the host of spiritual intelligence… A mind that branches out in many directions knows nothing; a mind that is not level is not acute; a mind that is divided is doubtful and confused. But for a mind with focused scrutiny, the myriad things can come together in its understanding; for in oneself is a unity that runs though all categories.[40]

As with the *Bai Xin*, the **Xin Shu Xia** shows that body alignment, if not sitting meditation, was in fact part of the early heart-mind cultivation techniques. Whereas the *Upper Xin Shu* begins by focusing on aligning the heart-mind so as to bring order to one's 'inner kingdom', the *Lower Xin Shu* begins by stating, "When the bodily form is not aligned (正: straight, aligned, upright), Virtue does not approach." So, just as one can bring peace and order to their nation by bringing peace and order to themselves, they can also bring peace and order to themselves internally by bringing peace and order (alignment) to their body, externally. The *Xin Shu Xia* further develops connections between internal and external government, focusing primarily on self cultivation as a means to establishing order in one's kingdom, both literally and figuratively.

Added to this metaphor is that of governing the heart-mind and body according to the patterns of Heaven and Earth. The *Xin Shu Xia* summarizes these analogies by closing with the saying "For what is above, study the Heavens; for what is below, study the Earth."

Most, though not all, of the *Xin Shu Xia* is found dotted throughout the *Nei Ye*, which appears to be either a redaction of the lower ("xia") *Xin Shu*, or to have developed out of the same oral tradition. The inclusion of the *Xin Shu Xia* in *Guan Zi*, regardless of its many similarities to the *Nei Ye*, was possibly due to it having many duplicates as a self-contained book, likely alongside the *Xin Shu Shang*. The *Nei Ye*, then, may have been collated by Liu Xiang, and assisting

---

[40] Please see my commentary on the opening lines of the *Xin Shu Shang* for more of this excerpt.

scholars, from a multitude of scattered book fragments on internal cultivation. This might explain why the *Nei Ye* (book 49) is separated from the *Xin Shu Shang* (book 36), *Xin Shu Xia* (book 37), and *Bai Xin* (book 38), which appear consecutively in the *Guan Zi*. It might also explain the drastic reconfiguration of shared lines, variations in terminology, and why the sequence of these shared lines is more fluid in the *Xin Shu Xia*, where ideas follow more readily from the developing support of their preceding lines. This sequence appears as follows, outlined by the line groupings in *The Thread of Dao*:

1) When the body is aligned, the Virtue of Dao approaches and the body fills with qi. The self is thereby transcended as the body and mind function like Heaven and Earth. (lines 1-20)
2) This transcendence of self brings all things together and makes them peaceful in their unity. Those who attain this unity within are blessed with an awareness of the causes of calamity and good fortune. (lines 21-31)
3) It is not through thinking that one attains this inner unity, but by consolidating qi like numinous beings. Through this unity, the junzi (gentleman) gains greater wisdom and can rule the myriad things. (lines 32-47)
4) By the same technique, the Sage brings about change, order, and balance through wu wei, both in the nation and in the heart-minds of the people, ensuring lasting peace. (lines 48-64)
5) In doing so, the Sage's techniques are nearly unnoticeable. (lines 65-69)
6) Describes advantages of practicing this technique: a healthier body and more acute perception. (lines 70-79)
7) Describes disadvantages of not practicing this technique: great difficulties in your interactions with others. (lines 80-99)
8) Explains the effect of strong emotions and how to mitigate them with poetry, music, courtesy, respect, and silence. (lines 100-108)
9) Explains the important role of intention in practicing the art of the heart-mind, reiterating the physical benefits of this technique and that it is was developed by studying Heaven and Earth. (lines 109-126)

The *Xin Shu Xia*'s very inclusion in the *Guan Zi*, despite so many resemblances to the *Nei Ye*, and being much shorter, suggests that it held a significant degree of import, and perhaps influence, in the philosophical history that produced the *Guan Zi*. If the *Nei Ye* was not compiled by Liu Xiang, it likely appeared a few decades after the *Xin Shu* so as to include additional teachings commonly associated with the "techniques of the heart-mind." Further suggesting that the *Xin Shu Xia* was the earlier of these two texts: by comparing lines 80-99 of the *Xin Shu Xia* to lines 216-230 of the *Nei Ye*, the *Nei Ye* appears to have been written from a corrupted copy of *Xin Shu Xia*, with the writer attempting to make sense of a typo by changing other words to fit the meaning. More analysis on this can be found in my comments on *Xin Shu Xia*, lines 80-99.

One other plausible theory may be that, while the *Xin Shu Shang* was later expanded upon with a commentary, the *Xin Shu Xia* was instead developed into a longer treatise as the *Nei Ye*.

Nei Ye (Internal Cultivation)

The *Nei Ye* conveys the same internal cultivation tradition transmitted by the *Bai Xin* and *Xin Shu I&II*, while going further into matters of physical longevity and spiritual awakening. All four of these texts teach "the heart-mind technique" of allowing the mind to settle in calm, through non-obstruction. This technique is the foundation that leads to the energetic and spiritual transformations described in nei gong and nei dan (internal elixer) traditions – transformations also largely intimated in the *Bai Xin* and *Xin Shu*.

The heart-mind technique, aside from its role in nei dan, is taught as a means to bring "spiritual intelligence" (shen ming) – a facet of consciousness in which greater perception, and unity with Dao, are made possible by the spirit's illumination of the mind. Another benefit of cultivating "spiritual intelligence" is increased emotional-intelligence – one's capacity to recognize their own emotions and mitigate the negative effect of these emotions in their lives. Such negative effects might include limitations on impulse control, on one's ability to differentiate sense and reality, and on self-actualization. Emotional intelligence is, of course, important for rulers, generals, and other leaders who must determine the reality of a situation before deciding appropriate courses of action or non-action. To see the situation clearly, and act according to the time, rather than according to anger or desire, leaders are advised to first uncover the clear and calm center within the heart-mind. From this center, spiritual intelligence may arise, and they will not only see with "clear vision (明 ming, enlightenment)," but will cultivate the virtue needed to lead successfully, and the physical longevity needed to realize this success.

According to the *Nei Ye* and later Daoists, reaching this enlightenment and "ultimate spiritual intelligence" requires the transmutation of essence (jing) to energy-breath (qi), and energy-breath to spirit (shen). This practice is referred to in modern times as 'nei *gong*, internal work/cultivation', sharing the same meaning as nei *ye*: internal occupation/work/cultivation. We see the ancient theory and practices of this tradition throughout the *Nei Ye*. For example, the cultivation of jing-essence in lines 91-99:

> If you can be aligned, you can be silent.
> Then you can be settled.
> When the heart-mind settles in its very center,
> The ears and eyes become acute and perceptive
> And the four limbs become solid and stable.
> You can thereby house the pure and vital essence.
> This pure essence
> Is the pure essence of energy-breath.
> The way of energy-breath is to flourish

In lines 135-145:

> There is a spirit that alights in the body.
> One moment it leaves, and one moment it arrives.
> No one can comprehend it.
> Losing it assures disorder;
> Obtaining it assures order;
> Respectfully purify its dwelling place,
> And the pure and vital essence will naturally return.
> If planning and thinking about vital essence,
> Calm any thoughts about governing it.

Straightening your form, revere and honour it.
Essence will then become settled.

And in lines 174-191:

When pure and vital essence remains, life-energy spontaneously emerges.
One is then externally peaceful and radiant,
(Allowing them to) conceal this surging wellspring within.
As a flood of harmony and peacefulness,
It becomes an abyss of energy-breath.
If this abyss does not dry up,
The four limbs solidify;
If this wellspring is not exhausted,
The nine bodily orifices are free and unblocked.
One can then absorb all of Heaven and Earth,
Covering the four seas.
Within, one's intention is not vacillating;
Externally, they are without affliction and calamity.
Their heart-mind is maintained, within,
And their body is maintained, externally.
They do not meet upon calamity,
Nor do they encounter hostile people.
We call them "Sages."

The transmutation of jing-essence into qi can be seen, for example, in lines 1-22:

It is invariably the essence of things
Which gives them life.
Below, it gives birth to the five grains;
Above, it aligns the stars;
Circulating between Heaven and Earth,
We call it ghosts and spirits;
Collected within the bosom,
We call them Sages.

Introduction

As a result (of essence), the *energy-breath* of common people (becomes):
Bright! As though rising up to the Heavens;
Dark! As though entering the depths;
Spacious! As though within an ocean;
Enclosed! As though entirely self-contained.
As a result, this energy-breath:
Cannot be stopped with effort
Yet can be made peaceful through virtue;
Cannot be called over with a shout
Yet can be welcomed with a harmonious tone.
Honour it and guard it within. Do not neglect it.
This is called ripening virtue.
When virtue has ripened, wisdom comes forth
And the myriad things attain fruition.

The cultivation of energy-breath into spirit-like wisdom and enlightenment can be said to correlate with the transmutation of energy into spirit.[41] This is also found throughout the *Nei Ye*. For example, in lines 235-240:

By consolidating energy-breath (and becoming) spirit-like,
The myriad things perfect their existence.
Can you consolidate it? Can you unify it?
Can you, without divining by yarrow stalks
Know what is fortunate and what is perilous?
Can you stop (peril from arriving)? Can you make it cease?

In lines 249-253:

When the four limbs are aligned,
The blood and energy-breath are tranquil;
When unifying intention and consolidating the heart,

---

[41] See, for example, the sayings attributed to Lu Dongbin (Ancestor Lu) translated in Thomas Cleary's *Vitality, Energy, Spirit: A Taoist Sourcebook* (Shambhala Publications Inc. Boston: 1991). In the *Qingwei Sanpin Jing*, we find, "Spirit.. in humans.. is wisdom and intelligence, innate knowledge and capacity; it is the government of vitality and energy, awareness and understanding."

The ears and eyes do not indulge,
Yet what is far off is as though near.

And lines 317-326:

Boldly expand the heart and mind;
Broadly expand energy-breath.
With your body peaceful and unmoving,
You can preserve unification and reject 10,000 annoyances.
Seeing profit, it will not seduce you;
Seeing danger, it will not frighten you.
Spacious, comfortable, yet attentive and considerate.
When in solitude, enjoying yourself,
This is called "qi floating like clouds."
Your intention then functions like that of Heaven.

To understand shen ming (spiritual brilliance/spiritual intelligence), it helps to think of shen-spirit as a divine essence, rather than an entity in the way that spirit is understood in the West. Essential to consciousness, shen is often translated for Chinese medical purposes as "mind," though it contains a wider applicability in Daoist traditions. Shen ming could be translated as spiritual enlightenment/illumination, though to avoid complicating the term with Buddhist notions of enlightenment, spiritual intelligence seems more fitting (*ming* means literally "to see clearly," and "the light of the sun and moon").

The term shen ming is found elsewhere as referring to guardian spirits, "spiritual lights," which act like emissaries from Heaven, protecting and developing those who cultivate "inner attainment" or "inner Virtue." While early Daoist definitions of shen ming are elusive, its function resembles the ancient Chinese theory of the three yang-spirits (hun) and seven yin-spirits (po) that all people are said to be born with. The hun and po spirits are integral to life within the physical body, while loss of these spirits causes spiritual and physical illness. Shen ming, on the other hand, is not intrinsic to each individual, but comes and goes according to how one keeps their inner domain, like small birds taking rest where it is peaceful, or Daoist gods visiting the sanctity of a Daoist temple. A similarity appears between the shen ming guardians and the shen ming awakening, as they both seem to take up residence when a person is purified of emotions and cravings. For example, Heshang Gong comments on chapter 16 of the *Dao De Jing*:

> *"The way of impartiality shows the way of a king"*
> Impartial, honourable, and unselfish, one can become king of all under Heaven. By governing and aligning the body, form is unified. Countless spiritual lights then assemble in the body.

It may also be this connection between spiritual intelligence and spiritual lights that the *Nei Ye* refers to in lines 129-150:

> The ultimate spiritual intelligence:
> Luminous! It understands the myriad things.
> When, in the center, righteousness is guarded without err
> And things do not disturb the senses,
> Nor do the senses disturb the heart.
> This is called inner attainment.
>
> There is a spirit that alights in the body.
> One moment it leaves, and one moment it arrives.
> No one can comprehend it.
> Losing it assures disorder;
> Obtaining it assures order.
> Respectfully purify its dwelling place,
> And the pure and vital essence will naturally return.
> If planning and thinking about vital essence,
> Calm any thoughts about governing it.
> Straightening your form, revere and honour it.
> Essence will then become settled.
> Obtaining it, do not give up.
> Do not indulge the ears and eyes.
> Keeping the heart and mind without any other designs,
> And an aligned heart-mind within,
> The myriad things will (then) fall into accord.

The *Xin Shu Shang* also advises this approach to inviting shen ming:

> Heaven is described as empty, earth is described as still.

From this, (one should learn) not to boast.
Purify the temple, open the gates,
Eradicate egotism, and do not speak.
Spiritual intelligence will then reside.
When scattered, it is as though a rebellion rises up within you;
When calm and still, order naturally arrives.
Force cannot widely establish such order.
Wisdom cannot formulate all strategies.
(*Xin Shu Shang*, lines 38-42)

We can see from these examples that the internal development practice (nei gong) of cultivating the "three treasures" (jing, qi, and shen) originated long before the first Daoist orders and temples appeared, following Zhang Daoling's creation of the Way of the Celestial Masters in 142 AD. These excerpts also show that the meditation styles of later Daoist orders are wholly connected to indigenous Chinese sources, and are not as influenced by Buddhist and other Indian traditions, as commonly believed.

Guan Zi's Influence on the *Guigu Zi* (*Ghost Valley Master*)

The *Guigu Zi* (鬼谷子), or "(The Teachings of) Ghost Valley Master," is another early text showing obvious links to the cultivation traditions found in the *Guan Zi* – one that uses language even more similar to the *Xin Shu* and *Nei Ye* than that found in the *Dao De Jing* or *Nei Jing*. This text is said to have been written by a late Warring States period hermit named Guigu Zi, and offers shrewd advice for political communications and strategy, interspersed with advice on Daoist self-cultivation, especially for the purposes of enhancing perception and mental capacity. Available evidence can only date the *Guigu Zi* to as early as the 4th century AD,[42] however, it borrowed a great deal, nearly word for word, from *Guan Zi's* book 55, *Nine Adherences*, in its own chapter 12, "[nine] Talismanic Sayings."[43] "Talismanic Sayings (chapter 12)" is followed by seven chapters enti-

---

[42] Broschat, Michael Robert. *Guiguzi: A Textual Study and Translation*. University of Washington Ph.D. Thesis, 1985
[43] Credit to Broschat (ibid) for pointing this out as well.

tled *Ben Jing Yin Fu Qi Shu*[44] (本經陰符七術), or *Foundational Text: Seven Techniques of Yin Talisman*.

The influence of Guan Zi's internal-cultivation texts is unmistakeable in the first three of the *Seven Techniques of Yin Talisman*, where the term "art of the heart-mind" (xin shu) is used to describe the technique of settling the mind in order to unify the will, much as the *Xin Shu* and *Nei Ye* recommend, alongside numerous mentions of attaining oneness. The *Guigu Zi* is useful for the study of the *Guan Zi*'s "art of the heart-mind," as it expands on these teachings and offers some confirmation as to the meaning of "oneness" in the *Guan Zi*, and elsewhere, where it refers to uniting facets of consciousness and energy. The first three chapters of the *Seven Techniques of Yin Talisman* appear below[45] as a supplement to further understand related passages in the *Xin Shu* and *Nei Ye*.[46]

From the *Ghost-Valley Master's (Guigu Zi's)*, "Seven Techniques of Yin Talisman"
Translated by Dan G. Reid.

盛神法五龍
Broadening the Spirit in Accordance with the Five Dragons[47] (technique #1)

盛神者，中有五氣，神為之長，心為之舍，德為之大；養神之所，歸諸道。

Within the broadened spirit are five energies. Spirit leads them; the heart-mind houses them; Virtue expands them. The place to cultivate spirit is, ultimately, Dao

---

[44] Note the similarity in title to the *Ying Fu Jing*, attributed to *The Yellow Emperor*.
[45] Translated by Dan G. Reid
[46] See, especially, *Nei Ye*, lines 91-128.
[47] While "five dragons" is a metaphor for the "five energies: will, thought, spirit, and virtue," mentioned in this chapter, it may also suggest the five clawed dragon which was symbolic of the emperor. As with *Xin Shu Shang*, the "five dragon" technique is based in the central authority of the heart-mind.

道者,天地之始,一其紀也。物之所造,天之所生,包宏無形,化氣先天地而成,莫見其形,莫知其名,謂之神靈。
Dao preceded Heaven and Earth. It unifies the many threads. It is the development of things, and the emergence of Nature. Without form, it contains all vastness. Its transformative energy precedes the formation of Heaven and Earth. Nothing can see its form; none can know its name. It is called Divine Power (Shen Ling).

故道者,神明之源,一其化端,是以德養五氣,心能得一,乃有其術。
Thus, Dao is the source of spiritual intelligence. It unifies the disparate transformations. Thereby, Virtue fosters the five energies, and the heart-mind can bring about their unification. This is the art (of the heart-mind).

術者,心氣之道所由舍者,神乃為之使。九竅十二舍者,氣之門戶,心之總攝也。
This art entails the method of housing the heart-mind's energy. Spirit, then becomes a functionary. The nine orifices[48] and twelve houses[49] are the gates and passages of energy and the collective assistants of the heart-mind.

生受於天,謂之真人;真人者,與天為一。而知之者,內修練而知之,謂之聖人;
Life as received from Heaven is called the true person. The true person is one with Heaven (Nature). Those who practice internal cultivation (nei xiu) according to this knowledge are called sages.

聖人者,以類知之。故人與生生一出於化物。知類在竅,有所疑惑,通於心術,心無其術,必有不通。其通也,五氣得養,務在舍神,此謂之化。
Sages understand through categories. Thus people live according to the unified life energy that transforms things. Categories are

---

[48] The eyes, ears, nostrils, mouth, genitals, and anus
[49] Apparently referring to the 12 organs and corresponding 12 major meridians used in acupuncture. These are: lungs, heart, pericardium, spleen, kidney, liver, large intestine, small intestine, triple burner, stomach, bladder, and gall-bladder.

known through the orifices. If they cause doubt and confusion, this can be transcended with the art of the heart-mind (xin shu). If the heart-mind is without this technique, it will not transcend (doubt and confusion). If it transcends (doubt and confusion), the five energies are successfully nurtured. The objective is housing spirit. This is called transformation.

化有五氣者，志也、思也、神也、德也；神其一長也。靜和者，養氣。氣得其和，四者不衰。四邊威勢無不為，存而舍之，是謂神化。歸於身，謂之真人。

Transformation involves five energies: will, thought, spirit, and Virtue.[50] Spirit is their unifying leader. Silence and harmony nurture energy.[51] When energy attains harmony, these four energies do not weaken. When there is nothing that the power and influence of these four facets does not do, they remain and take up lodging. This is called spiritual transformation. Returning (the five energies to their original state) within a person, we call them a true person.

真人者，同天而合道，執一而養產萬類，懷天心，施德養，無為以包志慮思意而行威勢者也。士者，通達之神盛，乃能養志。

The true person is merged with Heaven (Nature) and connected to Dao. Holding to the unity (of will, thought, spirit, and Virtue[52]), they nurture and produce the myriad categories of things. Carrying the heart-mind of Nature in their breast, they act with nurturing Virtue. Taking no action, they consolidate will and intention, thought and contemplation, before moving with force and power. The student who reaches this understanding broadens the spirit, and can then cultivate will.[53]

---

[50] The fifth energy is presumably that of the heart-mind, as mentioned in the following "spirit tortoise" technique.

[51] "Energy," here and in the following sentence, may also refer to the energy of the heart-mind.

[52] See above, "Spirit is their unifying leader."

[53] The description of "oneness" in this chapter, as it relates to power and transcending doubt, offers insight into the oral traditions behind chapter 39 of the *Dao De Jing*. DDJ39 reads:

The Thread of Dao

In the beginning was the attainment of Oneness

Heaven attained Oneness
And became clear
Earth attained Oneness
And became serene
Gods attained Oneness
And became spiritually powerful (ling)
Valleys attained Oneness
And became full
The myriad things attained Oneness
And were born
Lords and kings attained Oneness
And all under heaven became loyal

Then occurred the following

Heaven, lacking the cause of its clarity
Began to tremble and split open
Earth, lacking the cause of its serenity
Became fearful and began to gush forth
The gods, lacking the cause of their spiritual power
Became fearful and stopped moving
The valley, lacking the cause of its fullness
Became fearful and began to drain
The myriad things, lacking the cause of their life
Became fearful and began to die out
The lords and kings, lacking the cause of their being praised and elevated
Became fearful and began to fall

Therefore, value the lowest and treat it as the root source
Elevate the low and treat it as the foundation
This is why lords and kings call themselves orphans, widows, and "no hub-of-the-wheel"
Is this not treating the lowest as the root source?
Is it not?
Thus, they are sent several palanquins without a palanquin

Have no desires for fine jade
Nor for cheap necklaces and stones

(Translated by Dan G. Reid)

養志法靈龜
Cultivating Will in Accordance with the Spirit-Tortoise[54] (technique #2)

養志者，心氣之思不達也。有所欲，志存而思之。志者，欲之使也。欲多則心散，心散則志衰，志衰則思不達。

Develop the will when heart-mind-energy and thoughts do not reach (their goal). When you have a desire, the will appears as you think about it. Will is the envoy of desire. When there are many desires, the heart-mind is scattered. When the heart-mind is scattered, the will falters. When the will falters, thinking does not reach (the objective).

故心氣一則欲不徨，欲不徨則志意不衰，志意不衰則思理達矣。

Thus, when the heart-mind's energy is unified, desire is not wavering. When desire is not wavering, will and intention do not falter. When will and intention do not falter, thinking and reasoning reach (their objective).

理達則和通，和通則亂氣不煩於胸中，故內以養氣，外以知人。養志則心通矣，知人則職分明矣。

When reason reaches (its objective), knowledge is effective. When knowledge is effective, chaotic energy does not cause turmoil within the breast. Thus, internally, energy is cultivated; and externally, other people are understood. By cultivating the will, the heart-mind is effective. By understanding other people, (appropriate) divisions of labour are clearly perceived.

將欲用之於人，必先知其養氣志。知人氣盛衰，而養其志氣，察其所安，以知其所能。

If you wish (to know) the usefulness of others, you must first know their (ability to) cultivate the energy of the will. To know if others' energy is abundant or lacking, and if they cultivate the

---

[54] The tortoise may have been chosen to represent the steady perseverance of this technique.

energy of their will, examine their peace and stability. Thereby, know their ability.

志不養，則心氣不固；心氣不固，則思慮不達，思慮不達，則志意不實。志意不實，則應對不猛；應對不猛，則志失而心氣虛；志失而心氣虛，則喪其神矣；神喪，則彷彿；彷彿，則參會不一。

If will is not cultivated, the heart-mind's energy is not consolidated. If the heart-mind's energy is not consolidated, then thought and consideration is not penetrating. If thought and consideration are not penetrating, will and intention will not be genuine. If will and intention are not genuine, then response is not forceful. If response is not forceful, then will is lost and the heart-mind's energy is depleted. This destroys the spirit. If spirit is destroyed, there is aimlessness. If there is aimlessness, gathering together does not unify.

養志之始，務在安己；己安，則志意實堅；志意實堅，則威勢不分，神明常固守，乃能分之。

To begin cultivating the will, try to stabilize yourself in peacefulness. Stabilizing yourself in peacefulness, the will and intention will be genuine and firm. When the will and intention are genuine and firm, power and influence will not be separated. If spiritual intelligence is always firmly protected, you will be able to separate (others' power and influence over you).[55]

---

[55] Technique #4 is entitled "Dividing Power in Accordance with the Crouching Bear" and deals with dividing the power of others. The vast majority of the *Guigu Zi* addresses diplomacy and managing inter-personal power relationships.

實意法螣蛇
Consolidating Intention in Accordance with the Soaring Snake[56] (technique #3)

實意者，氣之慮也。心欲安靜，慮欲深遠；心安靜則神策生，慮深遠則計謀成；神策生則志不可亂，計謀成則功不可間。

Consolidating intention refers to contemplative energy. The heart-mind desires peace and quiet. Contemplation desires depth and breadth. When the heart-mind is peaceful and silent, spiritual foresight[57] arises. When contemplation is deep and broad, strategic plans are refined. When spiritual foresight arises, the will should not be disturbed. When strategic plans are refined, success will not be denied.

意慮定則心遂安，心遂安則所行不錯，神自得矣。得則凝。

When intention and contemplation are settled, the heart-mind becomes peaceful. When the heart-mind becomes peaceful, its tendencies are not problematic. The spirit is then contented. When the spirit is contented, it condenses.

識氣寄姦邪得而倚之，詐謀得而惑之；言無由心矣。故信心術守真一而不化，待人意慮之交會者，聽之候也；

If the energy of knowledge is relied upon, corruption creeps in and is then relied upon. Deceptive plans ensue, resulting in fear and doubt. Words then no longer follow from the heart. Thus, you must trust in the technique of the heart-mind (xin shu). Preserve true unity and do not change. Wait for others' intentions and contemplations to come together, and patiently listen to them.

計謀者，存亡之樞機。慮不會，則聽不審矣；候之不得，計謀失矣，則意無所信、虛而無實。故計謀之慮，務在實意；實意必從心術始。

---

[56] Xun Zi (d.238 BC) wrote: "The eyes cannot focus on two things clearly. The ears cannot listen to two things acutely. The soaring snake has no feet, yet flies, while the wu rodent has five feet yet fails."

[57] Ce (策) commonly referred to divining stalks in ancient texts and so also meant "forecast."

Strategic planning is the hinge between survival and peril. If ideas are not organized, their reception will not be thorough. Patient listening is then not obtained, and strategic planning is lost. Intention then loses trustworthiness, and becomes empty and disingenuous. Thus, in strategic thinking and plans, the aim is to have genuine intention. Genuine intention must begin with the heart-mind technique (xin shu).

無為而求，安靜五臟，和通六腑，精神魂魄固守不動，乃能內視反聽，定志慮之太虛，待神往來。
Seek, through non-doing, stable tranquility of the five internal organs,[58] and harmony throughout the six bowels.[59] When the vital-essence, spirit (shen), yang-spirits (hun), and yin-spirits (po) are steadfastly guarded and unmoving, you can internalize your gaze and return your listening; settle your will and contemplation on cosmic emptiness, and attend to the spirit's leaving and returning.

以觀天地開闢，知萬物所造化，見陰陽之終始，原人事之政理。不出戶而知天下，不窺牖而見天道；不見而命，不行而至；是謂道知。以通神明，應於無方，而神宿矣。
Thereby, observe the opening and closing of Heaven and Earth, understand the developing changes of the myriad things, see the beginning and end of yin and yang, and determine the source of governing human affairs. Without going out the door, know all under Heaven. Without glancing out the window, see the Dao of Heaven. Not seeing, yet commanding. Not travelling, yet arriving. This is called "knowing Dao." Thereby, spiritual intelligence pervades. Responding without rule, the spirit takes its lodging.

The above three chapters from the *Guigu Zi* provide a detailed description of embracing Oneness which will serve in helping to understand its meaning throughout the *Guan Zi*, *Dao De Jing*, *Heshang Gong Commentary on the Dao De Jing*, and other ancient Daoist writings.

---

[58] Liver, heart, spleen, lungs, and kidneys
[59] Stomach, small intestine, large intestine, gallbladder, urinary bladder, and "triple heater"

Having read these chapters, readers will no doubt find them elucidating while reading *The Thread of Dao*.

Will, Intention, and Thought

Also important to understanding these texts are the differences between will (志, zhi), intention (意, yi), and thought (思, si). As Guigu Zi points out, "will is a functionary of desire." Will is essentially the energy, power, and effort of resolve. It is associated with the kidneys – the same place where jing, the basic energy that fuels the body, develops. Will is also the energy associated with the drive to reach goals and improve one's station in life. It should not be imbalanced by the fire and joy of the heart, nor depleted by the spontaneity of the liver. Balanced and "genuine," the will is effective and lasting. As Guigu Zi points out in technique #2: *"When there are many desires, the heart-mind is scattered. When the heart-mind is scattered, the will falters. When the will falters, thinking does not reach (the objective)."* This is also reflected in Lao Zi's DDJ3:

> Therefore, the Sage's government
> Empties the heart-mind and enriches the stomach
> Softens the will and strengthens the bones
> People then remain uncontrived and without [excessive] desires
> While the scheming [mind does] not dare to act
> Act by not acting
> And everything will fall into place

While using similar semantics, the "softening" of the will mentioned here is part of reducing desires – softening the inner urge to satisfy one's desires – rather than weakening the will as an intrinsic capacity or faculty. Further, though Lao Zi uses the term "ruo (弱, literally 'weakening')," it should be understood that Lao Zi uses the terms "weak and strong" to suggest what would later be described as "yin and yang" respectively, favouring the "weak" – in other words "flexible" and adaptable – in every example of this contrast. The "weakening" here is more like a person relaxing their body in order to wriggle out of an attacker's hold, in this case the hold of their desires.

According to Wu Dang Chen,[60] the quality of intention is affected by one's desires and emotional stability, which will determine its positive or negative quality, i.e., whether one's intention is genuine, kind, etc. This may explain Lao Zi's comments in DDJ3 about emptying the heart-mind, enriching the *stomach*, and softening the will, for the intention is said to reside in the spleen,[61] associated with earth, the colour yellow, and perhaps the Daoist alchemical "yellow court" located at the same level as the spleen.[62] As Guan Zi's Xin Shu texts illustrate, 'unity' is attained by going beyond the thoughts and arriving at intention. This is to dissolve the heart-mind's "decisions" and allow it to again become spontaneous and open, rather than closed and subject to the limitations of thought. "Act by not acting, and everything will fall into place" – allow the intention to settle until it becomes "genuine" and naturally consolidates the qi, heart-mind, hun (internal yang-spirits), and po (internal yin-spirits). When this is achieved, thoughts may disappear like stars outshone by the morning sun.

While intention generally refers to awareness and focus, the *Ling Shu Jing (Hinge of the Spirit Classic)* volume of the *Yellow Emperor's Classic of Internal Medicine (Huang Di Nei Jing)* describes the relationship of intention and will as follows:

> That which relies on things is called the heart-mind (xin). What the heart-mind recalls is called intention (yi, notion). When the intention remains in a particular place, this is called will (zhi). What comes from the will as it processes and transforms is called thought (si). When thought travels a great distance (as though in search of its) beloved, this is called contemplation (lu). When contemplation arrives at its location, this is called wisdom (zhi).[63]

---

[60] 14th generation Wu Dang Zhang Sanfeng lineage holder; 25th generation Long Men (Dragon Gate) Daoist Priest; President and founder of the Daoist Association, USA. See Wu Dang Chen's youtube.com channel for weekly sermons.

[61] In Chinese medicine, the spleen and stomach are yin and yang counterparts, respectively.

[62] This is not to say that focus should be on the spleen, as transformation of the will and intention are naturally occurring benefits of clear-minded focus on the lower dantien (just below the navel), or simply on emptiness.

[63] See the commentary section on the *Nei Ye*, lines 1-22, below, for more of this excerpt. From Ling Shu Jing, chapter eight.

In this description of cognitive process, *yi* might be better translated as "perceiving" or "conceiving," while *zhi* seems closer to a static or accepted perception of reality, a sort of vague conception or "notion" that gives rise to thought, contemplation, and hopefully wisdom. Notably, wisdom and comprehension (zhi) is also associated with the kidneys in Classical Chinese Medicine – an association that could also be attributed to the power (will) of the mind to focus until reaching understanding.

Such a delineation of cognition is also found in Buddhist philosophies of cognition which seek to deconstruct our perceptions of reality in order to transcend the illusions of this cognition:

> Ordinary mentation is bound up with expectations, judgments, and desires. The Buddhist philosophical term used for describing the state of ordinary mentation is *prapañca* (lit. 'fabrication,' usually translated as 'conceptual proliferation')[see *Samyutta Nikāya*, IV, 72]. We don't simply apprehend an object. Rather, we apprehend it as the locus of a multiplicity of associations: in seeing a tree we perceive an entity made of trunk, branches, and foliage but also something that can provide shade and lumber. In perception we are ordinarily assailed by a stream of conceptualizing tendencies, which have their ultimate source in linguistic conventions and categorizing practices. These conceptualizing tendencies overwhelm and distort the perceptual experience… It is primarily on account of this proliferating tendency of the ordinary mind that notions such as self and other are superimposed upon the constant flow of phenomena. Such superimpositions are the main cause for the reification of perceptual content, leading to the all too familiar propensity to operate with notions such as existence and non-existence, self and other. As the Abhidharma traditions maintain, concepts are superimposed upon the constant flow of phenomena in dependence upon the presence or absence of stimuli at the sense-doors.[64]

---

[64] Coseru, Christian, "Mind in Indian Buddhist Philosophy", *The Stanford Encyclopedia of Philosophy* (Spring 2017 Edition), Edward N. Zalta (ed.), URL = <https://plato.stanford.edu/archives/spr2017/entries/mind-indian-buddhism/>.

The *Xin Shu Xia* and *Nei Ye* describe the process of intention, will, and thought somewhat differently than the *Huang Di Nei Jing*, though the model is similar. Note that the *Xin Shu Xia* (lines 113-119) uses the word *punishment* (刑)[65] to denote *decision* where the Ling Shu Jing uses *will* (志):

> At the center of the heart-mind, there is again another heart-mind.
> Intention precedes words;
> From intention follows decision (刑);
> From this formulation (形, form) follows thought;
> From thought follows knowledge.
> Invariably, the heart-mind's decisions
> Will supersede knowledge, even at the expense of one's life

The *Nei Ye* (which I believe was a later redaction developed from corrupted copies of the *Xin Shu* and *Bai Xin*) omits this phase of will/decision/intent-form in a similar passage (lines 97-104), perhaps due to the redactor's uncertainty as to the meaning of "punishment and form" in this description:

> This pure essence
> Is the pure essence of energy-breath.
> The way of energy-breath is to flourish.
> Flourishing, it becomes thoughts;
> Thoughts become knowledge;
> After knowledge, it stops.
> Invariably, mental formulations (心之形)
> Will supersede knowledge even at the expense of one's life.

A later passage in the *Nei Ye* (lines 165-173) more closely reflects the phases of development found in the *Xin Shu Xia* and *Ling Shu Jing*:

> Within the center of the heart-mind, there is another heart-mind.
> In this heart of the heart-mind,

---

[65] The similarity between 刑 and 形 has led some to believe that the former was a typo, meant to be the same as the latter. Given the significant and fitting meaning of 刑, I'm not convinced that this was the case.

There is a resonance (intention) which precedes words.[66]
Resonance (音) is followed by forms;
Forms are followed by words;
Words are followed by directives;
Directives are followed by order. (使然後治)
When there is disorder, there is sure to be confusion.
Confusion leads to death.

XSX, lines 9-15, also offer insight into intention and the role it plays in internal cultivation:

Therefore it is said: "When things do not confuse the senses,
And the senses do not confuse the heart-mind
This is called 'inner Virtue'."
Thereby, the energy of intention is settled;
Having settled, it returns to alignment.
Energy-breath then fills the body,
And one's conduct is righteous and upright.

Note the nature of this conduct as it relates to Guigu Zi's ability to determine whether or not one cultivates their will:

To know if others' energy is abundant or lacking, and if they cultivate the energy of their will, examine their peace and stability. Thereby, know their ability.

Finally, we see the continuation of this teaching on turning intention into form in the martial art, xingyi chuan (形意拳), translated as "form-intention-fist," which is often taught as part of the Daoist curriculum. The training of intention in this martial art is perhaps best described in Jin Yunting's *Xing Yi Boxing Manual*, in which he explains:

---

[66] "音 sound/tone," appearing in the 'received text', is usually replaced in translations of lines 167-168 with "意 yi, notion, intention, awareness." See *Nei Ye* line 224 which speaks of "wordless tone." That line also appears in XSX line 88 as "unspoken words." "音 Tone," therefore, may have had a significance regarding unspoken "sentiments," as in a "resonance" or feeling in the heart-mind that induces thought.

"The mind must be at ease: During training the mind cannot be flustered or hurried. When flustered, one has a frightened and fearful intention. When hurried, one has an anxious and hasty intention... If [the qi is] like on a normal day when not practicing, then internally one will be deficient and empty; in meeting situations one will be timid and shrinking. When approaching an enemy, one must not be fearful and frightened, [or] anxious and hasty. Therefore, the mind must be at ease and be full with trained qi externally and internally."[67]

The Zen of Guan Zi

Chinese Buddhism, quiet openly, drew a great deal from the *Dao De Jing* and *Zhuang Zi*, and thereby the cultural history that gave birth to these texts. When Chan masters speak of emptiness, no-mind, no form, and no self, they seem to be speaking of the Dao itself and providing keys to the mysteries spoken of by Lao Zi centuries earlier.[68]

For example, in the Zen teachings popular with Japanese samurai, focusing largely on maintaining an empty and agile mind, we see a later development of teachings found in *Xin Shu Shang*, lines 51-59:

> Therefore, the junzi does not dwell on what he likes, nor is he coerced by what he dislikes.
> Tranquil, pleasant, and effortless, he abandons wisdom, and it abides in him as a result.
> He responds, but does not initiate;
> Moves but does not possess.
> If one is excessively headstrong, they will err when adapting to changes.
> Thus, the ruler who has Dao
> Remains in the state of not knowing.
> He responds to things as though by coincidence.
> This is the Dao of tranquil means.

---

[67] Jin Yunting, Ling Guiqing, John Groschwitz (trans). *The Xingyi Boxing Manual*. Berkley: Blue Snake Books, 2015. p. 29
[68] Buddhism arrived in China from India in 80 AD.

Though Buddhist teachings have oftentimes been the vehicle that brought these indigenous Chinese teachings back around to Chinese followers of Daoism, the Daoist precedence of their philosophical commonalities tends to be egregiously overlooked, to this day.[69]

Oneness in Buddhism and the Guan Zi

When people speak of Oneness, in the modern world, they generally speak in terms of the unity of all phenomena. This is the understanding of unity commonly found in Buddhism, yet also put forth by Zhuang Zi in his chapter "The Talisman of Complete Virtue."

> Confucius replied: "Death and life are both great matters, yet are not considered as changes (to Wang Tai). If Heaven and Earth were to tumble over and sink into each other, he would not consider this any loss. His focus is on that which is without any falseness. He does not follow along with the changes of things, knowing that transformation is but their certain destiny. Rather, he guards the source of these changes within himself."
> Chang Ji asked: "What do you mean by that?"
> Confucius replied: "Looking at things from their differences, we find a liver and a gallbladder; a Chu State and a Yue State. Looking at things from their sameness, the myriad things are all one. As such, (Wang Tai) does not know what is meant for his eyes or ears, but simply allows his mind to float along in the harmony of Virtue. Things are seen as one, and so he does not see loss. When he lost his foot, he considered it as leaving behind a pile of earth."[70]

---

[69] The Buddha was born and raised in southern Nepal as Siddhartha Gautama. His year of birth is uncertain, but is said to be as early as 563 BC, and as late as 400 BC. The factual dates of Daoist timelines are also debated, but may go back to the oracle shamans of the Xia Dynasty (c.2000 BC). Either way, these teachings first existed in China, in indigenous sources, for centuries before Buddhism arrived there in 80 AD.
[70] Translated by Dan G. Reid

We find a similar discussion of unity in the 5th century Buddhist poem, *Xin Xin Ming,* 信心銘 – *Faith Mind Inscription*, by the Third Chinese Chan (Zen) Patriarch, Sengcan (d. 606).

[...]
眞如法界　In the realm of True Suchness,
無他無自　There is neither *other* nor *self*.
要急相應　When pushed and pulled to make differentiations,
唯言不二　Simply say, 'Not two.'

不二皆同　Not two, all is the same,
無不包容　There is nothing it does not contain.
十方智者　Sages in the ten directions
皆入此宗　All enter into this lineage.

宗非促延　This lineage is beyond hurry and delay.
一念萬年　A single recollection is ten thousand years;
無在不在　Beyond being and non-being,
十方目前　In all ten directions, it is right before your eyes.

極小同大　The infinitesimal is the same as the immense;
忘絕境界　Forget, and let vanish, external boundaries.
極大同小　Infinitely large is the same as small;
不見邊表　Outer surfaces are not seen.

有即是無　Where there is being, there is non-being;
無即是有　Where there is non-being, there is being.
若不如此　On what seems not like this,
必不相守　Be sure not to linger.

一即一切　In one is all;
一切即一　As all is one.
但能如是　If you can only proceed as such,
何慮不畢　What contemplation will not be fulfilled?!

信心不二　The mind of faith is not two,
不二信心　And not two is the mind of faith.
言語道斷　The path of words comes to a stop,

非去來今 For there is no past departing, no future arriving, and no present remaining

Support, and likely also inspiration, for the Faith Mind Inscription's teachings can be found in the traditions that gave rise to the *Dao De Jing* and *Guan Zi*. For example, in *Dao De Jing*, chapter two:

> … Existence and non-existence are born together
> Difficulty and ease result in each other
> Long and short are compared to each other
> Above and below are opposites of each other
> Noise and tone are harmonized by each other
> Front and back accompany each other…

And *Xin Shu Shang*, lines 45-48:

> (The Sage) knows yet does not speak, and serves without action,
> So that present and future generations may know the principles of Dao.
> Though having peculiar forms, and strange abilities, he does not follow the myriad things from their differences to their coherence.
> Thus, he can fathom the beginning of all under Heaven.

A link between the Chinese Buddhist and proto-Daoist traditions can also be seen in the use of the term "without division (無貳)" to say "without doubt or irresolution" in *Bai Xin*, line 206. The term xin (信), 'faith/confidence', in *Faith Mind Inscription* holds this same meaning. While the *Xin Xin Ming* speaks more to a view of existence, and the *Guan Zi* speaks more to a way of being, these two approaches are also 'not-two'.[71] Each approach ultimately begets the other,

---

[71] The Quan Zhen School of Daoism (founded circa 1167 AD) has long integrated seemingly Buddhist philosophies and practices into its own. As shown throughout *Thread of Dao*, many of these philosophies and practices existed in China for centuries, before Buddhism arrived there in 80AD, though it may have been their popularity in Buddhism which brought them to the attention of the Quan Zhen Patriarchs who found themselves quite a home in Buddhist teachings. A modern example of this: Quan Zhen Abbot Michael Rinaldini, founder of the American Dragon Gate Sect, teaches use of the 'break-through question' (called a hou-tou in

whether inner consolidation reveals ultimate unity, or the realization of ultimate unity settles one internally and allows their will and intention to naturally consolidate and 'become genuine'. Beyond these and other similarities, however, Buddhist and Daoist traditions hold many differences in theory, practice, and objectives, which this book will not venture to scrutinize.

Bringing together the concepts of 'the unity of existence' and 'inner consolidation' is the sense of "embracing Oneness" found in the *Dao De Jing* and *Heshang Gong's Commentary on Lao Zi's Dao De Jing*. While the sense of "holding Oneness" in the *Guan Zi* and *Guigu Zi* may be described as unifying will and intention, this description is more applicable to the *technique* of embracing Oneness, rather than a definition of Oneness itself.

To understand what the early Daoist masters meant by Oneness, we may find invaluable keys in Heshang Gong's commentary. For example, in his comments on Lao Zi's chapter 51, Heshang Gong appears to offer the meaning behind his frequent use of the term Oneness:

道生之，道生萬物。
"Dao actuates them"
Dao actuates the myriad things.
德畜之，德，一也。一主布氣而蓄養物形之，一為萬物設形像也。
"Virtue takes care of them"
"Virtue," here, means "Oneness." Oneness is the host of all things. It surrounds them with energy-breath, and gathers and rears things into form. Oneness establishes the form and image of all things.
勢成之。一為萬物作寒暑之勢以成之。
"Power completes them"
Oneness uses the power of hot and cold to complete all things.

As he reveals here, when Heshang Gong refers to Oneness, or holding Oneness, he refers not so much to unity and wholeness as he does to the power which spontaneously harmonizes and balances all

---

Zen) "What is not-two?" He uses this hou-tou to help students, and the Daoist priests that he trains, with Daoist zuowang ("sitting and forgetting") meditation.

things – otherwise often referred to as De/Virtue. Similar to the name of the Zheng Yi Daoist sect (often translated as "Orthodox Unity"), Oneness is the zheng yi – the "aligning oneness" to which all things are subject. The movement of De is the movement towards wholeness. Not an assimilation into oneness (though this literally translates "一"), but the cooperative diversity of wholeness. This is the nature of De/Oneness, and the expression of the all encompassing Dao. Chapters 51, 22, and 39, especially, reveal a force or *Virtue* that brings about this alignment, wholeness, balance and harmony. Lao Zi calls this force De, the Virtue (of Dao), while Heshang Gong tends to refer to it as Oneness. As chapter 51 explains:

> Dao actuates them
> Virtue takes care of them, extends their lifespans
> Teaches them, completes them
> Tests them, raises them
> And brings them back (to their pure natures)

Chapter 22 describes this process:

> That which is flexible is preserved
> That which is bent is straightened
> That which is empty is filled
> That which is broken is repaired
> That which is lacking acquires
> That which is excessive becomes confused
> Therefore, the Sage embraces Oneness
> So as to bring the world into alignment

Chapter 39 (which happens to follow the *Dao De Jing*'s defining chapter on Virtue – chapter 38) describes the effect of embracing Oneness, and provides ample support for Heshang Gong's equation of Oneness with Virtue. This connection in chapter 39 is more apparent knowing from chapter 51 that to Virtue is attributed the power of perfecting and completing life:

> In the beginning was the attainment of Oneness

> Heaven attained Oneness and became clear
> Earth attained Oneness and became serene
> Gods attained Oneness and became spiritually powerful
> Valleys attained Oneness and became full
> The myriad things attained Oneness and were born
> Lords and kings attained Oneness and all under Heaven became loyal
> (DDJ39)

Another helpful example to understand this equation is Heshang Gong's reference to chapter 39 in his comments on chapter 10:

> *"Embrace Oneness. Can you do this without letting (your coporeal spirits) flee?"*
> People who can embrace Oneness, and not let it leave them, extend their lives. In Oneness, Dao began to situate life by the supreme harmony of the vital energy-breaths. Therefore it is said: "Oneness covered the world with names."
>
> Heaven attained Oneness and became clear. Earth attained Oneness and became serene. Lords and kings attained Oneness and became upright and peace-loving. Going within, it is mind; going outwards it is actions; in covering all with its blessing, it is Virtue. All the names together are One. Referring to Oneness, it is said: "In a unified consciousness, there is no division (or doubt)."

To further this equation of De, the force which fosters and perfects life, with Oneness, we can also look to the ancient text, *The Great One Gave Birth to Water (Tai Yi Sheng Shui)*, found alongside the earliest known fragments of the *Dao De Jing* at Guodian, and dated to around 350 BC. The *Tai Yi Sheng Shui* describes "the Great One":

> The Great One gave birth to water. Water then returned to meet the Great One and thereby fashioned Heaven. Heaven returned to meet the Great One and thereby fashioned Earth. Heaven and Earth joined together and thereby fashioned spirit (conscious essence) and illumination. Spirit and illumination joined together and thereby fashioned Yin and Yang. Yin and Yang joined together and thereby fashioned the Four Seasons. The

Four Seasons joined together and thereby fashioned Cold and Hot. Cold and Hot joined together and thereby fashioned Moisture and Dryness. Moisture and Dryness joined together, thereby fashioning the year, and then stopped...

Thus, the Great One is found in water. It moves through the seasons, completes a cycle, and then begins again. Thus, the Great One is the mother of the myriad things. At once diminishing, at once filling, it uses itself as the thread (joining) all things. This is what Heaven cannot kill, what Earth cannot bury, and what Yin and Yang cannot fashion. Those of noble character who understand this, we call Sages.[72]

With these descriptions of the Great One, both in the *Dao De Jing*, and *Tai Yi Sheng Shui*, we can see that Virtue is, as Heshang Gong points out in chapter 51, another title for Oneness. Thus, in finding Heshang Gong's mentions of "embracing Oneness," we can understand this as embracing the power of Dao – Virtue (De) – and allowing it to spontaneously harmonize, purify, and align – to spontaneously (zi ran) "govern" us internally and bring about the Great Peace (tai ping) that Dao brings to a nation.

As Heshang Gong demonstrates throughout his commentary, the Dao of governing the body and the Dao of governing the nation follow the same principles, revealing that Lao Zi's verses speak simultaneously of three dimensions: 1) governing oneself; 2) governing the nation; and 3) the principles of Dao governing all existence and non-existence as implemented through Oneness – Virtue.

Translating the *Bai Xin*, *Xin Shu*, and *Nei Ye*

The translations and annotations for the *Bai Xin*, *Xin Shu*, and *Nei Ye* in *The Thread of Dao* make a case for retaining numerous characters that had been considered typos by various eminent scholars in the field. Annotations are provided where dispute of the translation is anticipated for this and other reasons, sometimes addressing the commonly suggested changes, or otherwise simply providing support

---

[72] Excerpt from *Tai Yi Sheng Shui* (anonymous) translated by Dan G. Reid

for my translation of commonly redacted characters. This approach was made in an effort to provide readers with a translation of the original text as it had been received in ancient times. Though it is possible that the texts have numerous errors, I have tried to keep an open mind as to how these characters made sense to the early scribes and authors, finding this exercise, coupled with additional research, to reveal functional and relevant meanings for the original characters in all but one or two occasions.

The following abbreviations are found throughout the commentary: DDJ (*Dao De Jing*), BX (*Bai Xin*), XSS (*Xin Shu Shang*), XSX (*Xin Shu Xia*), and NY (*Nei Ye*).

I have separated most of the syllables that are normally grouped together in pinyin spelling so as to render terms more recognizable to readers familiar only with Wade-Giles spelling.

The principle texts are presented below in numbered lines of Chinese characters appearing above their line by line translations. If readers wish to first read the principle texts in full, please simply skip over the paragraphs between these numbered lines. For comparing the below translation of the *Nei Ye* with that of Harold Roth, please see Roth's associated paragraph (zhang) numbers in the index, below.

The first paragraph following each section of the principle text is my own brief summary comment.

Where lines of the principle text are referenced in the commentary sections of *The Thread of Dao*, it is strongly encouraged to re-read the referenced lines (preceding the commentary) before continuing to read the commentary.

The Proto-Daoist Texts of the Guan Zi:

白心
Purifying the Heart-Mind
Bai Xin

心術上
Art of the Heart-Mind: upper volume
Xin Shu Shang

心術下
Art of the Heart-Mind: lower volume
Xin Shu Xia

內業
Internal Cultivation
Nei Ye

白心
Purifying the Heart-Mind
Bai Xin

1　建當立有,[73]
To establish long-standing order:
2　以靖為宗,
Take peace and tranquility as your revered ancestor,
3　以時為寶,
Treat opportune moments as precious jewels,
4　以政[74]為儀,
And treat political affairs as a matter of ceremony.
5　和則能久,
With harmony, there can be enduring continuity.

---

[73] Many scholars have decided, with near unanimity, that this opening phrase does not make sense as it appears, and have therefore made various changes to the characters jian dang li you 建當立有 (see Graziani). There are, however, examples from the same time period which combine these characters. The question of how to establish a stable order, using the same characters (建當), appears in the Han Shu when a prince inquires: "「建當云何？」How does one establish a stable order? 霸曰：「自大將軍出.. The leader of the princes replied: 'Enlarge yourself by deploying armies…"
"Li you (立有)" appears in many texts from the same era, though is usually followed by the subject that is established (立). You emphasizes li so as to say 'long-standing' or 'well-established.' Here, li you appears after that which is established, rather than before. Line five also suggests this reading.

[74] Wang Niansun suggests replacing "zheng, 政 political affairs" with "zheng, 正 rectitude," to say "treat rectitude as a matter of ceremony."

The *Bai Xin* (BX) begins by addressing matters of decorum and diplomacy; however, as soon becomes apparent, these strategies are not simply techniques to avoid conflict. Rather, they are offered by someone steeped in the Daoist Sage's tradition of cultivating longevity and spiritual evolution, seeking to impart this path to enlightenment upon those tasked with bringing peace and stability to China's Warring States Period.

The *Bai Xin* bears many resemblances to the *Dao De Jing* (DDJ), including the manner in which its guidance simultaneously shimmers with outer and inner meanings.[75] Heshang Gong's commentary on the *Dao De Jing* is considered an early confirmation of Lao Zi's hidden metaphors for internal cultivation in methods of government; however, these proto-Daoist texts in the *Guan Zi* show that this metaphor was well established by the time the *Dao De Jing* reached a wider audience, around 200 B.C.

This ability to speak with simultaneous exoteric and esoteric meanings is evident in the first five lines of *Purifying the Heart-Mind (Bai Xin)*. The treatise begins: "To establish long-standing order: take peace and tranquility as your revered ancestor." The essence of Daoist cultivation lies in longevity and a peaceful existence, attained by following nature and learning from, for example, the detachment of Heaven and patience of Earth. "Take peace and tranquility as your revered ancestor / yi jin wei zong" teaches that the basis of this master's diplomacy lies in the 'art of the heart-mind' – an art which can ensure, and even be used to describe, the most skillful policy in all matters of government. This sentence can also be read "consider silence as the origin," or "consider bringing peace to the world as a form of worship."

How should one take peace and tranquility as their revered ancestor? Line three reads: "Treat opportune moments as precious jewels."

---

[75] This sequence of external (behavioural) guidance later to be revealed as guidance on internal cultivation is also found in the earliest known complete copy of the *Dao De Jing*. The "Mawangdui" DDJ (168 BC) presents the De volume, focusing more on the external matters of state and society, before the Dao volume, which focuses more on internal matters, such as purifying and emptying oneself and cultivating Dao and De internally. The Dao volume was moved to the beginning of the text some 300-500 years later.

When appreciating a precious jewel, one may not even touch it, yet they will look at it deeply, considering its hues, and the hidden lines within it. If one wishes to shape such a jewel, they must find its soft and hard points so that their shaping of it neither destroys it, nor removes more than is necessary to reveal its full splendour. Above all, they give it their full attention, and do not cast it aside. This is, as line four states, to treat the moment as "a matter of ceremony." As line 5 continues, this is the path towards longevity, and peace.

"Treat opportune moments as precious jewels," refers to opportunities, both immediate and seasonal, with the word "shi, 時, season, timing." This line may intentionally corresponds with the last several lines of the *Bai Xin*, on timing and cultivation, while also speaking of the external factors of planning and acting according to agricultural seasons – planting, growing, ripening, harvesting, and storing – junctures with universal applicability to human endeavours.

6 非吾儀, 雖利不為。
That which goes against my standards of ceremony,
though it may bring (me) profit, I will not take such action.
7 非吾當, 雖利不行。
That which goes against what I find appropriate,
though it may bring (me) profit, I will not put forward.
8 非吾道, 雖利不取。
The (path) which runs counter to my true path,
though it may bring (me) profit, I will not take it.
9 上之隨天,
What (the sage) puts above all else is following Heaven;
10 其次隨人。
Only then will he follow men.
11 人不倡不和,
What others did not put forth,
he does not try to harmonize with.
12 天不始不隨。
What Heaven did not begin, he does not follow.

13 故其言也不廢,
Thus, his words are not wasted,
14 其事也不隨。
And his endeavours are not misguided

While these lines offer external, actionable, guidance, they reveal the actions of someone who holds to his or her practice of keeping the heart-mind undisturbed, cautiously making sure that their mind does not become muddied with thoughts, and emotionally entangled.

Evidently speaking as someone of high authority, the author explains here that leaders must conduct themselves, in these precious moments, in a calm and dignified manner so as to avoid setting a precedent for ungracious behaviour. After all, if those tasked with ensuring the greater good are impetuous and selfish, what more can be expected of those under them?

This circumstance provides a helpful model of what it means to be in accord with Dao. Encountering a situation of great potential gain or loss, the leader is not "the first to move forward" but remains earnest, considerate, and mindful of what is in accord with Dao. By suspending personal goals they can see more clearly what is in accord with Dao and so have the potential for success and longevity. As Lao Zi says in DDJ77:

> Who can have in excess, and care for all under Heaven?
> Only those who have Dao

and in DDJ67:

> … I have three treasures
> Which I hold close and protect
> The first is kindness
> The second is economy
> The third is not daring to be first (and take precedence over) the world…

While not indicating any familiarity with the *Dao De Jing*, the *Bai*

Purifying the Heart-Mind

Xin clearly illustrates Lao Zi's "third treasure" in lines 6-10. Rather than putting his own profit above following the Dao, the sage follows the path of Dao and Heaven, rather than the selfish path of man.

Similarities to the *Dao De Jing* also appear between BX11-14 and DDJ2:

> ... Noise and tone are harmonized by each other[76]
> Front and back accompany each other
> Therefore, sages handle affairs with non-action
> They practice wordless instruction
> And the myriad things all take their places...

At first glance, it may appear that these authors discourage initiative altogether; however, as the *Bai Xin* makes clear, their objective is accordance with Heaven, 天 Tian, often equated, perhaps rightfully so, to the Western notions of Nature and its manifestations – nature.

It should be noted that the nature of human beings, according to Daoists, is qing 靜: silence, tranquility, stillness. It is this state to which all things return. While humans have powerful emotions, like rainstorms, these emotions do not last, and are followed again by tranquility (see DDJ23). As these texts show, by cultivating tranquility, one can see things as they are, and thus act according to the time. So, by non-action, one knows the time; and when that precious timing arrives, it is embraced accordingly.

15 原始計實, 本其所生。
The true primordial strategy
is the root from which life springs.
16 知其象則索其形,
Knowing its image, one apprehends its form.
17 緣[77]其理則知其情。

---

[76] Heshang Gong comments on this line: "When a superior sings, those below him must harmonize."

[77] Reading yuan 緣 in the sense of "climb," eg: "緣木求魚 climb a tree to seek for fish"

Reaching to its principles, one knows its nature.
18 索其端則知其名。
Seeking its end, one knows its name.
19 故苞物眾者莫大於天地,
Thus, for producing many flourishing things,
nothing is greater than Heaven and Earth;
20 化物多者莫多於日月,
For transforming many things,
nothing can transform so many things as the sun and moon;
21 民之所急,莫急於水火。
For causing urgency in people,
nothing is more urgent than water and fire.

Here we see the emergence of a higher wisdom: the "clear vision" (明 ming: enlightenment) that accompanies one's ability to preserve Dao within.

While, again, not indicating any familiarity with the *Dao De Jing*, lines 15-18 of the *Bai Xin* show a striking correlation to the following lines from DDJ1, perhaps offering further insights into them:

DDJ1:
> The Dao that can be told is not the Eternal Dao
> The name that can be named is not the Eternal Name
> The Nameless is the origin of Heaven and Earth
> The Named is the mother of the myriad things…

BX15-20:
> The true primordial strategy is the root from which life springs.
> Knowing its image, one apprehends its form.
> Reaching to its principles, one knows its nature.
> Seeking its end, one knows its name
> Thus, for producing many flourishing things, nothing is greater than Heaven and Earth.
> For transforming many things, nothing can transform so many things as the sun and moon.

What the *Bai Xin* calls "the 原始 primordial 計 strategy (that is) 實 real," the *Dao De Jing* refers to as the Eternal Dao in the line "The Dao that can be told is not the Eternal Dao." Both texts begin this discourse by setting apart the *true* Dao. As will be seen later, the *Bai Xin* also uses the term 道 Dao much in the same way as Lao Zi.

The parallels continue:

DDJ1:
 ... Thus, always without desires
 Observing its inner subtlety
 Always with desires
 Observing its outer surface...

BX17-18:
 Reaching to its principles, one knows its nature.
 Seeking its end, one knows its name

Despite the stark similarities in these verses, the differences in their terminology and shifted sequences of development suggest that both texts were written records of a shared oral tradition, rather than one directly influencing the other. Their verse-like qualities further suggest an oral transmission aided by these mnemonic devices.

Lines 15-16 also shed light on DDJ35's "Hold forth the great image and all under Heaven will approach." The *Bai Xin* clarifies the meaning of "the image," here, as an indistinct sense of Dao, not yet revealing its principles. Holding to the image, then, is to "know without knowing;" in other words, to know Dao, "the true primordial strategy," without intellectualizing it. Heshang Gong (c. 200 AD) comments on this line from DDJ35:

> *"Hold forth the great image and all under Heaven will approach"*
> "Hold forth," here, means embrace. "Image," here, means Dao. The Sage embraces the Great Dao, and everything in the world shifts its heart to the way things once were. He governs his body, and Heaven sends down spiritual lights. (These spiritual lights go) back and forth between his body (and Heaven).[78]

---

[78] All excerpts from Heshang Gong's commentary found in *The Thread of Dao* are borrowed from:
Reid, Dan G., translator. *The Heshang Gong Commentary on Lao Zi's* Dao De Jing. Montreal: Center Ring Publications, 2015.

22 然而天不為一物枉其時,
As such, Heaven does not twist its seasons
in consideration of an individual thing.
23 明君聖人, 亦不為一人枉其法。
An enlightened Sage ruler does not twist the law
in consideration of an individual person.
24 天行其所行, 而萬物被其利。
Heaven moves according to its own movements,
and the myriad things arrange their own benefits.
25 聖人亦行其所行, 而百姓被其利。
The Sage also moves according to his own movements,
and the hundred clans arrange their own benefits.
26 是故萬物均既誇 眾矣。
For this reason, each of the myriad things all praise them.

Preserving Dao within, sages do not take counsel from the confused logic and surface understanding of those whose vision is blurred by desire, fear, ambition, and self-interest.

Lines 19-26 present a backdrop of ideas concerning Heaven, Earth, and the Sage that the author of DDJ5 may have presupposed a familiarity with when stating:

> Heaven and Earth do not act benevolently
> The myriad things are treated no differently than ceremonial grass-dogs
> Sages do not act benevolently
> The hundred clans are treated no differently than ceremonial grass-dogs

Wang Bi, a 2nd century commentator on the *Dao De Jing*, interpreted these lines to mean that all people are treated equally under the law, stating:

The myriad things are all governed together and managed in the same way. Thus, (Heaven and Earth) are not benevolent.

Ren, translated as "benevolence," carried a meaning, especially in ancient times, of diligent consideration for courtesy, manners, and hierarchies, following the culture of those who served in the court. One of the most significant contrasts between Daoists and Confucians was that Daoists had little value for complex and prescribed manners and courtesies which they felt must flow as a natural expression from people's sense of oneness with all things.

Heshang Gong comments on the first line of DDJ5:

"Heaven bestows, and Earth transforms. It is not because of benevolence or mercy that they do this, but simply because it is in their nature (ziran)."

Ziran (自然) translates literally to "as itself," and means "spontaneous, natural action." The *Bai Xin* describes ziran, here, without using the term, in lines 24-25: *"Heaven moves according to (行: moves, follows) its own movements…"* This line precedes another helpful explanation, this time of "not benevolent," with *"and the myriad things arrange their own benefits."* If Heaven was benevolent, it would arrange things on behalf of the myriad things, yet instead, it simply acts according to its nurturing nature (described in the *Dao De Jing* as De, "Virtue"), and this is enough for the myriad beings to arrange things for themselves. One might say that to give a fish is benevolent, but Heaven and the Sage are more like the lake itself. By simply acting according to their own nature, they provide all things the opportunity to reap these benefits.

By the same token, we also see that Heaven and Earth are impartial; they are unaffected by partisanship or privilege. The ancient texts taught that righteousness, virtue, and adherence to Dao will determine fortune. Though:

for producing many flourishing things, nothing is greater than Heaven and Earth; for transforming many things, nothing can transform so many things as the sun and moon (BX19-20)

those who contravene the Dao of Heaven may soon learn that

> for causing urgency in people, nothing is more urgent than water and fire (BX21).

As the *Bai Xin* is part of the teachings on the "art of the heart–mind," the integrity and stability described in lines 22–26 also allude to 'retaining the throne of the ruler' – a metaphor in the *Xin Shu Shang* (XSS) for not allowing the senses to wrest power from the heart–mind.

> 27 是以聖人之治也,
> Therefore, the Sage's method of government
> 28 靜身以待之,
> Is to still the body and wait.
> 29 物至而名自治之。
> Things then arrive at their names, (showing what they are,) and naturally fall into place.
>
> 30 正名自治之,
> As these names naturally order themselves,
> 31 奇身名廢。
> Those which do not fit are abolished.
> 32 名正法備, 則聖人無事。
> When names are corrected and laws perfected, the Sage is without further endeavours.

Impartial and unhurried, one can see what corresponds to reality, remove what is illusory, and further clarify the nature and shape of a given situation.

Given the similarity between lines 22-26 and DDJ5 (see above), lines 27-29 appear to reflect the end of DDJ5, while lines 19-20 also reflect its middle lines.

The second part of DDJ5 reads:

> ... The gate of Heaven and Earth
> Is it not like a bagpipe?
> Empty yet not finished
> It moves, and again more is pushed forth

BX19-20:
> Thus, for producing many flourishing things, nothing is greater than Heaven and Earth. For transforming many things, nothing can transform so many things as the sun and moon.

DDJ5:
> To speak countless words is worthless
> This is not as good as guarding balance within

BX27-32:
> Therefore, the Sage's method of government is to still the body and wait.
> Things then arrive at their names, (showing what they are,) and naturally fall into place.
> As these names naturally order themselves, those which do not fit are abolished.
> When names are corrected and laws perfected, the Sage is without further endeavours

Including lines 19-20 in this section, we see that all of DDJ5 is reflected in lines 19-29. The inexhaustible creative power of the "bagpipe" (often translated as *bellows*)[79] is an illustration of the inexhaustible power of Heaven and Earth, described in BX19-21, while Lao Zi's disregard for attempts to inflate reality with words is described in BX27-32. Again, the drastically different sequences in which these same ideas appear suggests that both texts were written from their authors' own contemplation of ideas circulating amongst their peers at the time.

DDJ3 can also be better understood through BX27-29.

---

[79] Literally "bag-flute." Heshang Gong's commentary seems to suggest a musical instrument, perhaps similar to the sheng: "The center of a bagpipe is hollow and empty, yet people can obtain more sound from it."

BX27-29:
> Therefore, the Sage's (method of) government is to still the body and wait. Things then arrive at their names and naturally fall into place."

DDJ3:
> ... Therefore, the Sage's government
> Empties the heart-mind and enriches the stomach
> Softens the will and strengthens the bones
> People then remain uncontrived and without desires
> While the scheming do not dare to act
> Act by not acting
> And everything will fall into place

This passage from the *Dao De Jing* has been a source of controversy, as many found it to suggest making the populace ignorant; however, the *Bai Xin*, and commentators such as Heshang Gong, show that "the Sage's (method of) government" simultaneously refers to self-cultivation and meditation.

The *Bai Xin* also makes clear the interest of the ancient sages in "names," and these names' true inclinations.[80] Knowing these inclinations helps sages to understand the roles (also a facet of meaning in "名 names") of various phenomena in the world. Giving names to things assigns their connection to other things. The use and origin of things is more open without their names. Imagine, for example, the way an animal sees the world without words, and how things are not so distinguished when they no longer have any names. As we understand how to use things, we differentiate them with names. This process of naming is at the basis of wisdom, and so is associated with the role of the Sage.

The characteristic sense of the word "names," as used ancient Chinese texts, can also be better grasped by looking at the *Tai Yi Sheng Shui*, found alongside the earliest known fragments of the *Dao De Jing*. In the *Tai Yi Sheng Shui*, we find the following:

> Below is soil, and we call it Earth. Above is energy-breath, and we call it Heaven. "Dao" is also simply a title. May I ask its

---

[80] See also lines 16-19 of the *Xin Shu Shang*.

name? Those who serve the Dao must rely on this name – thereby, their service is completed and they themselves live long.

The difference here between title and name provides an integral context to understanding the nuance of "name" (ming). Seeking one's name is to seek a deeper level of familiarity. For example, even writing the childhood name of an emperor was a capital offence in ancient China. Asking the name of someone with a ranking title is to ask "may I truly get to know you? May I know who you truly are?"

Further, this practice of seeing the true character of external things coincides with the practice of observing one's own internal phenomena, such as cravings and emotions, which are brought to stability and order by practicing "the Sage's method of government." Such considerations can be seen in *Dao De Jing*, chapter one:

> … The Nameless is the origin of Heaven and Earth
> The Named is the mother of the myriad things
> Thus, always without desires
> Observing its inner subtlety
> Always with desires
> Observing its outer surface
> These two were born together, yet differ in name
> Together, they are called Fathomless Mystery…

33 不可常居也,
The sage cannot always remain in his position
34 不可廢舍也,
Nor can he hastily abandon it
35 隨變斷事也,
He must follow the changes of circumstance when deciding on affairs,
36 知時以為度。
Knowing what is best according to the time.

The Sage is unattached to outcomes. Ego is just a responsibility that they would happily divest themselves of, given the opportunity. When they have done what needed to be done, the Sage returns to the freedom of namelessness, and enjoys the simplicity of nature.

Lines 33-36 also correlate to DDJ3 as it speaks of "softening the will." Heshang Gong's comment on this line helps to illustrate the proximity of these ideas as they were understood in the proto-Daoist culture:

> *"Softens the will"*
> Harmonious and soft, humble, modest, and accommodating, the Sage does not linger in positions of authority.

"Softens the will" refers to selfish willfulness and stubbornness, and so, as the *Dao De Jing* and *Bai Xin* point out, softening one's will to control reality is an important step towards seeing things as they truly are. When scheming desires and emotions stop trying to control situations (*"People then remain uncontrived and without desires, while the scheming do not dare to act"* – DDJ3), the 'heart of the heart-mind'[81] can attain sovereignty, and a new, enlightened, perception of reality.

This teaching on withdrawing (and willfulness) also appears in DDJ9. In the "Guodian" *Dao De Jing*, (the earliest known copy of the *Dao De Jing*, found in the Guodian tombs and dated to around 295 BC), chapter 9 reads:

困而盈之，	To accumulate until full
而不若已。	Is not as good as coming to a stop
湍而群之，	When rushing waters gather
不可长保也。	Nothing can be long protected
金玉盈室，	When gold and jade fill the halls
莫能兽（守）也。	Nothing can preserve them
贵福乔（骄），	When fortune and wealth bring arrogance
自遗咎也。	They bring the misfortune of their own loss
攻（功）述身退，	Having achieved the goal, withdraw yourself
天之道也。	This is the way of Heaven

---

[81] See *Nei Ye*, lines 154-165

As will be seen in the proceeding lines, the *Bai Xin* and *Dao De Jing* both warn extensively about the dangers of this selfish willfulness. Thus, it is better to soften one's willfulness, and forcefulness, so as to "follow the changes" and do what is best for the time.[82]

37 大者寬, 小者局。
When there is abundance, (the sage is) generous;
when there is little, (the sage is) studious.
38 物有所餘, 有所不足。
(This causes) things to be in surplus, or insufficient.
39 兵之出, 出於人,
Deploying an army is to send it out towards others;
40 其人入, 入於身。
But when others retaliate, they invade one's own territory.
41 兵之勝, 從於適。
The success of an army follows good fortune,
42 德之來, 從於身。
(And) the approach of virtue depends on the individual.
43 故曰祥於鬼者義於人,
This is why it is said that omens and apparitions (arrive to defend) the righteousness of others.
44 兵不義不可。
(Thus,) an army must never lack righteousness.[83]

Outcomes are unpredictable, but even more so when sought greedily, without considering the rights of others. Thus, the Sage relies on righteousness, and so avoids unexpected misfortunes that might arise from seemingly successful ventures.

---

[82] See *Bai Xin*, lines 35-36
[83] Ke 可, means "can" as in "may." Here it suggests "appropriate/deserving," rather than "capable." See DDJ67 on spiritual protection of the virtuous. Given its proximity to omens and spirits (line 47), ke takes on a similar meaning to "the mandate of Heaven," as in "one must never be undeserving."

Lines 37-44 go further into the dangers of arrogance, hinted at in the lines preceding and made more explicit in DDJ9 – "When fortune and wealth bring arrogance, they bring the misfortune of their own loss." This idea, also suggested in lines 39-48, above, show up as well in DDJ67:

> ... Now, if one neglects kindness in courage
> Neglects economy in generosity
> Neglects humility in being at the forefront
> They will die.
>
> So, kindness in times of war brings victory
> And protecting it brings strength and stability
> Heaven will bring its aid
> And kindness will be protected

And in DDJ69:

> In the employment of an army, there is a saying:
> "I dare not be the host, but I will be a guest
> I dare not advance an inch, but will step back a foot"
> This is called advancing without advancing
> ...
> Misfortune has no greater cause
> Than not respecting an enemy
> By not respecting an enemy
> How much do we risk destroying what is precious?...

45 強而驕者損其強,
Those who are forceful and arrogant,
their strength is decreased;
46 弱而驕者前死亡。
Those who are weak and arrogant,
death and destruction await them;
47 強而卑義, 信其強。

When strong, humble, and righteous, this is true strength;
48 弱而卑義, 免於罪。
If weak, yet humble and righteous, they will avoid calamity.
49 是故驕之餘卑, 卑之餘驕。
For these reasons, the excessively arrogant are humbled, and the excessively humble become arrogant.

By cultivating himself, but not over-estimating himself, the Sage invites good will, greater clarity, and greater opportunities for success.

The idea of arrogance leading to downfall appears in many chapters of the *Dao De Jing*. Notice, for example, the similarity between DDJ30 and lines 45-49.

DDJ30
    As for those who use Dao to counsel the king
    It is not by weapons that they have power in the world
    Such activities are reciprocated
    Where troops gather, thorns and brambles appear
    Following war, there is sure to be famine and misfortune
    Large armies are sure to bring sadness in the future
    Achieve your aim well, and then stop
    Do not dare to abuse power
    Achieve your aim, but do not boast
    Achieve your aim, but do not attack again
    Achieve your aim, but do not become arrogant
    Achieve your aim, but do not claim all the credit
    Achieve your aim, but do not abuse power
    Things thrive in their prime and then become aged
    This is called "not Dao"
    What is "not Dao" ends prematurely

50 道者，一人用之，不聞有餘。
When (only) one person applies Dao, sufficiency is unheard of;

51 天下行之，不聞不足，
When all under heaven practice Dao, insufficiency is unheard of.

52 此謂道矣。
This is the meaning of Dao!

53 小取焉，則小得福，
If a small amount is obtained through (Dao), then that small amount can bring good fortune;

54 大取焉，則大得福。
If a large amount is obtained through (Dao), then that large amount can bring good fortune.

55 盡行之而天下服，
If this were practiced throughout, all under Heaven could be provided for.

56 殊無取焉則民反，
Alternatively, if success is not obtained through (Dao), the people will rebel,

57 其身不免於賊。
And individuals will inevitably become deceitful.[84]

58 左者出者也，
Those of the left will go on the offence,

59 右者入者也，
And those of the right will be invaded.[85]

60 出者而不傷人，
The attack will not injure anyone,

---

[84] See DDJ 2, 3, 9, 29, 46, 73, 74, and 76 on "if success is not obtained through Dao."

[85] Possibly referring to those of high and low rank/authority, with high rank on the left side, that of the junzi (according to DDJ31), and low rank on the right side, that of the soldier (according to Heshang Gong's commentary on DDJ31). Left signifies yang, and right signifies yin according to Heshang Gong and later Daoist theory.

61 入者自傷也。
But those invaded will have injured themselves.[86]

62 不日不月而事以從。
Not by the day or the month, but by how affairs follow (Dao),
63 不卜不筮而謹知吉凶。
And not by prophesy or divination, but by how cautiously one follows (Dao), can you know fortune and misfortune.

Knowing that success for all means lasting success, the Sage is careful to ensure that he remains with Dao, like a coachman takes care not to lose his carriage.

To understand way of following Dao when orchestrating affairs, we can turn to Lao Zi's words in DDJ51:

> ... It actuates them but does not possess them
> Sets them in motion but does not expect of them
> It extends their lives without ruling and controlling them
> This is called Fathomless Virtue

Cultivating the Virtue of Dao, and the benefit to those who do, is referred to in DDJ54, where the term "Virtue" can otherwise be read as its synonym and homonym: "得 attainment":

> ... Cultivate this in the body and its Virtue will be true[87]
> Cultivate this in the home and its Virtue will be plentiful
> Cultivate this in the village and its Virtue will be long lasting
> Cultivate this in the nation and its Virtue will be abundant

---

[86] Guo Songtao suggests moving lines 58-61 so that they follow line 40. I find that they fit the flow of argument better as received.

[87] Reading "virtue" as "attainment," these lines would be translated:
"Cultivate this in the body and its attainment will be true
Cultivate this in the home and its attainment will be plentiful
Cultivate this in the village and its attainment will be long lasting..."

Cultivate this in the world and its Virtue will be widespread…

Lines 62-63 of the *Bai Xin* offer an explanation of the closing lines in DDJ38,[88] which also addresses the mistake of putting more importance on divination than intrinsic virtue (De):

> … Thus, when Dao is lost, virtue appears
> When virtue is lost, benevolence appears
> When benevolence is lost, righteousness appears
> When righteousness is lost, etiquette appears
>
> In etiquette, sincerity and selflessness are lacking
> And this is the beginning of chaos
> This trajectory can be recognized
> When people who don't know
> Display flowery appearances of the Dao
> And speak as though they know how to recognize what is coming
> This is the beginning of idiocy
> Therefore, great and noble men stay with what is substantial
> And not with what is slight
> They stay with the fruit
> And not with the flower
> They leave that and choose this

64 是謂寬乎形, 徒居而致名。
This means that while relaxed in his body and staying in place, good reputation comes to him.
65 去善之言, 為善之事,
Leaving skillful words, and taking skillful actions,
66 事成而顧反無名。
When his affairs are completed,
he seeks again to become nameless.

---

[88] Chapter 38 is the first chapter of the *Dao De Jing*'s "Virtue (De)" volume.

Purifying the Heart-Mind

67 能者無名，從事無事。
That which is effective and capable is nameless,
attending to affairs without affair.[89]

68 審量出入而觀物所載。
Investigating and measuring what goes out and what comes in,[90] observe the things that it brings.

69 庸能法無法乎？
Who can follow the laws of that which is without laws?

70 始無始乎？
Who can begin like that which is without beginning?

71 終無終乎？
Who can end like that which is without ending?

72 弱無弱乎？
Who can have the softness of that which is beyond softness?

The Sage's spiritual intelligence is elusive, but real. To focus on selfish endeavours would complicate his connection to the oneness of all, and so he places value on following Dao and lets its principles of renewal take care of his needs.

DDJ37 also discusses the tranquility of rejoining with the nameless:

> The Dao is always effortless yet without inaction
> When lords and kings can guard this within
> The myriad things eventually transform themselves
> Transforming, yet desiring to do so intentionally
> I pacify this desire with the simplicity of the nameless
> The simplicity of the nameless removes all desires
> When the tranquility of desirelessness is established
> The world stabilizes itself

---

[89] Lines 67-68 could also be read "Those who are effective and capable are nameless, attending to affairs without affair. Investigating and measuring what goes and what comes in, they observe the things that it brings."

[90] The same words for "出 deploying and 入 being invaded," used in lines 39-44, are used here, possibly referring to those lines.

Lines 69-72 help to explain why the term "the nameless" is used to describe the ineffable, and begin the transition into a more overt discourse on self-cultivation.

Lines 65-72 speak to taking action when necessary and then releasing the grip of control. This theme holds the surface meaning of managing affairs while allowing the nature of situations to reveal themselves. It also carries implications related to the heart-mind and the inner Sage of spiritual intelligence: when action is required, the heart-mind gives rise to thought and contemplation, but when understanding has been reached, the ruler (heart-mind) does not spin his wheels on the subject. Rather, the heart-mind returns to emptiness and practices the Sage's way of government, exemplified by Dao and "Fathomless Virtue." As explained in the ancient commentary section of the *Xin Shu Shang*:

> "Responding to things as though by coincidence."
> This is called "adapting to the season" –
> Like a shadow taking the shape of a form,
> Or an echo responding to a sound.
> Thus, when things reach them, (the junzi) responds.
> When these things move on, (the junzi) remains in place.
> This means (the junzi) reverts back to emptiness.
> (XSS 215-221)

73 故曰美哉弟弟。
Thus, it is said: "So beautiful are untrodden mountain paths."
74 故曰有中有中,
Thus it is said: "There is a center within the center."
75 庸能得夫中之衷乎？
Who can obtain the center within the depths of the heart?
76 故曰功成者隳,
Thus it is said: "Accomplishments are destroyed;
77 名成者虧。
Fame is lost."
78 故曰孰能棄名與功,而還與眾人同。

Thus it is said: "Who can abandon fame and accomplishments, and become like one of the masses?
79 庸能棄功與名，而還反無成，
Who can abandon accomplishments and fame and return to being as one without accomplishments?"
80 無成有貴其成也，
Those without accomplishments value accomplishments
81 有成有貴其無成也。
Those with accomplishments value being without accomplishments.

Our fear of losing something often gets in the way of obtaining it. The Sage is not afraid of continuing on as he is, and so is not afraid of failing to obtain something new. This, paradoxically, affords him success in obtaining something that escaped others of the same abilities.

Lines 73-75 lead the reader deeper into the nameless, the ineffable, arriving at the "untrodden" purity in the "depths of the heart (衷)." Such a description is reminiscent of what later Daoist teachings on cultivating the Internal Elixir (Nei Dan) referred to as the Mysterious Pass, perhaps the clearest description of which is found in Li Daochun's (circa 1300 AD) *Collected works on Central Harmony* (aka *The Book of Balance and Harmony*, circa 1300 AD).

> The Mysterious Pass (玄關, xuan guan) is the pass of the most mysterious, most subtle, of mechanisms... Why do none of the Nei Dan texts give the exact location of the Mysterious Pass? It is because it is difficult to describe, and no attempts to do so will succeed that they call it the "Mysterious Pass." Therefore, the sages simply wrote of it with the single character, "center," and had (students) understand that "center" referred to the Mysterious Pass. So "center" meant neither inside nor outside, upper nor lower. It was not this sort of center.
> When Buddhists say, "thinking neither good thoughts nor bad thoughts, see the face of your original self (不思善, 不思惡, 正恁麼時, 那箇是自己本來面目)," this is the "center" of

Chan Buddhism. When Confucians say, "when euphoria, anger, sadness, and pleasure have not yet come forth, this is called 'the center'," this is the door of Confucians (此儒家之戶) – their "center." When Daoists say, "the place where thinking does not arise is called 'the center'," this is the "center" of Daoism. This is how "the center" applies to the three teachings.

When the Yi Jing (I Ching) says "tranquil and unmoving," this refers to the "center." "Sensing and accomplishing," is the employment the center. Lao Zi says "Arrive at supreme emptiness; embrace deep silence. Myriad creatures arise together. I thereby observe them returning."

The Yi Jing says: "Returning, see the heart of Heaven and Earth." The Yi Jing hexagram "Returning" shows one yang line arising under 5 yin lines. Yin is stillness (and silence). Yang is movement. At the extreme of stillness there is movement. This point (before) movement is the Mysterious Pass.

Put your mind to the place from which thinking arises. Persevering in this, the Mysterious Pass will naturally appear. Upon seeing the Mysterious Pass, the medicinal substance, firing process, timely operation, subtracting and adding, and final release through emergence of the spiritual embryo, collectively come from nowhere but this single opening.[91]

The *Nei Ye* uses similar terminology to the *Bai Xin*, and describes the pristine oasis found in the "heart of the heart–mind" as such:

Within the center of the heart-mind, there is another heart-mind
In this heart of the heart–mind
There is a resonance (intent) which precedes words
(lines 165-167)

While sayings such as "Accomplishments are destroyed; fame is lost" likely carry an internal meaning meant to help one transcend the mind and find their way towards this Mysterious Pass, in characteristic proto-Daoist fashion, they carry additional wisdom in their surface meanings. Discovering and exploring the center of the heart requires

---

[91] Translated by Dan G. Reid

a purity and sincerity that can easily escape those who seek renown, and so the *Bai Xin* teaches the importance of first abandoning this superfluous interest. This is reflected in the opening lines of DDJ2, often interpreted to mean that when someone is appreciated by all, they become full of themselves and thus no longer merit such praise. These lines, again, read:

> When all know the beautiful to be beautiful
> This ends in ugliness
> When all know the good to be good
> In the end there is "not good"...

Note, too, the understanding shared between line 78, and the end of DDJ77:

> ... Heaven's Way diminishes what has excess
> And restores what lacks sufficiency
> The way of man, however, is not this way
> Diminishing what suffers lack
> And assisting where there is excess
> Who can have in excess, and care for all under Heaven?
> Only those who have Dao...

To borrow the conclusion from line 81, then: In action, heed what is 'beyond action.'

Lao Zi's DDJ48 helps to clarify these lines further:

> The pursuit of learning requires daily accumulation
> The pursuit of Dao requires daily reduction
> Reducing and reducing
> Until arriving at effortlessness
> Effortless, yet without inaction
>
> Conquering all under Heaven
> Is best done without the endeavour to do so
> Perpetually, this endeavour will continue without satisfaction
> Even when all under Heaven has been conquered

These lines serve to show that, while anxieties and insecurities compel the mind to bolster the ego with thoughts of achievement and strength, we can also simply focus on removing these thoughts of achievement from our minds, and allow all things to unify in the emptiness therein.

82 日極則仄，
The sun reaches its zenith and then declines;
83 月滿則虧。
The moon reaches fullness and then wanes;
84 極之徒仄，
The zenith is followed by decline;
85 滿之徒虧，
Fullness is followed by loss;
86 巨之徒滅。
Enormity is followed by elimination.
87 庸能己無己乎？
Who can cultivate in themselves an absence of self?
88 效夫天地之紀。
One who follows the guiding principles of Heaven and Earth.

The Sage is unencumbered by any need to be admired. He enjoys the long road of life, and does not try to win the race.

This imagery of the sun and moon's rise and decline was also used in Heshang Gong's commentary on the *Dao De Jing* to caution against the error and consequences of arrogance.[92] The *Bai Xin* can be read here as making the same point by suggesting that the rise and fall of nations and rulers follows the rise in their self-satisfaction. Thus, the

---

[92] See chapter nine of Heshang Gong's commentary

proceeding lines (89-96) provide guidance on avoiding this self-satisfaction.

Lines 87-88 bring to mind DDJ7, a chapter which might be further understood alongside the explanations of restraint and longevity in lines 82-86:

> Heaven has longevity, Earth has continuity
> Heaven and Earth have the power of longevity and continuity
> because they do not live for themselves
> This is how they can live for so long
>
> Therefore, sages leave themselves behind
> And they end up in front
> They do not cater to themselves
> Yet they persist
> Is it not because they are without selfishness and wickedness
> That they are able to fulfill themselves?

Parallels to this rise and fall are also apparent in DDJ2, as discussed above.

89 人言善, 亦勿聽。
When others speak highly of him, the sage does not listen;
90 人言惡, 亦勿聽。
When others speak poorly of him, he also does not listen.
91 持而待之, 空然勿兩之,
Holding firm while receiving these words, he remains empty and hollow with his attention undivided (by these compliments or insults).
92 淑然自清。
Remaining pure and true, he clears his mind.
93 無以旁言為事成。
Without taking words from the people at his side as to the completion of affairs,

94 察而徵之, 無聽辯,
He examines evidence without listening to eloquence.
95 萬物歸之,
All things come to him,
96 美惡乃自見。
And what is good or bad reveals itself to him.

The Sage does not wish to get caught up in narcissistic sentiments of his wisdom and perception. He only wishes to keep his virtue and perceptions pure. Being taken in by other's opinions about him, good or bad, will only diminish his ability to do this.

Lines 89-96 counsel self-reliance and not giving undue power to external validation and the opinions of others. They are particularly evocative of DDJ13 in light of the question "Who can cultivate in themselves an absence of self?" in line 87:

DDJ13:
>   Favour and disgrace are both startling
>   Appreciate the great worrying that both of these cause in your body
>   ... What does it mean to say "Appreciate the great worrying
>   That (favour and disgrace) cause in your body?"
>   The reason I have great worries is because I have a self
>   If I did not have a self, what worries would I have?
>
>   Therefore, those who (govern) the self as the world
>   And cherish it as such
>   On them the world can rely
>   Those who (govern) the self as the world
>   And love it as such
>   To them the world can be entrusted

Good words and bad words can be used to manipulate the ego and steer one's decisions according to the manipulator's agenda. Not guarding against this is like handing over executive passwords to anyone who knows how that leader would like to view themselves. Sages, therefore, for the safety of the masses who had vested their power in such leaders, took care to warn those with the virtue to lead of this common vulnerability, knowing that a leader who is not capable of ruling themselves will have great difficulty ruling the world.

DDJ81 ("True words are not beautified; beautified words are not true words …") could also be compared to lines 89–96.

97 天或維之, 地或載之。
Something always keeps Heaven together; something always supports Earth.
98 天莫之維則天以墜矣。
If Heaven was not held together, then Heaven would fall;
99 地莫之載, 則地以沈矣。
If Earth was not supported, then Earth would sink.
100 夫天不墜, 地不沈,
But Heaven does not fall and Earth does not sink.
101 夫或維而載之也夫。
They are always held together and supported!
102 又況於人,
It is the same for human beings.
103 人有治之,
There is something that governs them.
104 辟之若夫雷鼓之動也,
Much like rolling drums of thunder
105 夫不能自搖者,
Cannot incite themselves.
106 夫或搖之。
There is something always inciting them.

The Sage sees the larger picture. In his wisdom and perception, he knows that he is only taking orders from the higher order. He does not establish anything, but only helps return things to the natural state of balance demanded by laws of harmony.

Lines 97-101 are, in fact, largely supported by the theory of ether, held by Nikola Tesla, and also later held by Albert Einstein. Tesla quotes himself in a letter to the editor of the New York Times, April 21, 1908:

> What I said in regard to the greatest achievement of the man of science whose mind is bent upon the mastery of the physical universe, was nothing more than what I stated in one of my unpublished addresses, from which I quote: "According to an adopted theory, every ponderable atom is differentiated from a tenuous fluid, filling all space merely by spinning motion, as a whirl of water in a calm lake. By being set in movement this fluid, the ether, becomes gross matter. Its movement arrested, the primary substance reverts to its normal state. It appears, then, possible for man through harnessed energy of the medium and suitable agencies for starting and stopping ether whirls to cause matter to form and disappear. At his command, almost without effort on his part, old worlds would vanish and new ones would spring into being. He could alter the size of this planet, control its seasons, adjust its distance from the sun, guide it on its eternal journey along any path he might choose, through the depths of the universe. He could make planets collide and produce his suns and stars, his heat and light; he could originate life in all its infinite forms. To cause at will the birth and death of matter would be man's grandest deed, which would give him the mastery of physical creation, make him fulfill his ultimate destiny.

Einstein at first denied the existence of this ether, but later changed his position. In "Ether and the Theory of Relativity" (1922), Einstein wrote:

> Recapitulating, we may say that according to the general theory of relativity, space is endowed with physical qualities; in this sense, therefore, there exists an ether. According to the general theory of relativity, space without ether is unthinkable; for in

such space there not only would be no propagation of light, but also no possibility of existence for standards of space and time (measuring-rods and clocks), nor therefore any space-time intervals in the physical sense. But this ether may not be thought of as endowed with the quality characteristic of ponderable media, as consisting of parts which may be tracked through time. The idea of motion may not be applied to it.

107 夫或者何？若然者也。
What is this constant thing? It is present at all times.
108 視則不見,
Looking for it with the eyes, it will not be seen;
109 聽則不聞。
Listening for it with the ears, it will not be heard.
110 灑乎天下滿,
Scattered throughout, it fills all under Heaven.
111 不見其塞。
Though not seen on the surface,
112 集於顏色,
It is collected in the harmonious shape of the face;
113 知於肌膚。
It is known in the muscles and the skin.
114 責其往來,
Dutifully, it comes and goes,
115 莫知其時。
Yet no one knows its timing.
116 薄乎其方也,
So small, it is (within) the square (of Earth);
117 騖乎其圓也,
So expansive, it (exceeds) the circle (of Heaven).
118 騖騖乎莫得其門。
Expanding and expanding, no one can reach its gate.

The Sage recognizes order in harmony and thereby learns the laws and principles governing even the Imperial Emperor – the "Son of Heaven."

Lines 107-118 speak of the ineffability of Dao, a topic touched upon in many Daoist texts, including of course the *Dao De Jing*. This ineffability is said to manifest in the principles of harmony, noted throughout the myriad things, and likely suggested in DDJ1's discourse on finding the principles of Dao in "outer surfaces." Note too, the shared mention of an ever expanding gate in line 118, above, and DDJ1:

> … The Nameless is the origin of Heaven and Earth
> The Named is the mother of the myriad things
> Thus, always without desires
> Observing its inner subtlety
> Always with desires
> Observing its outer surface
> These two were born together, yet differ in name
> Together, they are called Fathomless Mystery
> This mystery, ever more mystifying
> Is a multitude of gates
> All leading to the subtlety within
> (DDJ1)

Similar language, in respects to the ineffability of Dao, is also found in DDJ14:

> By looking, it is not seen. It is known as Clear
> By listening, it is not heard. It is known as Inaudible
> What cannot be obtained when seized is known as Infinitesimal
> These three things cannot be inspected
> And are merged into one
>
> Above, it is not bright
> Below, it is not dark
> Immeasurable and unnameable
> It is again nothing
> This is called "having no form or appearance"

Without a materialized image
This is called "absent-minded"
Greet it and you do not see its front
Follow it and you do not see its rear
Hold to the ancient Dao and ride it until you possess the present
Then you will have the power to know the ancient beginning
This is called "the thread of Dao"

119 故口為聲也,
The mouth utters,
120 耳為聽也,
The ears listen,
121 目有視也,
The eyes observe,
122 手有指也,
The hands gesture,
123 足有履也,
And the feet walk.
124 事物有所比也。
These functions all have respective things (which enable them).
125 當生者生, 當死者死。
What must live, lives, and what must die, dies.
126 言有西有東, 各死其鄉,
This means that in both the East and the West, each will die according to its own situation.

There is a reason behind everything, even though it may not be apparent.

Lines 119-126 suggest an idea similar to the concept of interdependence in Buddhist philosophy, and also to the concept of origins mentioned earlier in lines 94-106. Just as listening is made possible by the ears, and observing is made possible by the eyes, all things depend on other things for their existence and operations. Awareness of this natural law is also evident when ancient Chinese texts speak of "names."

Name (ming) suggests more than simply appellations, but also the full development and *function* of a "thing" in the world, having reached a level of distinction from the things on which its existence depends. While a "name/ming" describes physical characteristics, it also signifies function, much the same as a "title" in English.

This maturation of "names" can be seen in other lines of the *Bai Xin*, for example:

Lines 16-18
>   Knowing its image, one apprehends its form;
>   Reaching to its principles, one knows its nature;
>   Seeking its end, one knows its name.

Lines 27-32
>   Therefore, the Sage's method of government
>   Is to still the body and wait.
>   Things then arrive at their names, and naturally fall into place.
>   As these names naturally order themselves,
>   Those which do not fit are abolished.
>   When names are corrected and laws perfected,
>   The Sage is without further endeavours.

And, further down, in lines 130-135
>   As for men of highest wisdom,
>   Their mouths are without empty chatter,
>   And their hands are without empty gesturing.
>   As things arise, they are destined to be heard of,
>   Assigned names and sounds,
>   And combined according to form and appearance.

Another word, at times useful to describe "names," would be "facts."

127 置常立儀, 能守貞乎？
By establishing a culture of etiquette, can you preserve sincerity?[93]
128 常事通道, 能官人乎？
By keeping affairs in accord with Dao, can you govern others?
129 故書其惡者, 言其薄者。
Thus, books are shunned, and words are cheap.[94]
130 上聖之人,
As for the sages of antiquity,
131 口無虛習也,
Their mouths were without empty chatter,
132 手無虛指也。
And their hands without empty gesturing.
133 物至而命之耳。
As things arose, orders were sent out,
134 發於名聲,
They issued names and sounds,
135 凝於體色,
And expressed themselves through body language,
136 此其可諭者也。
Like this they could express themselves.
137 不發於名聲,
What could not be expressed with name and sound,
138 不凝於體色,
Nor expressed through body language,
139 此其不可諭者也。
This they would not express.
140 及至於至者, 教存可也,

---

[93] Zhen 貞 often appears in the Yi Jing, translated as sincerity, and contains a number of nuances related to virtue and integrity.
[94] In other words, relying on advice written or spoken when Dao was not profuse is nothing compared to observing the way into which things settle when Dao is profuse, and thereby knowing how they ought to be.

For reaching the ultimate goal, it is the same whether these teachings survive,
141 教亡可也。
Or otherwise disappear.
142 故曰：濟於舟者和於水矣，
Thus, it is said: "Those who ferry across the river are in harmony with the water."[95]
143 義於人者祥其神矣。
"Those who are righteous towards others receive blessings from the spirits.

The constant thread of Dao is not dependent on teachings. Holding to righteousness, not allowing oneself to be seduced by egocentric fantasies, not placing egotistical concerns above the inborn virtue and that emptiness which connects us to everything in the universe — this is a practice much greater than the sum of its parts.

When Lao Zi described Dao, he did so by speaking of the things that arose from it, such as nature, humanity, Heaven, and Earth. He did not attempt to define Dao, but rather only spoke of how it transcends the limitations of any definition. As such, he would also contrast definitions, or "names," with their opposites to show that Dao is both, and so neither. As Dao is "the unborn," it cannot yet be described. We see this in DDJ4 where Lao Zi states:

> … Tranquil! As though having a life of its own
> I do not know whose child it is
> It appears to have preceded the primordial ruler (God)

Heshang Gong comments on DDJ1:

> The Eternal Name can only be like that of a child who has not yet spoken; like baby chicks which have not come out of their

---

[95] "濟 to ferry across the river" also means "to assist."

eggs; like a brilliant and precious pearl which is still within its oyster; like beautiful jade which is still between the rocks

Lines 142-143 refer to the commonly held belief that spirits hold much sway in orchestrating success or misfortune for humans in the physical realm. Heshang Gong often referred to shen ming, or "spiritual lights," as, for example, in chapter seven:

> All people love (sages) like their own mothers and fathers. The spiritual lights (shen ming) protect them like a newborn child. Thus, they always remain... Sages act with love towards people, and are protected by the spiritual lights. Is this not because they are fair, upright, and without selfishness?

We see here a spiritual equivalent to what Buddhists would ascribe to *karma*. As line 143 states: "To those who are righteous towards others, the spirits bring good fortune." While Daoists and Buddhists agree on the universal principles of balance, stretching through one's lifetimes in the case of Buddhism, Daoism also attributes the force and effect of this balance to agents of the spirit realm that mete out recompense and retribution.

144 事有適, 而無適,
Affairs have suitable and unsuitable (solutions),
145 若有適觿解, 不可解而後解。
For example, it is suitable to use an ivory bodkin[96] to untie (knots). What cannot be untied is then untied.
146 故善舉事者,
As for those who excel at improving situations,
147 國人莫知其解。
When the nation's people cannot figure out how to "untie" (a situation),

---

[96] Bodkins are sewing spikes that were often carried in decorative casings and worn at the waist for emergency fabric repairs

148 為善乎, 毋提提,
They apply their skill but do not hold onto the situation without letting go.
149 為不善乎, 將陷於刑。
This would be unskillful, for it submerges the situation in laws and punishment.
150 善不善, 取信而止矣。
Such ability is not skillful.
Attain trustworthiness and then stop.[97]
151 若左若右, 正中而已矣。
Bring left and right to align in the center, and then stop.[98]

When resolving conflicts, the Sage does not let his emotions direct his actions, but carefully observes a situation and the impulses of those involved. To avoid deepening the problem, he first identifies the opposing sides of the issue. He can then work his way towards the larger issue by resolving the many smaller ones along the way.

Lines 144-151 speak of using suitable actions to ameliorate a situation, and of not overusing the tools of power and prohibition. This lesson also appears in DDJ9:

> To take hold and continue filling
> Is not as good as coming to a stop
> If you obsessively refine a spear
> It will not be long enough to protect you
> If gold and jade fill the court
> Nothing can hold onto them
> When fortune and wealth bring arrogance
> They bring the misfortune of their own loss

---

[97] See also DDJ57
[98] Left and right may refer to upper and lower ranks or echelons of government or society. See lines 56-63 of the *Bai Xin*, and accompanying footnotes, which also discuss the disorder between "left and right," referred to in these lines.

When achievements are completed
Their recognition should continue
But the individual should withdraw
This is the way of Heaven

Note the common thread of *holding on for too long* (see BX line 148). The commonality here is also interesting in that the earliest copy of DDJ9, found at the Guodian tombs,[99] did not refer to "holding," while the edits made to later copies of this chapter reflect the lexicon found in the *Bai Xin*. Though DDJ9 is more lyrical, the same message is carried across, and lines 144-151 of the *Bai Xin* offer a more exact meaning to the *Dao De Jing*'s broader applicability.

The message in both texts can be traced back to an inner meaning of letting go rather than using force, and of unburdening the mind of worry and excessive thought. The Guodian copy of DDJ9 has the image of waters accumulating and then bursting forth and causing damage, rather than being allowed to circulate naturally and not build up a reservoir of potential disaster. This idea is discussed further in the *Bai Xin*'s following lines, which look at an obsession with prohibitions.

152 縣乎日月無已也
What about (governing) the districts? (As sure as) the sun and moon go on without stop,
153 愕愕者不以天下為憂,
Those who are alert and responsive will not cause the world to worry;
154 刺刺者不以萬物為筴,
Those who make longwinded speeches do not consider the myriad things in their plans.[100]
155 庸能棄刺刺而為愕愕乎?

---

[99] Please see the comments on BX lines 33-36 for a translation of the Guodian DDJ's chapter 9.
[100] 刺刺 is a compound word meaning "talkative." 筴, a type of grass, means "plan; urge."

Now, the question is, who can give up longwinded speeches while being alert and responsive?

156 難言憲術,
It is difficult to describe the method of creating rules and laws.

157 須同而出。
They must have consistency before being issued.

158 無益言, 無損言,
And be without saying too much or too little,

159 近可以免,
Otherwise, people can come close to yet evade them.

The Sage knows that words can be used to obscure the truth more easily than they can be used to reveal it. Thus, he is careful about over-limiting things with definitions of true and false, right and wrong.

Lines 152-159 of the *Bai Xin* also warn of promoting rules and expectations without restraint, much as in DDJ57:

> When aligned, the nation is well governed
> When aberrant, the military is effective
> It is by having no endeavour to do so
> That the world is conquered
> How do I know this to be the case?
> By this:
>
> When taboos are abundant in the world
> The people are extremely poor
> When the people have an abundance of sharp weapons
> The nation grows dark
> When people have an abundance of skill and ingenuity
> Irregular things flourish
> When laws and standards are increasingly publicized
> Thieves and robbers abound

Thus the Sage says:
I do nothing, and the people reform themselves
I love stillness, and the people regulate themselves
I do not endeavour, and the people enrich themselves
I am without desires, and the people are natural

These lines in the *Bai Xin* may also carry with them some of the context preceding DDJ81:

True words are not beautified
Beautified words are not true words
The skilled are not argumentative
The argumentative are not skilled
Those who (pretend to) know do not remain open-minded
The open-minded do not (pretend to) know...

160 故曰：知何知乎？
Thus it is said: "Know!" But what should you know?
161 謀何謀乎？
"Plan!" But what sort of plan?
162 審而出者, 彼自來。
To those who are careful in issuing orders, these (answers) naturally arrive.

163 自知曰稽,
Knowing oneself is called "investigating" (jī);
164 知人曰濟。
Knowing others is called "crossing the river" (jī).
165 知苟適可, 為天下周。
By knowing what is frivolous and what is necessary, one can bring the world into unison.[101]

---

[101] The final character here "make the world Zhou 周" (as in Zhou dynasty, also meaning circle; cycle; complete) is debated by scholars to be a typo for various words. However, given the context of 'making things fit,' I've maintained the origi-

166 內固之一，可為長久。
Internally, solidifying themselves into a unified whole, one may lengthen their lifespan.
167 論而用之，可以為天下王。
Discussing the application of this principle reveals the way to rule all under Heaven.[102]

Trying too hard to know can lead one away from their spiritual intelligence, and into the realm of pragmatic definitions, created to serve purposes that are no longer relevant. Better to just sit and wait, purifying the heart-mind of all "doing," until illumination arrives.

Lines 160-167 provide an important historical backdrop for the development of Daoist internal cultivation. We see here the suggestion to first find inner stability and unity before attempting to assist the world (lines 166-167). This ties into earlier passages which warned of wielding excessive control, and the text's opening lines on conduct in political affairs. By first finding inner calm, leaders can avoid impetuous decisions that create even more dissent and disorder – the exact opposite of a law's intended effect. The *Bai Xin*, here, points out the confluence of these internal and external endeavours:

> Internally, solidifying oneself into a unified whole, one may lengthen their lifespan.
> Discussing the application of this principle reveals the way to rule all under Heaven (lines 166-167)

The parallels between BX160-167 and DDJ47 give an idea of how these teachings travelled through various discussions at the time:

DDJ47:
   Without going out the door

---

nal character with perhaps moderate flexibility in its usage. The text's proceeding comment on unification also suggests the utility of this word choice.

[102] See also DDJ16 on knowing the eternal and thereby knowing the way of the king and lengthening life.

Know all under Heaven
Without glancing out the window
See Heaven's Way
The further out one goes
The less they know
Therefore, the Sage does not move
Yet he knows
He describes and names (things)
Without seeing (them)
He brings about perfection
Without acting

BX160-167 also tie into the ideas of DDJ57 (appearing in the commentary for lines 152-159, above), while showing a closer resemblance to DDJ65 (below) in their guidance on knowledge and the connection between strategies for self-government and state-government.

DDJ65:
[…]
Difficulty in governing people
Comes from a wealth of wisdom
Hence, when knowledge is used to govern the nation
This results in thievery from the nation
Not using knowledge to govern the nation
Blesses the nation
Understand the broader application of these two principles
There is an infinite understanding
Which can be found in these principles (see BX line 167)
This is called Fathomless Virtue
Fathomless Virtue, profound and far-reaching
Following it, things return back to their nature
Arriving at great submission

Note here, as well, the definition of Fathomless Virtue given in DDJ51, and the insight it gives into self-government and state-government in both DDJ65 and the *Bai Xin*.

(from DDJ51)
... (Dao) actuates them but does not possess them
Sets them in motion but does not expect of them
Extends their lives without ruling and controlling
This is called Fathomless Virtue

168 天之視而精。
By observing Heaven, realize your essence;
169 四璧而知請。
By the changing seasons, understand you inner feelings.
170 壤土而與生,
By the fertile soil, support your life energy.
171 能若夫風與波乎？
Can you be like the wind and waves?
172 唯其所欲適。
They desire only what is appropriate to the circumstance.
173 故子而代其父曰義也,
So, when a son replaces his father,
this is called righteousness.
174 臣而代其君曰篡也,
When the minister replaces the ruler,
this is called usurpation.
175 篡何能歌,
When do we sing of usurpation?
176 武王是也。
In regards to King Wu.[103]

---

[103] Likely referring King Wu (武王), the first King of the Zhou Dynasty who wrested power from the Shang Dynasty. This may suggest references to the Duke of Zhou in (unspecified) songs about King Wu. The Duke of Zhou took power from King Wu's heir, the teenage King Cheng, to protect the Dynasty from Cheng's inexperience. The Duke of Zhou is highly revered as a Chinese cultural hero, and so the usurpation here may, in fact, be spoken of in a positive light, and as a metaphor for energetic transformations described in directly preceding lines.

Purifying the Heart-Mind

177 故曰庸能去辯與巧,
Thus, it is said:
"Who can abandon argumentation and scheming,
178 而還與眾人同道。
And accompany common people on the same road?

When the mind submits to the spirit, peace reigns throughout the body.

In lines 168 to 172, the *Bai Xin* speaks of jing-essence in its original state as endowed by the Heavens – the basic seed of life. Just as the Daoist concept of De, Virtue, is that of an intrinsic perfection, this jing-essence from Heaven is uncorrupted and therefore holds the plan of Heaven within it. As lines 179-183 (below) show, when this jing-essence can genuinely expresses itself and individuals do not try to confine this expression within the limitations of intellect, this Heaven endowed jing-essence can bring them to the full expression of Heaven's plan in their lives, allowing them to be like the wind to the waves as their desires are suited to the plan of Heaven.

The *Nei Ye* begins by discussing how (primordial) jing-essence is the basis by which common people develop into Sages, and later shows that purifying the mind of thoughts is necessary for the cultivation of jing (see NY88-104). The *Bai Xin* also appears to imply clearing the mind in lines 160-167, and follows with this statement about the great transformative power of jing, suggesting that heaven packs qi and spiritual knowledge into jing, which is essentially 'unpacked' through heart-mind purification techniques. As the *Xin Shu Shang* (ancient commentary section), lines 90-97 state:

> What people occupy themselves with today is jing-essence.
> Getting rid of desires should be the priority.
> From this follows quiet stillness.
> Quiet stillness brings about jing-essence.

This reference may otherwise refer to King Wu (武王) of Chu (740-690 BC), the first king of Chu. Wu usurped power from the legitimate Zhou Dynasty viscount of Chu State, and later declared independence for Chu, with himself as King.

From jing essence, singularity is established.
Singularity brings about illumination.
Illumination brings about spirit.
As for spirit, this is reaching the treasure.

179 故曰思索精者明益衰,
Thus, it is said, "When thoughts search for essence,
brilliance further declines.
180 德行修者王道狹,
When virtuous actions are studied,
the path of the king narrows.
181 臥名利者寫生危,
To lay down (desires for) fame and profit
is to take command of what endangers one's life."
182 知周於六合之內者,
As for those with knowledge spanning everything within the six directions of the universe,
183 吾知生之有為阻也。
I know that this causes obstruction in their lives.

The knowledge of the spirit reigns supreme. The spirit thrives in virtue, and so the Sage knows that virtue is greater than fame and profit.

Lines 179 exemplify the Daoist principle of skillful "non-action" and clear minded meditation, illustrated in Lao Zi's chapter 11: "Door frames and windows are carved out to make a room, and in this emptiness the room is used."

Line 180 may be read in consideration of DDJ38 ("Highest virtue is not noticeably virtuous, therefore it has Virtue. Lower virtue is unmistakably virtuous, therefore it is without Virtue") and the hypocrisy that can arise from excessive focus on goodness and worthiness, as explained in DDJ3 ("Do not exalt the worthy and the people will not fight). Regarding "the path of the king" becoming narrow, this statement may reflect DDJ16, considering the intolerance and disconnection from intrinsic wisdom that can result from an obsession with demonstrable virtuous conduct. DDJ16 states:

> The way of impartiality shows the way of a king
> The way of a king shows the way of Heaven
> The way of Heaven shows the way of Dao
> The way of Dao shows the way of longevity
> And for the body to be without peril

Lines 179-181 may further explain Lao Zi's intent when rejecting the Confucian approach to self-cultivation: seeking a name as someone who has attained true virtues brings with it the tendency to backslide in one's cultivation of jing-essence – the pure life-force endowed by Heaven (Nature) which is truly responsible for our ultimate potential and development.

As Heshang Gong comments on DDJ27:

> *"Excellent counting does not use counting devices"*
> Those who are excellent at finding a strategy to attain Dao simply guard Oneness within and do not shift from it. Their strategies are not numerous, and so they do not use counting devices to know them all.

For further reference on this approach, see also DDJ19:

> Quit sageliness
> Abandon wisdom
> And the people will benefit one hundred fold
> Quit benevolence, abandon right-conduct
> And the people will return to caring for their parents
> Quit cleverness, abandon profit
> And robbers and thieves will not exist
> These three
> Are only ornamental, and not satisfactory
> Thus, we have the following:
> Observe the natural state
> Embrace the unaltered

Minimize self-importance
And have few desires

184 持而滿之, 乃其殆也。
If you continue filling something (without stopping), you endanger it.
185 名滿於天下, 不若其已也。
For name and reputations to fill the world is not as good as coming to a stop.
186 名進而身退, 天之道也。
When the name goes forth, the self retreats. This is the Dao of Heaven.[104]
187 滿盛之國, 不可以仕任。
In a nation that is excessive, one should not accept office.
188 滿盛之家, 不可以嫁子,
To a family that is excessive, one should not marry off a child.
189 驕倨傲暴之人, 不可與交。
When people are proud, arrogant, and violent, it is not right to associate with them.

The Sage finds nourishment in the simplicity of nature. He knows that filling a room with too many things makes it uninhabitable, just

---

[104] This saying appears in various forms in the DDJ, though appearing here, it shows how it is tied to "names," and perhaps knowledge of "everything in the six directions." The *Bai Xin* seems to have a view which accords closely with Buddhism, in that, returning from the attachments and trappings of life, the wise sages also detached from the need to be recognized, accepting that they are a part of the whole, though acting and appearing separate and distinct. "Returning to the nameless" is to return to the state before distinction, and before the competition and desires of the "named."

as filling the mind with too many ideas makes it unaccommodating to a full and true experience of the present.

Lines 184-189 may be the most complete reflection of DDJ9 in the *Bai Xin*. Note, especially, the similarity between lines 184-185 and the beginning of DDJ9, as well as that between line 186 and the end of DDJ9. Here is chapter nine again, for comparison:

> To take hold and continue filling
> Is not as good as coming to a stop
> If you obsessively refine a spear
> It will not be long enough to protect you
> If gold and jade fill the court
> Nothing can hold onto them
> When fortune and wealth bring arrogance
> They bring the misfortune of their own loss
>
> When achievements are completed
> Their recognition should continue
> But the individual should withdraw
> This is the way of Heaven

BX184-189 further clarify the underlying reference to reputation suggested throughout DDJ9 and presented more fully in its last four lines. Tirelessly seeking reputation is like grinding down a spear. One can only do so for so long before they have nothing left to sharpen. Having a great and widespread reputation invites people to test and attack it, and if this doesn't destroy it, one can bring shame on themselves simply by "believing their own hype" and becoming arrogant. Thus, Lao Zi counsels to simply do marvelous things and then move on without demanding recognition. The Sage is content to remain undefined, like the Dao, rather than speaking of his or her strengths, achievements, or anything that may garner the admiration or sympathy of others. This is the Sage's way of both survival and enduring success.

190 道之大如天,
Dao encompasses the vastness of Heaven,
191 其廣如地,
The span of the Earth,
192 其重如石,
The heaviness of stone,
193 其輕如羽,
And the lightness of a feather.
194 民之所以知者寡,
Those with knowledge of it amongst the people are few.
195 故曰何道之近 而莫之與能服也。
Thus it is said: "How is it that Dao is so close, yet none can live by it?"[105]

196 棄近而就遠, 何以費力也。
By rejecting what is close and chasing after what is far, how can one but squander their power?
197 故曰：欲愛吾身, 先知吾情
Thus it is said: "Desiring to take care of myself, I must first know my true inner state.
198 君親六合以考內身。
By observing the universe, I investigate my own body."
199 以此知象, 乃知行情,
As such, comprehending this image, one thereby understands the tendencies of their true inner state.
200 既知行情, 乃知養生。
Knowing the tendencies of their true inner state, they will know how to nourish life.

Dao is right there, within everyone and everything, every moment and every circumstance. By training the mind to look within and notice the heart-mind's many activities, one can begin to rein in its

---

[105] Literally, "yet none can wear it."

many affairs and consolidate focus. They can then move forward in a positive and meaningful direction.

Lines 190-200 follow the same set of ideas running through DDJ70, 71, and 72, and which might be summarized as follows:

While people seek to make great names for themselves, Dao surpasses all yet is known to so very few. Such names are external, existing in the minds of others, whereas Dao is found within, in emptiness, seemingly non-existent.

In the same way that Dao is not acknowledged by those who chase after renown, the virtue of those who live by Dao goes unnoticed. They are simply natural, and seemingly "nothing special," not seeking to display their progress for others; instead, they work on themselves in obscurity.

Lines 196-200 bear a striking resemblance to the lesson of DDJ47, which reads, again:

> Without going out the door, know all under Heaven
> Without glancing out the window, see Heaven's Way
> The further out one goes, the less they know
> Therefore, the Sage does not move, yet he knows
> He describes and names (things) without seeing (them)
> And brings about perfection without acting

While, on the surface, the *Dao De Jing* may suggest that the Sage transcends time and space to see physical things and circumstances, the *Bai Xin* explains that what is perceived is internal. Thus, comparing these two texts brings our attention to early Chinese traditions of mindfulness. A central practice of mindfulness is to observe one's inner state, and pay attention to phenomena such as emotions, urges, and feelings by becoming aware of their "arising, abiding, declining, and ceasing." The *Bai Xin* adds to this, in lines 179-200, a Daoist practice of recognizing the unity of our inner (microcosmic) and outer (macrocosmic) worlds, and perhaps also recognizing subtle environmental influences on our inner state. As the *Bai Xin* states:

> "Desiring to take care of myself, I must first know my true inner state.

By observing the universe, I investigate my own body."
As such, comprehending this image, one thereby understands the tendencies of their true inner state.
Knowing the tendencies of their true inner state, they will know how to nourish life.

Lao Zi states this in DDJ47 (above) as:

... Therefore, the Sage does not move, yet he knows
He describes and names without seeing
And brings about perfection without acting

"He describes and names without seeing" may refer to closing the eyes and looking inwards at what has no shape or sound, referred to vaguely in the *Bai Xin*, line 199, as "the image." As explained in my commentary on *Bai Xin* line 16, above, "the image" is essentially another term for Dao. Here, "the image" can be likened to *dharma*. As with the term "Dao," dharma can mean a principle of cosmic order, a way of living, and/or phenomena. While phenomena seem separate, they are empty of independent existence; they are illusory, and simply a part of the one principle. Phenomena such as feelings, emotions, thoughts, ideas, beliefs, mental and social constructs, etc., when allowed to reveal their "names,"[106] eventually simply disappear, returning to the one principle – emptiness; Dao.

As part of Daoist mindfulness practice throughout the day, one can pay attention to the movement of the qi (energy-breath) as it is affected by emotions. *The Huang Di Nei Jing, Su Wen*, chapter 39, describes these movements as follows:

The hundred diseases are generated by qi.
When one is angry, their qi rises
When euphoric, their qi relaxes
When sad, their qi dissipates
When fearful, their qi descends
When cold, their qi collects

---

[106] See BX27-32 for an example of how the art of purifying the heart-mind reveals the true nature of "names."

When over-heated, their qi leaks out
When startled, their qi is chaotic
When exhausted, their qi is wasted
When pensive, their qi is knotted

While it takes time to dissolve the internal triggers that set our emotions off and put the heart-mind at risk of usurpation, by noticing, for example, the rising qi of anger, one can see the roots of their reactions and employ the energy-moderating power of the lungs[107] to even out their qi.

Buddhist teacher Pema Chodron (1936-present) reveals that the path outlined in BX190-200 continues to this day:

"If your everyday practice is to open to all your emotions, to all the people you meet, to all the situations you encounter, without closing down, trusting that you can do that – then that will take you as far as you can go. And then you'll understand all the teachings that anyone has ever taught."

201 左右前後，周而復所，
Turning to the left, right, front, and back, running full circle, return to the place (at the center).
202 執儀服象，敬迎來者。
Holding to a ceremonious outward appearance, respectfully welcome that which approaches.
203 今夫來者必道其道，

---

[107] See Nei Jing Su Wen, chapter eight, in the Introduction: Internal Cutlivation in the Guan Zi, Xin Shu Shang:
　The heart holds the office of the ruler;
　It brings forth spiritual intelligence.
　The lungs hold the office of the grand tutor;
　They bring forth order and moderation.
　The liver holds the office of the general;
　It brings forth ambitions and planning…

Those today who seek its approach require this method to (invite) Dao.

204 無頡無衍, 命乃長久。
Without soaring (into the sky), without spilling over,
the destined life-force (ming) will be extended.

205 和以反中, 形性相葆。
Harmonize by returning to the center,
where both body and pure nature (xing) are preserved.

206 一以無貳, 是謂知道。
Be unified and without (doubt or) division.[108]
This is called "knowing Dao."

207 將欲服之, 必一其端, 而固其所守。
Wishing to be enveloped by it,[109] you must unify to the furthest extent, and solidify that which is protected within.

Aligning the body helps to align the heart-mind and perceptions, connect the nerve pathways and improve the circulation of vital essences. This enables the unhindered intuitive response of the body's movements and the innate functions of the internal organs. The Sage understands the importance of following the natural laws of harmony, and so is mindful of the natural harmony of his body.

This section of the *Bai Xin* is amongst the clearest descriptions of meditation from texts of this time, including parables in the *Zhuang Zi*. "A ceremonious outward appearance" (line 204) suggests an upright yet relaxed and dignified posture. "Respectfully welcome that which approaches" suggests that this posture should be calm and dignified, but not prideful and stiff, putting the ego aside and being open to the guest. In both meditation and welcoming guests, the mind should be bright, open, and attentive (internally and singularly

---

[108] "Undivided," more commonly meant "無貳爾心 without doubt (undivided) in your heart," but its literal meaning is emphasized within the context of these lines of the *Bai Xin*.
[109] Literally "clothed, covered, by it"

attentive for the case of Daoist meditation). Guests are not welcomed ceremoniously with dull and lethargic minds, nor inattentive minds. The *Bai Xin* also points out that, with the busy life and busy minds of most people, "those today who seek its approach require this method to (invite) Dao" (line 205). This image of being upright at attention is reinforced in the opening lines of the *Xin Shu Xia*:

> When the bodily form is not aligned, Virtue does not approach;
> When the center is not pure and clear, the heart-mind is not stable.
> An aligned bodily form is adorned with Virtue

Line 204 counsels simplicity and inner balance in this practice, and warns against "soaring" and "spilling over." A similar sentiment can be seen in DDJ15:

> ... Who, by the power of their stillness
> Can make clouded water slowly become clear?
> Who, by the power of their serenity
> Can sustain this progress until life slowly arises?
> Those who maintain this Dao do not desire fullness
> It is because they are not full that they can remain covered
> And not let what is new come to an end

Lines 205 and 201 describe an inward gathering of energies, which the *Nei Ye* shows to include the energy of thoughts, and a "returning to the center" — a singularity of mind and attention, not scattered on myriad interests, but focused on the present. DDJ5 refers to this inner returning with the lines "To speak countless words is worthless. This is not as good as guarding the center." Such descriptions resemble the practice of *stabilizing jing* found in the *Nei Ye*, (especially) lines 135-150.

Lines 205-207 provide some direction on how to proceed from this inner silence and inner gathering: "Left, right, front, and back, running full circle, they return to the place (at the center)" (line 201). This is the blending of yin and yang into Oneness. The place at the center could also refer to the lower-dantien, considered the body's center of gravity, and located about two finger-widths behind and below the navel. This gathering of focus to the center resembles, further, advice found in Heshang Gong's commentary. For example, compare line 206 with the following comments by Heshang Gong on DDJ1, and DDJ10:

> "*Thus, always without desires, observing its inner subtlety*"
> The "subtlety," here, means the key. People who maintain the absence of desire will be able to observe the key to Dao. "The key" is Oneness.
> ...
> "*(Is a) multitude of gates, all leading to the subtlety within*"
> Heaven can return to the Heaven within itself, and dispense energy-breaths which are either potent or weak. Eliminating strong emotions, abandoning desires, and guarding balance and harmony within: this is called "knowing the gate-key to the door of Dao."
> (DDJ1)
> All the names together are One. Referring to Oneness, it is said: "In a unified consciousness, there is no (doubt or) division."
> (DDJ10)

If lines 206-207 were to precede lines 201-205, the sequence of ideas in this section (unifying to the fullest extent, returning, and preserving ming) would be the same as in DDJ16:

> Arrive at supreme emptiness
> Embrace deep silence
> Myriad creatures arise together
> I thereby observe them returning
> So many things blossoming
> And each returns back to its roots
> Returning to the roots is called silence
> This means returning to one's destiny-life-force (ming)
> Returning to one's destiny-life-force is called eternality...

Quite significantly, the *Bai Xin* refers to both pure nature (xing) and destiny-life-force (ming), whereas the DDJ does not mention xing in any of its chapters. Xing and ming later become perhaps the most fundamental, and mysterious, elements of Daoist meditation texts. Ming, more literally translated as 'destiny', and 'mandate', has particular meanings associated with the life-preservation practices of Daoist cultivation – an association made especially clear in the *Bai Xin*, lines 204 and 205.

> 208 責其往來, 莫知其時,
> If one advances and retreats in this requirement,
> they cannot understand the opportune moment.
> 209 索之於天, 與之為期。
> Seek it from Heaven, and follow its timing.
> 210 不失其期, 乃能得之。
> If you do not neglect the timing,
> you can attain fulfillment.[110]
> 211 故曰吾語若大明之極。
> Thus it is said: I speak of the great ultimate enlightenment.

Paying attention to the changes and transformations that take place within, the Sage is aware of when to go deeper, when to hold fast, when enough is enough, and when to begin again.

In lines 208-211, the direct words of the *Bai Xin* appear once again to be cut from the same cloth as the *Dao De Jing*. DDJ41 begins in a pattern similar to BX208:

> When the highest student hears the Way
> Diligently, he treads the path
> *When the mediocre student hears the Way*
> *At first present, he falls back* [see line 208]
> When the lowest student hears the Way
> He breaks into a great laugh
> If he did not laugh

---

[110] This goes back to the opening lines of the *Bai Xin* which speak of the importance of timing.

It wouldn't be the path[111]

The *Bai Xin* then goes on to speak of the elusive opportune moments (lines 209-210), known by following the timing of Heaven. This timing leads to fulfillment and "ultimate enlightenment," but how does one follow the timing of Heaven and know the opportune moment? As the rest of DDJ41 goes on to show, this might not be so simple, for the ways of Heaven are not easily delineated.

... Thus, such sayings have been established:
The illuminated path appears dark
The path forward seems to go back
The level path appears uneven
The highest virtue, low as a valley

Great purity appears disgraced
Magnanimous virtue appears insufficient
Deep Virtue appears easily detached
True substance seems to change

Great squares are without corners
Great vessels develop slowly
Great voices rarely speak
Great images are without form
The Way is hidden and without name
Yet kindly lends itself
To our fruition

The importance given to "the timing of Heaven" in this section of the *Bai Xin* reveals yet another level of depth in this text, showing that it truly is an early ascendant of Daoist "Internal Alchemy" (Nei Dan) texts. Much of the later cryptic writings on this esoteric tradition use metaphors of seasonal and cosmic timing to describe the

---

[111] There are conflicting theories as to why the lowest student laughs — that he is actually a sage, laughing at attempts to describe Dao; or that he is simply arrogant. Either way, it appears that the following descriptions of the Dao are so seemingly topsy turvy that they make the lowest student laugh; yet, if they were not like this, they would not describe the Dao.

internal energetic processes of internal cultivation. Liu Yi Ming (1734-1821), an 11th generation master of the Complete Reality (Quan Zhen) School's "Dragon Gate Sect," wrote many books clarifying these metaphors. One example of this is his commentary on Chang Boduan's *Four Hundred Words on the Golden Elixir* (c. 1050 AD), in which he states:

> "The firing process does not call for set times; the winter solstice is not in December. As for the rules of bathing, spring and autumn are also metaphors without reality."
> … when a point of yang light appears in the body, it is like the winter solstice in December… The time of the horse [month of May, hour of noon] is taken to be the time for repelling the yin convergence because the arising in darkness of a point of yin energy in the body is like the summer solstice in May of the lunar calendar. When one yin comes to join, one should quickly work to repel it, suppressing this bit of false yin, evaporating it as it grows, not letting up for a moment.[112]

In light of Chang Boduan and Liu Yi Ming's words, lines 194-211 of the *Bai Xin* clearly point to an early existence of Nei Dan. Here these lines are again, uninterrupted:

> Those with knowledge of it amongst the people are few.
> Thus it is said: "How is it that Dao is so close, yet none can live by it?"
> By rejecting what is close and chasing after what is far, how can one but squander their power?
> Thus it is said: "Desiring to take care of myself, I must first know my true inner state.
> By observing the universe, I investigate my own body."
> As such, comprehending this image, one thereby understands the tendencies of their true inner state.
> Knowing the tendencies of their true inner state, they will know how to nourish life.

---

[112] Chang Po-Tuan, commentary by Liu I-Ming. *The Inner Teachings of Taoism*. Translated by Thomas Cleary. Shambhala Publications Inc. Boston: 1986.

> Turning to the left, right, front, and back, running full circle, return to the place (at the center).
> Holding to a ceremonious outward appearance, respectfully welcome that which approaches.
> Those today who seek its approach require this method to (invite) Dao.
> Without soaring (into the sky), without spilling over, the destined life-force (ming) will be extended.
> Harmonize by returning to the center, where both body and pure nature (xing) are preserved.
> Be unified and without (doubt or) division. This is called "knowing Dao."
> Wishing to be enveloped by it, you must unify to the furthest extent, and solidify that which is protected within.
> If one advances and retreats in this requirement, they cannot understand the opportune moment.
> Seek it from Heaven, and follow its timing.
> If you do not neglect the timing, you can attain fulfillment.
> Thus it is said: I speak of the great ultimate enlightenment.

Behind the later Nei Dan texts' cryptic style is the fact that this tradition had to be kept between teachers and disciples. Carving its teachings into bamboo for those who hadn't already shown a sincere interest would have drawn the wrong sort of attention – as Lao Zi imparts, many would not have been ready for such marvels, and would have simply laughed them off.

> 212 大明之明，非愛人不予也，
> The brilliance of great illumination
> does not nurture those who do not accept it.
> 213 同則相從，反則相距也。
> To those who join with it, it also joins.
> From those who are in opposition to it, it also separates.
> 214 吾察反則相距，吾以故知古從之同也。

*I have witnessed this opposition, and subsequent separation.
Thereby, I know that the ancients joined with it in unity.*

As the sage follows Heaven rather than man (and human desires that lead to obstinate actions), he recognizes when Heaven/nature/ziran offers the time, the opportunity, to be seized. He waits on Heaven's hand in emptiness and tranquility, and follows when beckoned by the right timing and opportunity. He must be open, listening, and changing according to what is naturally offered. Doing so, he proceeds with the chariots of "all things being aligned" – the "action of no action" (wei wu wei) that allows all things to fall into place. Virtue is the power within action of no-action. When Virtue abides, Dao naturally follows, for "Virtue is the abode of Dao."[113] Though we are still, many processes continue on inside of us. The Daoist art of stillness – the art of stillness in movement and movement in stillness – allows for these processes to proceed at a higher capacity and functionality than simple inertia. Like King Yu's waterways, the Daoist art of stillness finds the path of least resistance and highest attainment. As such, this practice reduces the potential for harm caused by obstinate force, and so naturally bestows longevity, effortlessness, and competence, whether in our physical body or in our endeavours.

These closing lines of the *Bai Xin* emphasize the techniques of lines 201-207, above, which can be understood as a method to welcome Virtue in light of the *Xin Shu Xia*'s opening lines (see my comments on lines 201-207, above). These closing lines also share in common with DDJ23 the idea of sympathetic resonance. Lao Zi's words in DDJ23 impart the very same thoughts as BX212-214, while mentioning Virtue, directly:

> Those who are one with Dao
> Dao is also happy to have them
> Those who are one with Virtue
> Virtue is also happy to have them
> Those who are one with loss
> Loss is also happy to have them

---

[113] See *Xin Shu Shang*, lines 113-122

We might take from the connection between these stanzas that the beginning of DDJ23 (see below) also suggested the importance of tranquility when welcoming Virtue – whether during quiet stillness, or when conducting affairs. This ideal of conduct is found in the opening lines of the *Bai Xin*, and in BX130-132:

> As for the sages of antiquity,
> Their mouths were without empty chatter,
> And their hands without empty gesturing.
> As things arose, orders were sent out

DDJ23 begins:

> To speak rarely is natural
> Gusting wind does not last in the early morning
> Sudden rainstorms do not last all day
> Who acts in this way? Heaven and Earth
> If Heaven and Earth cannot continue in such a way
> What then, should be the case for men?
> They should follow the method of Dao!

For a better understanding of early Daoist references to Virtue, it helps to look at the early commentary attached to the *Xin Shu Shang*, lines, 116-119:

> Thus, Virtue (De) also means "attainment (de)."
> As for this attainment, it is called "attaining the causality."
> The effortlessness of this (causality) is called "Dao."
> When abiding in things, we call it "Virtue."

Synonymous with "obtaining the causality," Virtue is what put things into order so that they accord with Dao. So Virtue is within, a power obtained that brings about balance and harmony. Wu wei is also to not resist this change, this reversion back to balance and harmony. The *Xin Shu* and *Nei Ye* both describe the way of attaining Virtue, while the ancient commentary appended to the *Xin Shu Shang* explains that Virtue implies its homonym (de) meaning attainment – when Virtue is attained, Dao naturally follows as Dao resides within

Virtue. As such, all of the Daoist arts, from internal cultivation, to martial arts, to painting, music, and healing practices, apply the technique of inviting virtue, balance, and harmony using the technique of wu wei (no action) – relaxation in action that allows Dao to naturally arise in the subject, whether that subject is a work of art, a patient, or oneself.

心術上
Art of the Heart-Mind: upper volume
Xin Shu Shang

1 心之在體,
  In the body,
2 君之位也。
  The heart-mind holds the throne of the ruler;
3 九竅之有職,
  The nine apertures hold offices
4 官之分也。
  Of various public servants.
5 心處其道,
  When the heart-mind remains with Dao,
6 九竅循理。
  The nine apertures act reasonably;
7 嗜欲充益,
  When desires and euphoric feelings are plentiful,
8 目不見色
  The eyes don't see appearances
9 耳不聞聲。
  And the ears don't hear sounds.
10 故曰：上離其道,
   Thus it is said: When those above lose the Way,
11 下失其事。
   Those below neglect their duties.

The Sage counsels the ruler, and shows him the way of peace, like the spirit counsels the heart-mind. The Sage is not given executive powers by the ruler, but can help the ruler make the right decisions if the ruler is open to the Sage's counsel. Following this counsel, the ruler centers himself and secures the loyalty and dedication of his ministers.

Political metaphors for stabilizing the heart-mind give early Chinese teachings on mindfulness much of their essential character. Contained in this metaphor is the Daoist method of government, defined by the Sage's ability to bring stability and harmony without forced intervention. By emptying the heart-mind of desires, the Sage brings all things into balance. For example, DDJ37 states:

> The Dao is always effortless yet without inaction
> When lords and kings can guard this within
> The myriad things eventually transform themselves
> Transforming, yet desiring to do so intentionally
> I pacify this desire with the simplicity of the nameless
>
> The simplicity of the nameless removes all desires
> When the tranquility of desirelessness is established
> The world stabilizes itself

And in DDJ2:

> ... Sages handle affairs with non-action
> They practice wordless instruction
> And the myriad things all take their places without responding
> Given life, but not possessed
> Acted for, but not expected of
> Perfection is cultivated, and not dwelled upon
> Surely, what is not dwelled upon
> Does not leave

What the *Xin Shu Shang* immediately reveals about the *Dao De Jing*, is that the Sage is not only a wise counsel to the nation's presiding authority, but is also within, guiding the ruler – the heart-mind – towards sovereignty over "all under Heaven" and "the myriad things" –

ie., the senses, emotions, desires, stress, impulses, and anything else which must be stabilized in order to preserve inner unity. When these things are disordered, confusion reigns, and the sovereignty of the heart-mind is imperiled. The Sage is to the ruler what the spirit's illumination is upon the heart-mind. She brings clarity, perception, and peace to the ruler. To invite the Sage, the ruler must first become stable and orderly, kind and genuine. Then the Sage will find it safe to convene with him, seeing that the ruler is capable of giving up tyrannical power and instead following Dao. The art of the heart-mind is not simply a way to find peace, but a way to bring forth the spiritual intelligence – the Sage.

The *Xin Shu Shang* further provides an important example of mindfulness teachings in ancient China, appearing long before Buddhism arrived from India in 80 AD. While Buddhist mindfulness teachings may focus more directly on attention to inner phenomena (sensations, emotions, thoughts, etc.), both Buddhist teachings and the ancient Chinese "art of the heart-mind" seek to lead students towards a clear perception of their inner state. As Lao Zi says in DDJ33:

>Those who know others, are wise
>Those who know themselves, are clear-sighted
>Those who overpower others, have strength
>Those who overpower themselves, have fortitude
>Those who know contentment, are rich
>Those who exercise this fortitude, have will-power
>Those who do not lose their station, continue
>Those who die but do not disappear, live long

XSS, lines 7-9, show that when the heart-mind is stirred-up, the eyes and ears no longer function as loyal servants of the heart-mind. As a political metaphor, this suggests the beginnings of usurpation, and so warns against letting the desires of the senses disturb, and thereby overthrow, the heart-mind. This is at the very basis of mindfulness practice in everyday life, and may be summed up as: Maintain focus while not relinquishing "the throne of the ruler" (the heart-mind).

Lines 1-11 may also provide some background for understanding DDJ12, which, in light of XSS7-9, appears to have implied "desiring" at the beginning of its first three lines[114]:

(Desiring) the five colours blind(s) the eyes
(Desiring) the five tones deafen(s) the ears
(Desiring) the five flavours numb(s) the mouth
The intensity of the hunt makes the mind go mad
Goods which are difficult to obtain interfere with one's journey
Thus, sages are guided by their stomachs
And not by their eyes
Leaving that
They take this.

In Chapter 10 of the Diamond Sutra (a passage which later became one of the most influential in Chinese Buddhism), a nearly identical admonition can be found, helping to unravel the expressions of the proto-Daoists:

> Therefore, bodhisattvas and mahasattvas should give rise to a clear and clean mind. They should not linger on appearances arising in the mind. They should not linger on sounds, smells, sensations, or dharma (lit. laws) arising in the mind. They should, abiding nowhere, give rise to (the clear and clean) mind.[115]

In a passage of great proximity to the meaning and (likely) the era of the Xin Shu Shang, Xun Zi (313-238 BC) writes in his chapter "Removing Obstacles":

> The mind is the ruler of the body, and the host of spiritual intelligence. It gives commands but does not take commands. It restricts itself, allows itself, takes from itself, overcomes itself, moves itself, and stops itself. You can force someone's mouth

---

[114] Heshang Gong also interpreted DDJ12 in this way, suggesting that the desires of the senses inhibit and damage them.

[115] 是故須菩提。諸菩薩摩訶薩。應如是生清淨心。不應住色生心。不應住聲香味觸法生心。應無所住而生其心。 Translated by Dan G. Reid.

to be silent, you can force their body to scrunch up or stretch out, but you cannot force their mind to change their ideas. What it finds to be true, it accepts, and what it finds to be false, it rejects.

For this reason I say: what the mind apprehends, allow it to do so without restraining it. Allow things to spontaneously appear to the mind in their breadth of diversity, with the extent of the mind's nature remaining not-two.

The *Book of Poetry* says:

Picking and gathering burdock roots
The basket is not full yet the roots fall out
I sigh for the man in my heart
As I let it go to and fro

A basket is easy to fill, and burdock is easy to gather, but not when the mind is divided in every which way. This is why I say: A mind that branches out in many directions knows nothing; a mind that is not level is not acute; a mind that is divided is doubtful and confused. But for a mind with focused scrutiny, the myriad things can come together in its understanding; for in oneself is a unity that runs though all categories.[116]

It may be of value to understanding the Xin Shu and Nei Ye that Xun Zi's above discourse describes the (heart-)mind as the host, or lord, of spiritual intelligence.[117] If we are to understand the Sage as the spiritual intelligence, it may also help to understand that the Sage holds no executive power, nor goes where the powerful would try to control him. The ruler, as with the heart-mind, has the power to do as he wishes, but he cannot force the Sage's allegiance. To earn that, he must show that he is capable of acquiescing to higher wisdom, of practicing kindness, of being content with frugality, and of transcending self-interest; further, he must show that he can unite with Dao and allow its power, De, to fill his sails. In this way, the ruler

---

[116] From *Xun Zi* (c. 250 BC), by Xun Zi, chapter 21. Translated by Dan G. Reid.
[117] Please also see the section on the *Xin Shu Shang* in the Introduction ("Internal Cultivation in the Guan Zi") where similarities are shown between XSS1-11 and *The Yellow Emperor's Classic on Internal Medicine*, chapter eight. For more on spiritual intelligence, please see the section on the *Nei Ye* in the Introduction.

(the heart-mind) may rule with the expertise of the Sage (spiritual intelligence).

12　毋代馬走,
　　Do not attempt to do the running for a horse.
13　使盡其力,
　　Let it exhaust its strength.
14　毋代鳥飛,
　　Do not attempt to do the flying for a bird.
15　使獘其羽翼。
　　Let it collapse its wings.
16　毋先物動,
　　Do not precede the movements of other things,
17　以觀其則。
　　But rather, observe their inclinations.
18　動則失位,
　　By moving you lose the throne position (of the heart-mind),
19　靜乃自得,
　　But when still, you naturally obtain it.

The Sage has control over his impulses, like the ruler has control over his ministers. He does not act rashly, but observes the time, thereby achieving maximum effect with minimal effort at opportune moments.

As lines 1-11 indicate above, the desires of the senses give rise to impulses which may coerce and dethrone the heart-mind. Lines 12-19 explain that these impulses should not be given reign, as this would compel the heart-mind to "attempt to do the running for a horse" and "the flying for a bird." Such efforts are both futile and dangerous. Instead, the heart-mind (ruler) must not be pushed forward, away from the "throne position," but rather observe these inclinations, 'letting the horse exhaust its strength – letting the bird collapse its wings.' Through this stillness, the throne of the heart-mind is naturally reclaimed.

Zhuang Zi expands on this teaching in chapter four, "The Human World Today":

> You have heard of flying with wings, but you have not yet heard of flying without wings. You have heard of knowing with knowledge, but you have not yet heard of knowing without knowledge. Look at the closed room. In an empty room, brightness blooms and good fortune stops to visit. If you do not also come to a stop, this is called sitting and racing about. If you allow the ears and eyes to penetrate within, while keeping the mind's knowledge outside, gods and spirits will naturally come to dwell with you. How much more will other people! This is to transform the myriad things. It is the pivot of (legendary rulers) Yu and Shun, and that which Fuxi and Jiqu practiced to the end of their days. How much more should we all do the same![118]

20 道不遠而難極也。
The Path is not far off, yet people are unable to reach it.

21 與人並處而難得也。
It follows men, dwelling in the same place,
yet is difficult to obtain.

22 虛其欲, 神將入舍。
When you are empty of desires,
the spirit goes forth into the house.

23 掃除不潔, 神乃留處。
If you sweep away and cleanse impurities,
the spirit will remain settled.[119]

---

[118] Translated by Dan G. Reid
[119] One must sweep out the temple to invite spiritual lights. One must sweep the dust out of the heart-mind in order to invite spiritual light. Feng Shui advocates this as well, saying that a clean and tidy house invites fresh energy.

Sweeping away desires, the Sage makes a place to receive what is truly valuable.

XSS22-23 might be further clarified by Heshang Gong's comments on DDJ11 (containing the line "The surrounding clay makes a pot, and by its emptiness the pot is used").

"When governing the body, one should eliminate strong emotions and abandon desires so that the five organs are hollow and empty, and their spirits can return."

Lines 22-23 also reflect an idea common to Daoist meditation, and found in Heshang Gong's commentary on DDJ10. Note that Heshang Gong's comment here (below) also resembles the Buddhist mindfulness technique of impartially observing the mind's engagements.

"Looking deeply, purify and eliminate"
One should wash the heart-mind until it is clean and pure. The heart-mind lives in the fathomless depths of emptiness. Investigate. Know its myriad engagements. This is called "investigating the fathomless."

While Heshang Gong's commentary on the *Dao De Jing* may appear to reflect Buddhist influences, the proto-Daoist texts of the *Guan Zi* show that Heshang Gong was, in fact, pointing out the early indigenous Chinese meditation traditions underlying Lao Zi's teachings.

The saying "the Dao is not far off, yet people are unable to reach it" (line 20) bears a close resemblance to statements in the *Dao De Jing* describing the ineffable quality of Dao. For example, DDJ14[120] reads:

... Greet it and you do not see its front
Follow it and you do not see its rear
Hold to the ancient Dao and ride it until you possess the present
Then you will have the power to know the ancient beginning
This is called "the thread of Dao"

---

[120] Please also see DDJ41, quoted in the commentary for the *Bai Xin*, lines 208-211.

In the *Xin Shu Shang*, however, "the Dao is not far off, yet people are unable to reach it" appears in the context of lines 12-19 (above) which show how to attain the throne position of the heart-mind. The statement is then followed by an illustration of how this position is lost to futile pursuits (see lines 24-27, below). Piecing these statements together, we see that Dao also refers to the state of inner unity and sovereignty, and that the method to attain this state is to sweep out the dust of the heart-mind (lines 22-23).

Dao, literally "the Path," should thus be understood not only as a process, but also as a place at which to arrive, or "得 attain to." Such a definition is significant to the lexicon of proto–Daoist philosophy, especially in regards to "De, 德, Virtue," as shown in the ancient *Xin Shu Shang* commentary:

> Virtue is the abode of Dao.
> When things attain (Virtue), they live.[121]
> Being alive, they can know the office of Dao's essence.
> Thus, Virtue also means "attainment."
> As for this attainment, it is called "attaining the causality."
> The effortlessness of this (causality) is called "Dao."
> The abode of Dao is called "Virtue."
> Thus, between Dao and Virtue, there is no space.
> For this reason, it is said "they are not separate."
> The principle of this space is called "their abiding place."
> (*Xin Shu Shang*, lines 113-122)

24　人皆欲智，而莫索其所以智乎。
　　All men desire wisdom,
　　yet none can find (the Path) through wisdom!
25　智乎智乎，投之海外無自奪，
　　Wisdom! Wisdom! Cast it out into the ocean,

---

[121] See the excerpt from the Ling Shu Jing, found in the commentary on lines 1-22 of the Nei Ye: "Qi Bo replied: That which Heaven gives an individual is De (intrinsic virtue). That which Earth gives an individual is qi (energy-breath). When De and qi intermingle, there is life…"

Do not attempt to capture it outside of yourself.
26 求之者不得處之者,
In those who seek it, it takes up no lodging.[122]
27 夫正人無求之也, 故能虛無,
By aligning themselves and not seeking it,
they can arrive at empty-nothingness
28 虛無無形謂之道。
What is empty-nothingness, and without form,
is called Dao.
29 化育萬物謂之德。
What transforms and gives life to all things is called Virtue.

Those who think they are clever often lack the virtue to invite success. Because they think they are wise, they are oblivious to the truth.

Just as teachings on mindfulness advise focusing on the present moment and not getting caught up in illusory creations of the mind, the *Xin Shu Shang* explains that engaging our intellects to attain stillness and wisdom will only lead us further from the all embracing emptiness of Dao – like closing our eyes in an attempt to better see the moon. Heshang Gong's commentary suggests that Lao Zi alludes to this strategy of effortless attainment in chapter 27 of the *Dao De Jing*.[123]

> Excellent walking leaves no trail of footprints
> Excellent speech is without fault or blame
> Excellent counting does not use counting devices
> Excellent closing requires no bolts
> Yet the seal cannot be broken
> Excellent binding requires no rope to secure it
> Yet cannot be unbound…

---

[122] See also DDJ47: "Without going out the door, know all under heaven…"
[123] HSG's commentary on DDJ27 is provided, in part, in my comments on lines 297-316 of the Nei Ye.

In lines 12 through to 29, the *Xin Shu Shang* discusses matters of 1) guarding stillness, 2) sweeping clean the heart-mind, 3) retaining spirit, 4) transcending wisdom, and 5) practicing non-action. In doing so, its author transmits proto-Daoist techniques for self-cultivation in the same sequence as preserved in DDJ10:

> Guard the fortress of your bodily spirits
> Embrace Oneness
> Can you do this without letting them flee?
> Gather together the energy-breath and become soft
> This is the power of an infant
> Looking deeply
> Purify and eliminate
> Can you be without flaw?
> Caring for the people and governing the nation
> Can you be without effort?
> Heaven's gate opens and closes
> Can you act the part of the female?[124]
> With your awareness shining on every corner
> Can you be without knowledge?
> Giving them life and cultivating them
> Giving them life yet not possessing them
> Acting for them yet not expecting of them
> Leading them forward but not managing them
> This is called Fathomless Virtue

Following chapter 10, while speaking of the space within an empty vessel, DDJ11 states: "So substance is gained, and emptiness is used." By emptying one's heart-mind of negative emotions and attachments, one may use this spaciousness, or "empty vessel," to attain Virtue. Virtue transforms things and brings about their completion and perfection. Thus, one uses "what is not there," the emptiness of the heart-mind, to gain Virtue. Then, what is there (Virtue), may be used to bring about completion and perfection. This process, of Virtue

---

[124] According to Heshang Gong "Heaven's gate opens and closes" refers to both an area near the North Star, and also to inhalation (opening) and exhalation (closing). "Can you act the part of the female?" may suggest receiving primordial essence from Heaven, spoken of in the beginning of the *Nei Ye*.

fostering transformation, is further developed in the *Nei Ye*, especially lines 1-22, and the *Ling Shu Jing*, chapter eight (see commentary on NY1-22).

30 君臣父子人間之事謂之義。
   The duties between ruler and minister, father and son, and neighbours: this is called righteousness.
31 登降揖讓, 貴賤有等, 親疏之體, 謂之禮。
   Rising and kneeling, bowing and yielding, respecting the hierarchy within the family: this is called courtesy.
32 簡物小未一道,
   To simplify things, humbling them before the one Dao,
33 殺僇禁誅謂之法。
   Reducing offenses with prohibitions and punishment: this is called law.
34 大道可安而不可說,
   The Great Dao can bring peace and stability,
   yet it cannot be explained.
35 直人之言, 不義不顧。
   (If) the correct man's words did not refer to righteousness, or filial duties,
36 不出於口, 不見於色,
   If they did not leave his mouth, nor did his face reveal them,
37 四海之人, 又庸知其則。
   All people within the four seas would return to their commonalities and understand these rules.

Having learned rules of conduct, and not how to cultivate inner stillness and harmony, people often use these rules for self-serving purposes and become callous judges of others' behaviour. This has the opposite effect as teaching them to find inner stillness, from which they can empathize with, and truly care for the needs of, others.

The proto-Daoists are often regarded as the first anarchists, or otherwise the first to have written down a philosophy of anarchism. Both philosophies are, in fact, far more complex and multi-faceted than such comparisons take into account; however, there are some intrinsic similarities in the political facets by which proto-Daoists and anarchists were distinguished from their contemporaries. For Daoists, this political facet can be seen in their rejection of involuntary obedience to tradition, especially concerning obligations towards arbitrary hierarchies. The proto-Daoists felt that such obsession with authority was antagonistic to the development of both society and the individual. Mikhail Bakunin, an influential Russian anarchist, reflects this same ideology in tenets of his "Revolutionary Catechism" (1866). You might note that, like most of the early Chinese philosophers, Bakunin also addresses the definitions of justice, duty, and virtue.

> II. Replacing the cult of God by *respect and love of humanity*, we proclaim *human reason* as the only criterion of truth; *human conscience* as the basis of justice; *individual and collective freedom* as the only source of order in society.
> III. Freedom is the absolute right of every adult man and woman to seek no other sanction for their acts than their own conscience and their own reason, being responsible first to themselves and then to the society which they have *voluntarily* accepted.
> ...
> V. The *freedom* of each is therefore realizable only in the equality of all. The realization of freedom through equality, in principle and in fact, is *justice*.
> VI. If there is one fundamental principle of human morality, *it is freedom*. To respect the freedom of your fellowman *is duty;* to love, help, and serve him is *virtue*.[125]

---

[125] Mikhail Bakunin, Sam Dolgoff (editor, translator?). Bakunin on Anarchism. Black Rose Books, 1980.

Reading these words from Bakunin, it is easy to see how many came to the conclusion that the proto-Daoists were also anarchists upon finding the following statements from Lao Zi in DDJ19:

> Quit sageliness
> Abandon wisdom
> And the people will benefit one hundred fold
> Quit benevolence, abandon right-conduct
> And the people will return to caring for their parents
> Quit cleverness, abandon profit
> And robbers and thieves will not exist
> These three
> Are only ornamental, and not satisfactory
> Thus, we have the following:[126]
> Observe the natural state
> Embrace the unaltered
> Minimize self-importance
> And have few desires

Zhuang Zi (Chuang Tzu) also illustrates the inadequacy of prescribed morality in many of his parables, including the following from his chapter entitled "Horses Hooves":

> Yes, in the age of perfect virtue, men lived in common with birds and beasts, and were on terms of equality with all creatures, as forming one family – how could they know among themselves the distinctions of superior men and small men? Equally without knowledge, they did not leave (the path of) their natural virtue; equally free from desires, they were in the state of pure simplicity. In that state of pure simplicity, the nature of the people was what it ought to be. But when the Sagely men appeared, limping and wheeling about in (the exercise of) benevolence, pressing along and standing on tiptoe in the doing of righteousness, then men universally began to be perplexed. (trans. Legge)

---

[126] For a further similarity in the continuity of thought between DDJ19 and the *Xin Shu Shang*, please also note the resemblance between the four following lines in DDJ19, and XSS lines 39-40: "Purify the temple, open the gates, eradicate egotism, and do not speak."

Re-reading the entire *Dao De Jing* through the lens of this key concept – of returning to our spontaneous and intrinsic virtue rather than conforming to authorized prescriptions – one could, advantageously, see its influence in nearly every verse.

38 天曰虛, 地曰靜, 乃不伐。
    Heaven is described as empty, earth is described as still.
    From this, (one should learn) not to boast.

39 潔其宮, 開其門,
    Purify the temple, open the gates;

40 去私毋言, 神明若存。
    Eradicate egotism, and do not speak.
    Spiritual intelligence will then reside.

41 紛乎其若亂, 靜之而自治。
    When scattered, it is as though a rebellion rises up;
    when calm and still, order naturally arrives.

42 強不能遍立, 智不能盡謀。
    Force cannot widely establish such order.
    Wisdom cannot formulate all strategies.

In their balance of emptiness and stillness, Heaven and Earth have lasted four and a half billion years. In this time, they have supported the lives of innumerable spiritual vessels. The Sage, therefore, takes Heaven and Earth as his teachers in the cultivation of life and longevity.

If we hope to regain our ancient intrinsic virtue, we would be remiss not to heed the wisdom of our oldest living ancestors – Heaven and Earth. From Heaven, the Daoists say, we can learn emptiness and non–attachment to self. From earth: stillness, silence, and groundedness. As the *Xin Shu Xia* ends by stating: "For what is above, study Heaven. For what is below, study the Earth." This can, in part, be understood to mean "make your heart–mind empty, like Heaven, and your body stable, like the Earth." By doing so, we can truly transcend the need for moral dictates and even free the mind of the confounding limits of human knowledge. The ancient commentary on the *Xin Shu Shang* (beginning at line 60, below) comments on line 39, "*The temple* refers to the heart-mind. The heart-mind is the abode of wisdom. Therefore it is called 'the temple.' To purify it is to get rid of liking and rejecting" (XSS, lines 161–164).

Zhuang Zi describes the master who has shed these limitations to his or her self–actualization in the following story from chapter 19, The Total Comprehension of Life:

> Artisan Chui made things round with more accuracy than a compass, for his fingers followed the transformation of things without investigating them in his mind. Thus, his spirit tower (heart-mind) was unified and unfettered. The foot is forgotten when the shoe fits properly. The waist is forgotten when the belt fits properly. Knowledge forgets right and wrong when the heart-mind fits properly. There is no inward alteration, nor outward following when the confluence of affairs is fitting. Once fitting, and there is no longer any sense of not-fitting, forget both fitting and not-fitting.[127]

Lao Zi explains the path to this state, similar to what is today often called "the flow state," with the following from DDJ48:

> The pursuit of learning requires daily accumulation
> The pursuit of Dao requires daily reduction
> Reducing and reducing
> Until arriving at effortlessness
> Effortless, yet without inaction…

Echoing lines 39–40, "Purify the temple, open the gates, eradicate egotism, and do not speak," Lao Zi states in DDJ19:

---

[127] Translated by Dan G. Reid

... Observe the natural state
Embrace the unaltered
Minimize self-importance
And have few desires

43 物固有形，形固有名，
Things which have solidified have forms.
Forms which have solidified have names.

44 名當謂之聖人。
Those who give them appropriate names are called sages.

45 故必知不言無為之事，
Thus, he knows yet does not speak, and serves without action,

46 然後知道之紀。
So that present and future generations may know the principles of Dao.

47 殊形異執，不與萬物異理，
Though having peculiar forms and strange abilities, he does not follow the myriad things from their incongruity to their coherence.

48 故可以為天下始。
Thus, he can fathom the beginning of all under Heaven.

Knowing that even Heaven and Earth have an origin, he looks to the oneness of all things. Though seeming to have arisen separately, they all draw from the same source.

The term "names (名 ming)" contains many connotations in early Chinese philosophy, including those shared in English, such as *appellation* and *reputation*, but also *concept*, *fact*, and *definition*. Lines 43-48 show a connection between the pursuits of the Chinese sage and the Western philosopher in their searches for truth – for understanding how things work and thus how they should be defined. In understanding this pursuit, we also see how the Chinese sage arrives at "the nameless" – the eternal which is without any final state and thus without definition, yet from which all things arise. In the Daoist technique of "sitting and forgetting" (zuowang), one leaves all definitions until arriving at clarity, dwelling in emptiness, going back to where no distinctions have yet arisen, where there are no "names" but simply the undifferentiated Oneness. Heshang Gong remarks on this outlook in his commentary on DDJ10:

"Embrace Oneness. Can you do this without letting (your bodily spirits) flee?"
People who can embrace Oneness, and not let it leave them, extend their lives. In Oneness, Dao began to situate life by the supreme harmony of vital energy-breath. Therefore it is said: "Oneness covered the world with names."

Heaven attained Oneness and became clear; Earth attained Oneness and became serene; lords and kings attained Oneness and became upright and peace-loving. Going within, it is mind; going outward, it is actions; in covering all with its blessing, it is Virtue. *All the names together are One.* Referring to Oneness, it is said: "In a unified consciousness, there is no division."

Through this Oneness, the Sage attains greater clarity of mind and perception. As lines 12-19 and line 45 explain, in this stillness, one should simply observe phenomena without interfering. In doing (or 'not-doing') so, they can truly see phenomena for what they are, and avoid becoming subject to, or caught up in, them.[128] As explained throughout Guan Zi's self-cultivation texts, this technique can bring about a tranquil sovereignty of the heart-mind over the senses, and thereby initiate the spontaneous alignment and nourishing of life.

Lines 47-48 explain that it is not by the external appearances or differences of things that sages find "the beginning of all under Heaven," but by instead returning to the nameless – their common beginning.

---

[128] See XSS line 210, below "If not empty, one becomes the same as other 'things'."

This teaching also appears in DDJ47,[129] and DDJ14 (below):

By looking, it is not seen. It is known as Clear
By listening, it is not heard. It is known as Inaudible
What cannot be obtained when seized is known as Infinitesimal
These three things cannot be inspected
And are merged into one

Above, it is not bright
Below, it is not dark
Immeasurable and unnameable
It is again nothing
This is called "having no form or appearance"
Without a materialized image
This is called "absent-minded"
Greet it and you do not see its front
Follow it and you do not see its rear
Hold to the ancient Dao and ride it until you possess the present
Then you will have the power to know the ancient beginning
This is called "the thread of Dao"

49 人之可殺, 以其惡死也,
   People face execution because they hate death,
50 其可不利, 以其好利也。
   And they face financial loss because they adore profit.
51 是以君子不休乎好, 不迫乎惡,
   Therefore, the junzi does not dwell on what he likes,
   nor is he coerced by what he dislikes.
52 恬愉無為, 去智與故。
   Tranquil, pleasant, and effortless, he abandons wisdom,
   and it abides in him as a result.
53 其應也, 非所設也,

---

[129] DDJ47 is translated above, in the commentary on *Bai Xin*, lines 196-200.

He responds, but does not initiate;
54 其動也，非所取也。
Moves but does not possess.
55 過在自用，罪在變化。
If one is excessively headstrong,
they will err when adapting to changes.
56 是故有道之君，
Thus, the ruler who has Dao
57 其處也，若無知。
Remains in the state of not knowing;
58 其應物也，若偶之。
He responds to things as though by coincidence.
59 靜因之道也。
This is the Dao of tranquil means.

[End]

Maintaining contentment, the Sage is not drawn into danger.

The proto-Daoists' focus on preserving and nourishing life led them to re-assess the value of common pursuits, finding that so many of them had the opposite intended effect. Seeking to be above others often makes them despise you; fame is often followed by disgrace; storing up treasures invites thieves; succulent foods often damage one's health. This realization guides much of the Daoist lifestyle, and is intimated by Lao Zi in DDJ75:

> ... The people are careless towards death
> Because they seek fullness of life
> This causes carelessness towards death
> So then, only those without regard for their lives
> Will strive for fullness of life
> Therein resides the virtue of valuing life

Such a realization is also profoundly important to Zen Buddhism, which teaches students to meditate on the temporality of the body, and the interdependence between mind and external objects. While also helping students to see the underlying reality of life, this practice reduces their attachment to false values and meaningless pursuits.

Lines 51-52 describe this non-attachment by showing that the junzi[130] does not dwell on gain and loss, likes and dislikes, nor on wisdom – on knowing and not knowing. In this way, the junzi can remain "tranquil, pleasant, and effortless," while moving unobstructedly through the snares of life. This practice of remaining in a learned obliviousness to one's own likes and dislikes ushers the junzi into an awareness of the present, and helps them adapt appropriately to the time (see line 55).

To better understand what the *Xin Shu Shang* means by "the ruler who has Dao remains in the state of not knowing," we can also look at an influential passage from the Zhuang Zi on "heart-mind fasting" (xin zhai), a term synonymous with "purifying the heart-mind" (bai xin):

> Yan Hui said: "… By doing what other's do, they have no basis to blame me. This is called being a fellow disciple. Maintaining the ways of antiquity is to be a disciple of antiquity. Though my words of instruction may point out the ruler's errors, they will be the words of antiquity and not my own. As such, though being direct, they will not be insulting. This is called being a disciple of the ancients. Will this suffice?"
>
> Confucius replied: "Most certainly not! You have too many conditions and policies. You plan to go to [the tyrannical ruler of Wei] having yet to learn anything about him. Though your plan is firm, you will only avoid transgression. Stopping at that, how can you successfully convert him? You are only using your mind as the teacher."
>
> Yan Hui said: "I have no way to proceed. May I be so bold as to ask the method?"
>
> Confucius replied: "Fasting. I will tell you how, but having the method and putting it into action – is this easy? If you act as

---

[130] A person of character, more literally "the noble"

though it is easy, radiant Heaven will not find you suited to the task."
Yan Hui said: "My family is poor. We've drunk no alcohol, nor eaten pungent vegetables for several months. Could this be considered fasting?"
Confucius replied: "This is fasting in preparation to offer sacrifice. It is not the fasting of the heart-mind."
Yan Hui said: "May I be so bold as to ask about the fasting of the heart-mind?"
Confucius replied:[131] "You must be of singular focus. Do not listen with the ears, but listen with the heart-mind; do not listen with the heart-mind, but listen with the breath. Listening (then) stops in the ears, and the heart-mind stops in its verifications. As for the breath, it is the emptiness which receives all things, and it is Dao which brings (all things) toward emptiness. *Emptiness* is the fasting of the heart-mind."[132]

While heart-mind fasting is an integral part of Daoist sitting practice, it is also integral to the Daoist way of being in the world, or "being in the moment." By emptying the mind of expectations and predeterminations, one can then perceive and adapt to reality. By following the breath, as students are taught in Taiji and Qigong (Tai Chi and Chi Kung), one's body and mind-intent draw in and push forward with no dissociation. Listening at the level of the heart-mind, and at the level of inter-being where one's very breath is in communion with their surroundings, allows one to purify the heart-mind and accord with Dao in all embracing emptiness. As the *Xin Shu Shang* describes, such openness allows one to be in the world with wisdom, equanimity, and effortless responsiveness. Doing so also requires a transcendence of doubt and of one's impulses to wield control. Rather, they must learn to observe from a state of equanimity. This is shown in lines 49-59, which explain that likes and dislikes, just as they are used to wield control over a population through rewards and

---

[131] 仲尼曰：「若一志，无聽之以耳而聽之以心，无聽之以心而聽之以氣。聽止於耳，心止於符。氣也者，虛而待物者也。唯道集虛。虛者，心齋也。」

[132] From *Zhuang Zi*, chapter four. Translated by Dan G. Reid.

punishments, wield control over our equanimity and ability to travel gracefully through life.

The potential for likes and dislikes to be turned into rewards and punishments also applies to inner cultivation. A common admonishment by Daoist teachers is that students will progress quicker if they give their energy to the present, to what they are doing at the time, rather than to hopes and dreams of higher levels and achievements. These aspirations, noble as they may be, hold the power to distract and lead one away from actualization in the present, just as desires and fears provide a handle by which others can lead them away from their best interests.

> Thus, the ruler who has Dao
> Remains in the state of not knowing.
> He responds to things as though by coincidence.
> This is the Dao of tranquil means. (XSS, lines 56-59)

To rule their own heart and mind, the Daoist is as though oblivious to rewards and loss, but rather, cherishes the benefits of living by Dao. Lao Zi expressed these sentiments with his natural eloquence, in chapter 20 of the *Dao De Jing*:

> Stop learning
> And there will be no grief
> Is reluctant acceptance so different from rejection?
> What is the difference between good and evil?
> People in a fearful place cannot be without fear
> Uncultivated! They have not been centered!
>
> The crowd is joyous and buoyant
> As though having caught a massive beast
> Or celebrating spring rites
> I alone am like the clearness of still water
> Alas, in this way, making no predictions
> Nor making myself predictable
> Like a newborn baby
> Not yet able to make these distinctions
> Roaming! As though having no home to return to

The people in the crowd all have more than they need
But I alone am as one who has lost everything
I have the mind of a simpleton, indeed
Clouded and muddy!
It is customary for people to have clear and cutting perception
I alone am as though in a twilight of understanding
It is customary for people to be fascinated
I alone am as though distant and forlorn
Quick! I am like the ocean
Drifting! As though without any place to stop
The multitudes of people all have purpose
Yet I alone seem stubborn
And unsophisticated

I alone seem strange to others
For I cherish the nourishment of the mother

By not thinking of rewards and punishments or benefits and losses during their stillness practice, students allow the natural process, Dao, to unfold.

(Ancient Commentary Section of the *Xin Shu Shang*, appearing in the *Guan Zi*)

60　心之在體，君之位也。
　　"In the body, the heart-mind is the throne of the emperor.
61　九竅之有職，官之分也。
　　The nine apertures hold offices of various public servants."
62　耳目者，視聽之官也，
　　The ears and eyes hold the offices of looking and listening.
63　心而無與視聽之事，
　　The heart-mind is therefore not occupied with the duties of looking and listening.
64　則官得守其分矣。
　　Thus, these offices preserve their functions.

65　夫心有欲者，
　　When the heart-mind holds a desire,
66　物過而目不見，
　　Things pass by, but the eyes do not see it;
67　聲至而耳不聞也，
　　Sounds arrive yet the ears do not hear them.
68　故曰：上離其道，下失其事。
　　Thus, it is said: **"When those above depart from the Way, those below neglect their duties."**
69　故曰，心術者，無為而制竅者也。
　　Thus it is said: "With the heart-mind method, one is effortless and uncontrived, yet the apertures are regulated."[133]
70　故曰：
　　Thus it is said:
71　君，無代馬走，無代鳥飛，
　　**"Do not attempt to do the running for a horse.
　　Do not attempt to do the flying for a bird."**

---

[133] This quote is not from the texts in the Guan Zi, suggesting perhaps a common oral teaching, or simply a paraphrase of the *Xin Shu Shang*.

72 此言不奪能,
These words do not deny the ruler of his power.
73 能不與下誠也。
It is simply that his power should not meddle in what is truly the domain of those below him.

74 毋先物動者,
"Do not precede the movements of other things."
75 搖者不定,
What is agitated does not stabilize.
76 趮者不靜,
What is temperamental does not bring stillness.
77 言動之不可以觀也。
(Thus) it is said that movement does not allow for observation.

78 位者, 謂其所立也,
"Throne" refers to one's established place.
79 人主者立於陰, 陰者靜。
The ruler is established in Yin. Yin is found in stillness.
80 故曰動則失位。
Thus it is said that movement results in one losing their throne.
81 陰則能制陽矣,
Yin has the power to overcome Yang.
82 靜則能制動矣, 故曰靜乃自得。
Stillness has the power to overcome movement.
83 靜則能制動矣, 故曰靜乃自得。
Thus it is said, "when still, you naturally obtain it"

84 道在天地之間也,
The Dao exists between Heaven and Earth.
85 其大無外, 其小無內,
It is so large that it is without an exterior, it is so small that it is without an interior;
86 故曰不遠而難極也。

Thus it is said, "The Way is not far off, yet people are unable to reach it."

87 虛之與人也無間。
Between emptiness and human beings, there is no space,

88 唯聖人得虛道,
Yet only sages attain the emptiness of Dao.

89 故曰並處而難得。
Thus, it is said, "dwelling in the same place, yet is difficult to obtain."

90 世人之所職者精也,
What people occupy themselves with today is jing-essence.

91 去欲則宣,
Getting rid of desires should be the priority.

92 宣則靜矣,
From this follows quiet stillness;

93 靜則精,
Quiet stillness brings about jing-essence;

94 精則獨立矣。
From jing essence, singularity is established.

95 獨則明,
Singularity brings about illumination;

96 明則神矣。
Illumination brings about spirit;

97 神者至貴也,
As for spirit, this is reaching the treasure.

98 故館不辟除,則貴人不舍焉,
Hence, when public offices are not emptied, neither treasures, nor people, will occupy them.

99 故曰不潔則神不處。
Thus it is said "If (the residence) is not pure, then the spirit will not reside (there)."[134]

---

[134] The author paraphrases line 23 here, suggesting that this commentary was written from memory.

100 人皆欲知而莫索之,
"All people desire knowledge, yet none can find it."[135]

101 其所以知彼也, 其所以知此也。
There is something by which "that" is known, and something by which "this" is known.

102 不修之此, 焉能知彼?
If you do not study "this," how can you know "that?"[136]

103 修之此, 莫能虛矣。
For studying "this," nothing is as capable as emptiness.

104 虛者無藏也。
Emptiness is absent of accumulation.[137]

105 故曰: 去知則奚率求矣,
Thus it is said: "If you relinquish 'knowing,' what is there to seek after?[138]

106 無藏則奚設矣,
Without accumulating, what is there to establish?"[139]

107 無求無設, 則無慮。
Seeking nothing, and establishing nothing, there is nothing to worry about.

108 無慮則反覆虛矣。
Without worries, one reverts to emptiness.[140]

---

[135] The exact quote, above, is "All people desire wisdom (智), yet none can find it through wisdom"

[136] In the *Dao De Jing*, "this" versus "that" commonly suggests internal and external reality, respectively. See, for example, chapters 12, 38, and 72.

See also *Bai Xin*, line 196 "By rejecting what is close and chasing after what is far, how can one but squander their power?"

[137] Similar to chapter 81 of the *Dao De Jing*, "The skilled are not argumentative; the argumentative are not skilled. Those who (presume to) know do not remain open-minded. The open-minded do not (presume to) know. Sages do not hoard. Having helped others, oneself gains more." This describes "the beginner's mind" often spoken of in Zen.

[138] See DDJ12, "the intensity of the hunt drives the mind mad." Perhaps this line in DDJ12 also alluded to an over-reliance on knowledge.

[139] The quote in lines 105-106 does not appear in the *Xin Shu*, possibly suggesting a different copy, a different text, or an oral tradition.

109 天之道，虛其無形。
　　The Dao of Heaven is empty and without form.
110 虛則不屈，
　　Because it is empty, it is not exhausted.[141]
111 無形則無所位赶，
　　Because it is without form, it is without location,
112 無所位赶，故遍流萬物而不變。
　　Without a (central) throne, it is thus everywhere, circulating amongst the myriad things, yet never changing.

113 德者道之舍，
　　Virtue is the abode of Dao.
114 物得以生。
　　When things attain (Virtue), they live.[142]
115 生知得以職道之精。
　　Being alive, they can know the office of Dao's essence.
116 故德者得也，
　　Thus, Virtue (De) also means "attainment (de)."[143]
117 得也者，其謂所得以然也，
　　As for this attainment, it is called "attaining the causality."[144]
118 以無為之謂道，
　　The effortlessness of this (causality) is called "Dao."
119 舍之之謂德。
　　When abiding in things, we call it "Virtue."

---

[140] Discussions of emptiness take on various forms in the DDJ. Compare, for example, chapters 5, 9, 10, and 11. Chapter 9 speaks of "gold filling the halls" which could be understood as thoughts and knowledge which can overtake and burden the mind, or pleasant feelings widely sought after which can turn into burdens of craving and desires.

[141] See DDJ5 虛而不屈，動而愈出 "Empty yet not exhausted. It moves and again more is pushed forth."

[142] See the excerpt from the Ling Shu Jing, found in the commentary on lines 1-22 of the Nei Ye: "Qi Bo replied: That which Heaven gives an individual is De (intrinsic virtue). That which Earth gives an individual is qi (energy-breath). When De and qi intermingle, there is life…"

[143] "Virtue" and "obtain," Dé, are homonyms and sometimes used as synonyms.

[144] 所以然 means "the reason why"

120 故道之與德無間。
Thus, between Dao and Virtue, there is no space.

121 故言之者不別也。
For this reason, it is said "they are not separate."

122 間之理者, 謂其所以舍也。
The principle of this space is called "their abiding place."[145]

123 義者, 謂各處其宜也。
Of right conduct (yi, aka righteousness), it is said, "each circumstance has an appropriate response."

124 禮者, 因人之情,
Social customs (li, aka etiquette) are based on (considering) the feelings of others,

125 緣義之理, 而為之節文者也。
And pertain to principles of right conduct and cultured formalities.

126 故禮者謂有理也,
Thus, of social custom, it is said that there are principles.

127 理也者, 明分以諭義之意也。
These principles are for clearly perceiving differences, and explaining the aims of right conduct.

128 故禮出乎義,
Thus, social customs come from right conduct;

129 義出乎理,
Right conduct comes from principles;

130 理因乎宜[146]者也。
Principles are based on appropriateness;

131 法者所以同出,
And law[147] is what causes all of these to mutually arise.

---

[145] Very similar to "the Mysterious Pass," a principle in Daoist Nei Dan meditation

[146] Scholar Guo Moruo suggests replacing "宜 appropriateness," here, with "道 Dao." "Appropriateness" also makes sense here, however.

[147] "法 Law," here appears to refer to something more akin to "the laws of physics" rather than written and agreed upon laws of right conduct. Such usage of "fa 法 law" may provide context for its later, Buddhist, usage as "Dharma 法," a term which could be explained as the Buddhist equivalent of Dao, meaning both teachings and universal laws and principles.

132 不得不然者也。
We would not have one if not for what preceded it.

133 故殺僇禁誅以一之也,
Thus, murder is despised, prohibited, and punished for the same reason.

134 故事督乎法,
And thus, affairs are supervised by law.

135 法出乎權,
Law come from authority,

136 權出乎道。
And authority comes from Dao.[148]

137 道也者,
As for Dao,

138 動不見其形,
It moves yet its form is not seen.

139 施不見其德,
It provides, yet its virtue is not seen.

140 萬物皆以得,
The myriad things all obtain through it,

141 然莫知其極。
Yet still nothing knows its limits.

142 故曰可以安而不可說也。
Thus, it is said: **"(The Great Dao) can bring peace and stability, yet it cannot be explained."**

143 (直)人, 言至也;[149]
"The correct man" refers to one who is refined.

144 不宜, 言應也。

---

[148] As Lu Dongbin stated "one cannot achieve Dao without observing precepts." As this stanza shows, these principles ultimately come from Dao.

[149] In the principle text, "yet it cannot be explained" is followed by 直人之言. Thus, the received copy of the *Xin Shu Shang*, which here reads 莫人, 言至也, has been adjusted to fit the principle text. See also, Wang Niansun.

"(If his words) did not refer to propriety" speaks of responding.[150]

145 應也者，非吾所設，
Because this response (meant to teach propriety) is not for me to give,

146 故能無宜也。
(People) can do without such teachings on propriety.[151]

147 不顧，言因也。
"(If he did not speak of) filial duties" refers to the basis.[152]

148 因也者，非吾所顧，
The basis is not my filial duty.

149 故無顧也。
Thus, (the people would be better off) without (such talk of) filial duties.[153]

150 不出於口，不見於色，
"If (these words) did not leave his mouth, nor did his face reveal them"

151 言無形也。
Refers to formlessness.

152 四海之人，庸知其則，
"All people within the four seas would return to their commonalities and understand these rules"

153 言深囿也。
Refers to (all people within) the furthest limits.

---

[150] The principle text reads "不義 not (refer to) righteousness" rather than "不宜 not (refer to) propriety." As the author of this commentary may have had an alternate copy of principle text, I have retained "propriety" here.

[151] Heshang Gong comments on DDJ38:
"People are taken by the arm and forced to obey"
Etiquette causes many unnecessary tensions. When people are taken by the arm and forced to obey these rules, it creates hostility and competition between authorities and subordinates.

[152] See lines 204-205 below "This is called 'the basis.' The basis is to reside in one's own, while according with other things."

[153] See DDJ2 and DDJ18 on praising superficial virtue

154 天之道虛,
  The way of Heaven is to be empty.
155 地之道靜,
  The way of Earth is to be quiet and still.
156 虛則不屈,
  Empty, it is not exhausted.
157 靜則不變,
  Quiet and still, it does not change.
158 不變則無過,
  Unchanging, it is without excess.
159 故曰不伐。
  Thus, (the text) says **"(from this, one should learn) not to boast."**

160 潔其宮, 闕其門,
  "Purify the temple, unblock the gates,"[154]
161 宮者, 謂心也。
  "The temple" refers to the heart-mind.
162 心也者, 智之舍也。
  The heart-mind is the abode of wisdom.
163 故曰宮,
  Therefore it is called "the temple."
164 潔之者, 去好過[155]也。
  To purify it is to get rid of liking and rejecting.
165 門者, 謂耳目也,
  "The gates" refer to the ears and eyes,

---

[154] The line quoted here reads above as "開其門 open the gates," rather than "闕其門 unblock the gates." Que 闕 means, literally, "watchtower," but was also used in place of "缺 gap" to say "unblock, release" as though standing down and doing nothing. For example, the Art of War states: "歸師勿遏, 圍師必闕 Do not interfere with an army that is returning home. When you surround an army, leave an outlet free" (trans. Giles).

[155] Ding Shihan suggests replacing "過 excess, error, pass over" with "惡 dislike," to say "get rid of 好 likes and 惡 dislikes." This may have been the intention of the received character, as 過 also suggests "passing over" or rejecting something that one does not like.

166 耳目者, 所以聞見也。
And therefore listening and hearing.

167「物固有形,
"Things which have solidified, have forms.
168 形固有名」。
Forms which have solidified, have names."
169 此言不得過實,
This is to say that (names)[156] do not penetrate to the reality,
170 實不得延名。
Nor does this reality defer to names.
171 姑[157]形以形,
Thus, forms takes shape,
172 以形務名,
And the form provides the name.[158]
173 督言正名。
(This is how) words are overseen, and correct names are given.
174 故曰「聖人」。
Thus, (the text) says "(Those who give them appropriate names are called) sages."
175「不言之言, 應也」。
"Their unspoken words (are heard like cracks of thunder)" refers to responding.
176 應也者, 以其為之人者也。
Their response is to the actions of others.

177 執其名,
Holding the name (in mind),
178 務其應, 所以成之,
They deeply consider the appropriate response, and thereby manifest it.

---

[156] Though omitted, "names" is implied here as it appears in the preceding quote. (Wang Niansun, and Yasui Ko)
[157] 姑 appears to be a typo for "故 thus"
[158] May suggest that, just as the name can only reflect the form, the form can only reflect something else.

179 應之道也。
This is the Dao of responding.

180 「無為之道」,[159] 因也,。
"The Dao of non-action" is to animate.
181 因也者,無益無損也。
This is to animate without increasing or decreasing.
182 以其形,因為之名,
Taking the form as impetus to create the name –
183 此因之術也。
This is the art of animation.
184 名者,聖人之所以紀萬物也。
It is with names that sages arrange the myriad things.[160]

185 人者立於強,
Of people, there are those who are firmly established,
186 務於善,
Those who are skilled in their professions,
187 未於能,
Those who are not yet capable,
188 動於故者也。
And those who are making progress.
189 聖人無之,
The Sage is without these (categories).

190 無之,則與物異矣,
Being without them, he is unusual amongst the myriad things.
191 異則虛,
Unusual because he is empty.
192 虛者萬物之始也,
Emptiness is the origin of all things.
193 故曰可以為天下始。

---

[159] The received principle text reads "無為之事 serving without action."
[160] Suggesting that sages organize society by determining names, roles, and definitions.

Thus, (the text) says **"he can fathom the beginning of all under Heaven."**

194 人迫於惡, 則失其所好,
When people are coerced by what they dislike, they lose what they like.

195 怵於好, 則忘其所惡,
Intimidated by what they like, they forget (and thus endure) what they dislike.

196 非道也。
This is not the Way.

197 故曰：「不怵乎好, 不迫乎惡」,
Thus it is said: **"(The junzi is) not intimidated[161] by what he likes, nor coerced by what he dislikes."**

198 惡不失其理,
In the presence of what is disliked, he does not neglect logic.

199 欲不過其情,
In the presence of what is desired, he does not have excessive emotions.

200 故曰：「君子恬愉無為,
Thus it is said, **"The junzi is tranquil, pleasant, and effortless,**

201 去智與故」
He abandons wisdom, and it abides in him as a result."

202 言虛素也。
This is to say that he is empty, and in the original unaltered state.

203「其應非所設也, 其動非所取也」
"He responds, but does not initiate; moves but does not possess."

204 此言因也,
This is called "the basis."

205 因也者, 舍己而以物為法者也。
The basis is to reside in one's own, while according with other things.

---

[161] The received principle text reads "不休乎好 does not dwell on what he likes".

206 感而後應，非所設也，
(The junzi) responds to feelings, yet does not initiate them.[162]

207 緣理而動，非所取也。
Following the principle, he moves (things), but does not possess (them).[163]

208「過在自用，罪在變化」，
"If one is excessively headstrong, they will err when adapting to changes."

209 自用則不虛，
If headstrong, one cannot be empty.

210 不虛則仵於物矣。
If not empty, one becomes the same as other "things."

211 變化則為生，為生則亂矣。
With change and transformation, there is growth. With growth, there is bound to be confusion.

212 故道貴因，因者，因其能者，言所用也。
Thus, the treasure of Dao is the basis (of responding and not initiating; moving yet not possessing).[164] On this basis rests ability.[165] This is called usefulness.[166]

213 君子之處也「若無知」，

---

[162] Similar to Zhuangzi (Chuang Tzu) chapter 15:
不為福先,不為禍始；感而後應，迫而後動，不得已而後起 "He does not take the initiative in producing either happiness or calamity. He responds to the influence acting on him, and moves as he feels the pressure. He rises to act only when he is obliged to do so." (trans. Legge)

[163] Similar to DDJ34

[164] See lines 203-204

[165] In the Ziran ("naturalness") chapter of the Neo-Confucian "Lunheng," is found the following: "In the State of Song a man carved a mulberry-leaf of wood, and it took him three years to complete it. Confucius said 'If the Earth required three years to complete one leaf, few plants would have leaves'. According to this dictum of Confucius the leaves of plants grow spontaneously, and for that reason they can grow simultaneously. If Heaven made them, their growth would be as much delayed as the carving of the mulberry-leaf by the man of the Song State." (trans. Albert Forke, 1911)

[166] DDJ11 states: "But it is where there is nothing that the room is used. So, substance is gained, and emptiness is used."

The junzi remains in the state **"of not knowing."**
214 言至虛也。
This is called "arriving at emptiness."
215 「其應物也若偶之」,
"Responding to things as though by coincidence."
216 言時適也。
This is called "adapting to the season" –
217 若影之象形,
Like a shadow taking the shape of a form,
218 響之應聲也,
Or an echo responding to a sound.
219 故物至則應,
Thus, when things reach them, (the junzi) responds.
220 過則舍矣, 舍矣者,
When these things move on, (the junzi) remains in place.
221 言復返於虛也。
This means (the junzi) reverts back to emptiness.

心術下
Art of the Heart-Mind: lower volume
Xin Shu Xia

1 形不正者德不來
When the bodily form is not aligned,
Virtue does not approach;

2 中不精者心不治。
When the center is not pure and clear,
the heart-mind is not stable.[167]

3 正形飾德,
An aligned bodily form is adorned with Virtue;[168]

4 萬物畢得。
The myriad things (thereby) attain completion.

5 翼然自來,
When these wings (of Virtue and the heart-mind)[169]
naturally come together,

---

[167] *Xin Shu Xia* lines 1–3 correspond to *Nei Ye*, lines 122-127, with the exception that the *Nei Ye* reads "when the center is not 靜 tranquil,." rather than "when the center is not 精 pure and clear,"

[168] XSX line 3 corresponds to the NY, line 126, which reads "when the bodily form is aligned, it 攝 absorbs Virtue" rather than "is 飾 adorned with Virtue."

[169] "These wings" may otherwise refer to spirit and qi, said by Ma Danyang to be the underlying meaning of pure nature (xing) and destiny-life-force (ming), the combination of which is central to the Daoist Nei Dan (internal elixer) tradition.

6 神莫知其極。
The spirit knows no limits.

7 昭知天下,
Illuminated, it's comprehension of the world

8 通於四極。
Spans throughout the four directions.

9 是故曰,無以物亂官
Therefore it is said: "When things do not confuse the senses,

10 毋以官亂心
And the senses do not confuse the heart-mind –

11 此之謂內德。
This is called 'inner Virtue'." [170]

12 是故意氣定
Thereby, the energy of intention is settled;

13 然後反正。
Having (settled), it returns to alignment.

14 氣者,身之充也。
Energy-breath then fills the body,

15 行者正之義也。
And one's conduct is righteous and upright. [171]

16 充不美,則心不得。
If this fullness (of energy-breath) is not pleasant, the heart-mind does not benefit.

See Komjathy, Luis. *The Way of Complete Perfection: A Quanzhen Daoist Anthology.* Albany: State University of New York Press, 2013.

[170] XSX lines 9-11 correspond to NY, lines 132-134, which read:

不以物亂官　　And things do not disturb the senses
不以官亂心　　Nor do the senses disturb the heart–mind
是謂中得　　　This is called inner attainment

The correspondence between these lines demonstrates the synonymous use of "zhong 中, center, inner" and "nei 內, inner, internal," as well as the synonymous use of "de 得, attain, achieve" and "de 德, Virtue." The correlation between de 得 and de 德 was referred to in the *Xin Shu Shang*, line 116: "Thus, Virtue also means to attain. As for this attaining, it is called 'attaining the causality.'"

[171] A very Daoist description of De, in that outer virtue follows inner harmony combined with robust energy which nourishes the organs.

17　行不正, 則民不服。
　　If one's conduct is not upright,
　　the people will not be provided for.[172]
18　是故, 聖人若天然, 無私覆也;
　　Therefore, sages resemble Heaven during such times:
　　They are without thought of self when sitting above all.
19　若地然, 無私載也。
　　They resemble Earth during such times:
　　They are without thought of self when supporting all.
20　私者, 亂天下者也。
　　As for thought of self, it puts the world in chaos.[173]

Aligning the body according to Earth and Heaven, stable and aligned, energy and spirit naturally reach throughout and find balance.

The *Xin Shu Xia* (XSX), while not referring to the *Dao De Jing* or *Nei Ye*, bears many resemblances to these texts, suggesting a larger tradition of teachings and practices in which these texts were situated. As is often said of the *Dao De Jing*, the *Xin Shu Xia* appears to have been written for rulers, while providing universal wisdom applicable to all. Its teachings, therefore, likely grew in consensus amongst a community of sages, before being preserved in writing for the Sovereign by one or more members of the proto-Daoist community. Having found consensus, the practices and worldviews in these texts would also be transmitted verbally to nephews, siblings, scholars, and the like, accumulating various experiences and developing into longer

---

[172] The health of the internal organs determines virtues associated with them. Heshang Gong explains in DDJ6 that the organs and virtues (the organ spirits) must be nourished by breathing like a valley, nourishing the spirits. "The valley with a spirit does not die." The *Xin Shu Xia*, here, shows that having full breath brings balanced circulation, and thus the people will be provided for. The internal health brings the manifest virtue and actions of generosity when the breath is full and the body is nourished with the balanced circulation of energy that fills it like a surplus of grain stores for the population.

[173] XSX12-20 do not correspond directly to any lines in the *Nei Ye*, though similar ideas do appear. XSX18-20 are entirely unique, in the *Guan Zi*, to the *Xin Shu Xia*.

treatises. This seems to have been the case in the development of the *Bai Xin, Xin Shu Shang, Xin Shu Xia, Nei Ye,* and *Dao De Jing,* a process which likely began long before any of these texts were committed to writing.

The *Xin Shu Xia* shares a number of passages and expressions with the *Nei Ye,* leading some to conclude that the XSX was based on the *Nei Ye.* While plausible, this theory does not account for the unique directions the XSX takes before and after these shared sayings, nor the unique and calculated sequences in which these sayings appear in the XSX. The inclusion of the *Xin Shu Xia* in *Guan Zi* may, otherwise, be due to it having appeared in many duplicates as a self-contained book when Liu Xiang consolidated the many duplicates found in the 564 book bundles that he pared down into the 86 books of the *Guan Zi.* The *Nei Ye* seems more likely to have been an expansion of the *Xin Shu Xia,* bringing together additional and valuable teachings from the proto–Daoist internal cultivation tradition, and so presented as a separate book. This would make the *Xin Shu Xia* one of the principle, and first, documents of this tradition.

The opening lines of the *Xin Shu Xia* present a clear description of the Daoist approach to cultivating virtues. Not by adjusting their external behavior, but by settling themselves internally and pacifying their desires do people cultivate a true and lasting inner virtue. A comparison can be seen in lines 14–17 between breath filling the body and conduct filling the world. When one is full of positive and aligned qi, they express this outwardly with positive conduct, filling the world with social harmony and contributing to the realization of the great peace of Dao in the world. Added to this teaching of inner attainment outwardly expressing itself, is the technique of aligning the body to bring about internal alignment and balance. Just as one can cultivate peace and order in their nation by maintaining peace and order in themselves, they can cultivate internal peace and order by maintaining this alignment in the body.

Lines 18-20, which are entirely unique to the *Xin Shu Xia,* further demonstrate what it means to follow Heaven and Earth. Similar to lines 38-40 of the *Xin Shu Shang,* we see here that to be "above, like Heaven, and below, like Earth" involves transcendence of the self. Heaven is not aware of its Heaven-ness, and Earth is not aware of its

Earth-ness. They have transcended this notion of self and self-interest. In their stillness, sages also transcend their notion of self-ness. As explained in line 206 of the *Bai Xin*: "Be unified and without division. This is called 'knowing Dao.'"

The notion of transcending the self is prominent in Buddhism, where the self's absence of independent existence is described thoroughly to help one overcome their attachment to the "illusion of self." The proto-Daoist texts take a different approach to a similar end, convincing one to overcome attachment to self by showing the freedom that can be known by doing so. Chapter seven of the *Dao De Jing* states:

> Heaven has longevity, Earth has continuity
> Heaven and Earth have the power of longevity and continuity
> because they do not live for themselves
> This is how they can live for so long
> Therefore, sages leave themselves behind
> And they end up in front
> They do not cater to themselves
> Yet they persist
> Is it not because they are without selfishness and wickedness
> That they are able to fulfill themselves?

DDJ13 adds:

> What does it mean to say "Appreciate the great worrying
> That both (favour and disgrace) cause to your person?"
> The reason I have great worries is because I have a self
> If I did not have a self, what worries would I have?

Finally, DDJ33 states:

> Those who know others, are wise
> Those who know themselves, are clear-sighted
> Those who overpower others, have strength
> Those who overpower themselves, have fortitude
> Those who know contentment, are rich
> Those who exercise this fortitude, have will-power

Those who do not lose their station, continue
Those who die but do not disappear, live long

The last line of DDJ33 is often considered a reference to the Daoist notion of spiritual immortality; however, with this common thread of transcending the self, it may also suggest that those who overcome the petty concerns of the ego can live longer and achieve lasting accomplishments.[174]

In the *Huainan Zi* (139 BC), another compendium of Daoist thought which, like the *Guan Zi*, was initiated by an ascendant of Liu Bang, founder of the Han Dynasty, we find a continuation of teachings found throughout the *Guan Zi*'s proto-Daoist texts. In chapter one of the *Huainan Zi* appear instructions for attaining "inner Virtue," spiritual intelligence, and the constant accompaniment of Dao. Though the *Xin Shu Xia* and *Nei Ye* are never quoted in the *Huainan Zi*, common themes throughout these texts help one to uncover and clarify their essential underlying motifs. Not wishing to deprive readers of making these connections for themselves, the following excerpt, from the *Huainan Zi*, chapter one, is provided below without annotation:

> Now, those who use their ears and eyes to hear and observe strain their bodies to understand correctly. Those who use knowledge and deliberation to govern correctly abuse the mind and achieve nothing. Therefore, sages use a single measurement, complying with what has been well established. They do not alter its acceptability; they do not change its regularity. Thus, they can determine what accords to the level, knowing what is crooked by what is just.

> Euphoria and anger are deviations from Dao;
> Anguish and sorrow are losses of Intrinsic Virtue.
> Likes and dislikes overtax the mind;
> Cravings and desires disturb Pure Nature.

---

[174] For further comparison of XSX1-20 with the *Dao De Jing*, please see DDJ10, found in my commentary on the *Xin Shu Shang*, lines 24-29.

Intense anger ruins the yin;
Intense euphoria collapses the yang.
Weakened qi renders one mute;
Fear and terror causes insanity.
If one is anxious, sorrowful, and frequently angry,
Sickness will accumulate.
If likes and dislikes grow numerous,
Misfortunes will also follow.

Thus, when the mind is neither anxious nor jubilant, Intrinsic Virtue is refined.
When the mind is far reaching yet unchanging, tranquility is refined.
When cravings and desires do not burden the mind, emptiness is refined.
When the mind is without likes and dislikes, equanimity is refined.
When the mind is not scattered about on things, purity is refined.
If the mind can succeed in these five (refinements), it will break through to spiritual intelligence. To break through to spiritual intelligence is to attain what lies within.

Therefore, using the internal to control the external,
Your many endeavours will not fail.
If, internally, you can attain it,
Externally, you can harvest it.
With this inner attainment (中之得則),
The five major organs will be peaceful;
Thoughts and worries will be stabilized.
The tendons will be strong, and your strength will be powerful;
Your ears and eyes will be acute and clear.
Though relaxed in your efforts, you will not be wayward
Though firm and strong, you will not bring regret.
There is nothing you will overshoot
And nothing you will fall short of.
Dwelling in the small, you will not be cramped;
Dwelling in the large, you will not be extravagant.
Your yang-spirits (hun) will not be agitated;
Your shen-spirit will not be distracted.
Calm and collected, quiet and still,

You will be amongst the world like an owl.

The Great Way is level and smooth.
Though it may leave a person, it is never far away.
Seeking it nearby,
Though moving ahead, you can continually return to it;
As it presses you, you can be responsive;
As you feel it, you can move;
When things are impressive, they do not deplete you;
Though things change, you remain without form or image.
When you give (Dao) free reign and roam with it to the furthest reaches
You will be like its echo and shadow.
Climbing up high or descending into depths,
You will not lose your grip.
When walking through dangers and traversing narrow paths
You will not lose this mysterious companion.

If you can be like this, its Virtue will not retreat. As the myriad things scatter and blend together, you can follow their shifts and transformations, listening to the world as though it were a wind at your back moving you swiftly onwards. This is called "refined Virtue." With refined Virtue, there is true happiness.[175]

21 凡物載名而來,
All things uphold their names and come together.
22 聖人因而財之,
Sages hold to the basis[176] and cherish it.
23 而天下治,
The world is then orderly and peaceful.
24 實不傷不亂於天下

---

[175] From the *Huainan Zi* (edited by Liu An, 139 BC), chapter one. Translated by Dan G. Reid.
[176] See *Xin Shu Shang* lines 203–212 for more on the "因 basis."

The true state of things does not cause injury,
or put the world in chaos,
25 而天下治。
But makes the world orderly and peaceful.
26 專於意，一於心,
Consolidate the intent. Unify the heart-mind.
27 耳目端，知遠之證,
By bringing the ears and eyes to the beginning,
know what is confirmed far away.
28 能專乎？能一乎？
Can you consolidate? Can you unify?
29 能毋卜筮而知凶吉乎？
Without divining by yarrow stalks,
can you know what is perilous and what is fortunate?
30 能止乎？能已乎？
Can you stop it? Can you bring it to a halt?
31 能毋問於人,而自得之於己乎？
Can you do this, not by asking others,
but by achieving this within yourself?[177]

Seeking the constant within, that which obscures clear vision is removed.

While the *Xin Shu Xia*, here as well, carries sentences similar to the *Nei Ye* (NY), its focus is uniquely centered on both inner and outer unity – on inner peace resulting in social harmony. This topic begins in the preceding lines (see XSX 14–20), which segue into the discussion of unity, stating:

All things uphold their names and come together.
Sages hold to the basis, and cherish it.

---

[177] The following correspondence of lines occurs between *Xin Shu Xia* and the *Nei Ye*: XSX 26-27 to NY 251-253. XSX 28-36 to NY 237-248

The world is then orderly and peaceful.

This unity requires a return to that state of mind which precedes distinctions or 'names'. Line 26 states, "Consolidate the intent. Unify the heart-mind." As shown later in both the *Xin Shu Xia* (line 114) and *Nei Ye* (line 167), intent (*yi*) precedes words and thus the distinction of 'names'. By consolidating intent, the heart-mind finds the Oneness of "the beginning" mentioned in line 27. Such an understanding will be helpful when encountering lines 32-47, below, which also speak to unification, and the transcendence of thought, leading to wisdom.

Heshang Gong speaks of the originating Oneness in his comments on DDJ10:

"Embrace Oneness. Can you do this without letting (the bodily spirits) flee?"
People who can embrace Oneness and not let it leave them, extend their lives. In Oneness, Dao began to situate life by the supreme harmony of vital energy-breath. Therefore it is said: "Oneness covered the world with names."

Heaven attained Oneness and became clear. Earth attained Oneness and became serene. Lords and kings attained Oneness and became upright and peace-loving. Going within, it is mind; going outwards, it is actions; in covering all with its blessing, it is Virtue. *All the names together are One.* Referring to Oneness, it is said: "In a unified consciousness, there is no division (or doubt)."

"Gather together the energy-breath and become soft"
Gather and embrace the vital energy-breath within. Then it will not be chaotic and the body will become soft and pliant.

"This is the power of an infant"
Have the power of an infant. Be, internally, without a thought or worry, and externally, without official duties. Then the vital spirits will not leave.

Line 22, "Sages hold to the basis, and cherish it," can be further explained by reading *Xin Shu Shang*, lines 203–212, which define "the basis (因, cause, reason)."

> "He responds, but does not initiate; moves but does not possess."
> This is called "the basis."
> The basis is to reside in one's own, while according with other things.
> (The junzi) responds to feelings, yet does not initiate them.
> Following the principle, he moves (things), but does not possess (them).
> "If one is excessively headstrong, they will err when adapting to changes."
> If headstrong, one cannot be empty.
> If not empty, one becomes the same as other "things."
> With change and transformation, there is growth. With growth, there is bound to be confusion.
> Thus, the treasure of Dao is the basis (of responding and not initiating; moving yet not possessing). On this basis rests ability.
> This is called usefulness.

Lines 26-31 could be variously interpreted, either as consolidating the thoughts and minds of the people to create a unified and familial nation, or otherwise as consolidating one's own thoughts and mind so as to attain clarity, peace, and perception. Lines 32-47 confirm the latter as the ultimate significance of these verses.

A connection between thoughts and the beginning of peril (XSX29-36) is made clear in the *Nei Ye*, lines 103–104, with the statement "Invariably, mental formations will create excessive knowledge, even at the expense of one's life." Similar statements about divination also appear in the *Bai Xin* 62-63:

> Not by the day or the month, but by how affairs follow (Dao), and not by prophesy or divination, but by how cautiously one follows (Dao), can you know their fortune or misfortune.

And in DDJ38:

When people who don't know
Display flowery appearances of the Dao
And speak as though they know how to recognize what is coming
This is the beginning of idiocy
Therefore, great and noble men stay with what is substantial
And not with what is slight
They stay with the fruit
And not with the flower
They leave that and choose this

32 故曰,
Thus it is said
33 思之思之不得,
"Thinking and thinking does not attain.
34 鬼神教之。
Ghosts and deities teach this.
35 非鬼神之力也,
(Thinking) is not the strength of ghosts and deities;
36 其精氣之極也。
Their (strength) is the essence
of extremely refined energy-breath."[178]
37 一氣能變曰精。
Unified energy-breath can bring transformation.
This is called "essence."
38 一事能變曰智。
Unified endeavours can bring transformation.
This is called "wisdom."
39 慕選者, 所以等事也。
Desirable selection according to candidate's abilities
is the reason for classifying affairs;

---

[178] XSX lines 33-36 correspond to NY, lines 243-248. XSX lines 37-42 correspond, loosely, to NY, lines 105-114.

40 極變者，所以應物也。
Ultimate transformation
is the reason for responding to things.
41 慕選而不亂，
To make desirable selections according to candidates' abilities,
do not be chaotic and confused;
42 極變而不煩。
To make the ultimate transformation, do not be agitated.

43 執一之君子，
The junzi holds to Oneness.[179]
44 執一而不失，
Holding to Oneness and not losing it,
45 能君萬物。
He can rule the myriad things.
46 日月之與同光，
A companion of the sun and moon,
their lights unite (within him);
47 天地之與同理。
A companion of Heaven and Earth,
their principles unite (within him).

By removing thoughts and concepts, the heart can unite its ministers; finding truth within, truth can be recognized externally.

Here again, the *Xin Shu Xia* bears great similarity to the *Nei Ye* while differing significantly in meaning. The *Nei Ye* (lines 235-262) speaks of unification as a way to extend and preserve life, whereas the *Xin Shu Xia* is unique in lines 39-42 where it gives attention to wisely managing political affairs, as per the *Dao De Jing*'s double entendres

---

[179] See *Nei Ye*, lines 105-121, in comparison to XSX lines 43-64. While only a few of these lines use near exact wording, the progression of thought corresponds. XSX 46-47 do not appear in the *Nei Ye*.

for the nation and the individual. This dual focus continues in the XSX until line 64.

The *Xin Shu Xia* further elaborates on the meaning of inner unification by connecting it with the cessation of thoughts (lines 32-36) in the process of refining qi (energy-breath), furthering its earlier instructions to consolidate the intention and unify the heart-mind (XSX, line 26) so as to make the consciousness "unified and without (doubt or) division" (BX, line 206), and thereby eliminate scattered thoughts (see XSS, line 41).

This 'technique of the heart-mind (xin shu)' extends itself to managing affairs by fostering decisiveness, certitude, and focus in endeavours, honing the strength of the mind to eliminate inner distractions.

Lines 41-42 make a comparison between guarding the power of the heart-mind, and guarding the power of a ruler. In both cases, to ensure that only those meriting positions of influence attain them, the Sovereign must not be confused or agitated.

Understanding the teachings in these verses helps one to understand the backdrop of tradition in which the *Dao De Jing* was written, and to see with greater clarity the implications of its metaphors. Consider, for example, the above teachings on the cessation of thought, along with lines 43-47, in regards to DDJ28:

> … Return to Wuji, Supreme Nothingness
> Knowing praise, hold onto reproof
> And be a valley under Heaven
> Being a valley under Heaven, Virtue will always fulfill you
> Return to your unaltered substance
> Unaltered wood is shaped into vessels
> Sages make use of this model
> When acting in positions of leadership
> Thereby, the greatest establishment is undivided

When line 46 speaks of uniting the lights of the sun and moon, this evokes the meaning of 明 ming. Ming is translated as "enlightenment," yet means more literally "clear vision." It is written by combining the characters for 日 sun and 月 moon. This could also be understood as suggesting that the junzi embraces the yin and yang energies of the sun and moon, and the emptiness and stillness of

Heaven and Earth. The practice of "ingesting the essence of the sun and moon" became a part of Daoist visualization meditations closer to the 3rd century AD, but as we see, may find its beginnings in proto–Daoism.

Lines 46-47 also show underlying currents of thought evident in DDJ25:

> ... Dao is immense, Heaven is immense
> Earth is immense, and the Emperor is also immense
> From the periphery to the center
> There exists the Four Immensities
> And the Emperor represents their unification
>
> Man is regulated by Earth
> Earth is regulated by Heaven
> Heaven is regulated by Dao
> Dao is regulated by its own spontaneous nature

48 聖人栽物,
Sages shape things,
49 不為物使。
But they do not control them.
50 心安,是國安也。
A peaceful heart and mind makes for a peaceful nation;
51 心治,是國治也。
An orderly heart-mind makes for an orderly nation.
52 治也者心也。
That which is ordered, is the heart-mind;
53 安也者心也。
That which is made peaceful, is the heart-mind.[180]
54 治心在於中,

---

[180] XSX52–53 correspond to NY, lines 162-163

When the orderliness of the heart-mind reaches to the very center,
55 治言出於口,
Orderly words leave the mouth,
56 治事加於民;
And orderly affairs increase amongst the people.
57 故功作而民從,則百姓治矣。
Thus, as accomplishments flourish, the people follow in kind, and the hundred clans are also orderly.
58 所以操者非刑也,
What keeps them in order is not punishments;
59 所以危者非怒也。
What threatens them is not anger.
60 民人操,百姓治,
With the common people in order, and the hundred clans well governed,
61 道其本至也。至無不至。
Dao reaches to the very root foundation. Reaching (to this root), there is nothing which does not arrive (at Dao).[181]
62 非所人而亂,
Then it will not be individuals who bring disorder,
63 凡在有司執制者之利,
But the collectivity of those who seek to take charge, and control the system for their own profits.
64 非道也。
This is not Dao.

For a ruler to find the path towards peace in the kingdom, he need look no further than the path to internal peace. As the body resonates with a peaceful heart-mind, the words and actions of a peaceful ruler will resonate this stability and order throughout all under

---

[181] There appears to be a typo here, in that 至不至無 should appear as 至無不至. Credit to Xu Weiyu for this correction.

Heaven. Just as a bowl cannot be fully washed with contaminated water, a nation cannot be fully settled by a chaotic or corrupt leader.

Contrasting lines 43-64 of the *Xin Shu Xia* (beginning in the previous section) with lines 105-121 of the *Nei Ye* helps to reveal some of the more esoteric language within the *Nei Ye*. For example, the *Nei Ye* reads in lines 115-121:

> When the orderliness of the heart-mind reaches to the very center
> Orderly words leave the mouth
> And orderly affairs increase amongst the people
> As such, all under Heaven will be orderly!
> When one word is grasped, all under heaven fits together
> When one word settles (in the heart), all under Heaven cooperates
> This is the meaning of 'serving the greater good.'

Contrasting this excerpt with lines 54-64 of the *Xin Shu Xia*, "one word" can then be understood as referring to "Dao" in the lexicon of these writers, noting this difference in the *Xin Shu Xia*, line 61. Further, "serving the greater good" can be understood as the prevalence of Dao, rather than disorder being brought about by "the collectivity of those who seek to take charge, and control the system for their own profits" (line 63). "The greater good" (gong, 公) also means "public interest, impartial, unselfish" as opposed to "私 private, selfish," and is said to lead one towards Dao in DDJ16:

> ... Know how to embrace eternality
> This embrace shows the way of impartiality (公)
> The way of impartiality (公) shows the way of a king
> The way of a king shows the way of Heaven
> The way of Heaven shows the way of Dao
> The way of Dao shows the way of longevity
> And for the body to be without peril

A number of corresponding ideas on the use of force, abuses of power, and what is "not Dao" (see XSX, line 64), can be found by comparing XSX48-64 with DDJ30:

As for those who use Dao to counsel the king
It is not by weapons that they have power in the world
Such activities are reciprocated
Where troops gather, thorns and brambles appear
Following war, there is sure to be famine and misfortune
Large armies are sure to bring sadness in the future
Achieve your aim well, and then stop
Do not dare to abuse power
Achieve your aim, but do not boast
Achieve your aim, but do not attack again
Achieve your aim, but do not become arrogant
Achieve your aim, but do not claim all the credit
Achieve your aim, but do not abuse power
Things thrive in their prime and then become aged
This is called "not Dao"
What is "not Dao" ends prematurely

It may appear that the author of the *Nei Ye* (lines 105-121) condensed lines 43-64 of the *Xin Shu Xia* so as to focus more on the subject of internal cultivation, or that the author of the *Xin Shu Xia* expanded on the words of the *Nei Ye*; however, this is to assume that both texts were not simply based on the mutual influence of earlier teachings.

65 聖人之道，若存若亡。
   The way of sages is to be as though being and not being.
66 援而用之，殁世不亡。
   Aided by the employment of this (way), until the end of time they do not die.
67 與時變而不化，
   Following the time, they adapt, yet do not change.
68 應物而不移，
   They respond to things,

yet do not move from their places.¹⁸²

69 日用之而不化。
Daily employing this way, they are not transformed.

Action and inaction exist because of one another; black and white appear in opposition to one another; high and low exist in relation to one another. These differences appear, yet their distinction and separateness is also illusory. Like the Dao, sages contain both all and nothing within.

Lines 65-69 provide an early example of Chinese writings on immortality. This illustration of 'stillness in motion' appears before a description of the physical form becoming more durable as a result of "aligning and quieting" oneself (XSX70–73). XSX67-69, "不化 (They) do not change.. they are not transformed," therefore, departs from earlier notions of immortality which referred only to the words and deeds of a person living on in perpetuity.¹⁸³

Lines 65-69 also continue the trend of connecting longevity with the elusive qualities of Dao, a tenet which likely influenced DDJ35:

> Joyful music and sweets entice passing travelers to stop
> When Dao appears in the mouth
> Like water, it is without taste
> Looking at it, it is not seen
> Listening to it, it is not heard
> Using it, it is not used up

70 人能正靜者,
Those who can align and quiet themselves

---

[182] XSX67-71 correspond to NY89-95.
[183] See *Spring and Autumn Annals* in Chan's *A Source Book in Chinese Philosophy*. New Jersey: Princeton University Press, 1963. p. 13

71 筋肕而骨強。
(Make their) muscles flexible, and bones strong;
72 能戴大圓者
Those who can support the great circle (Heaven/the head)
73 體乎大方。
Their body is like the great square (Earth),
74 鏡大清者
They mirror the great clarity;
75 視乎大明。
Their vision is greatly illuminated.
76 正靜不失,
When alignment and stillness are not lost,
77 日新其德,
They daily refresh their virtue.
78 昭知天下,
Their knowledge illumines all under Heaven,
79 通於四極。
Spreading out to the four directions.

With the body stable and aligned like the Earth, and the head sitting atop like Heaven, the great circle, floating in emptiness, cornerless, almost shapeless, the natural Virtue of Heaven and Earth will bring health and wholeness to the body and spirit.

Lines 7-79 are another example of proto-Daoist instructions on attaining longevity by learning from Heaven and Earth. These lines can also be found, with slight alterations and additions, in the *Nei Ye*, lines 192-204.

80 金心在中不可匿。
A golden heart within cannot be hidden.[184]
81 外見於形容,
Externally, it is observed in the physical form
82 可知於顔色。
And can be recognized in the appearance of the face.[185]
83 善氣迎人,
Welcoming others with an energy-breath of goodness
84 親如弟兄。
Is like embracing them with the affection of brothers and sisters;
85 惡氣迎人,
Welcoming others with an energy-breath of wickedness
86 害於戈兵。
Is like injuring them with a soldier's spear.
87 不言之言,
Unspoken words
88 聞於雷鼓。
Are heard like the drums of thunder,
89 金心之形,
While manifestations of a golden heart[186]
90 明於日月,
Illuminate like the sun and moon.
91 察於父母。
They are perceived as though by one's own parents.
92 昔者 明王之愛天下,
The ancient enlightened kings' love for all under Heaven

---

[184] Similar to *Nei Ye* 216-217, where "A golden heart within" is replaced with "全心在中 Keeping the heart-mind centered." "金心 Golden heart" is used again in line 89, and fits the imagery in line 90. If one were to "correct" one of these passages in light of the other, the *Xin Shu Xia* seems more fitting and likely to be the original.

[185] *Nei Ye*, line 219, reads "it is seen in the skin's colour."

[186] Replaced with "心氣之形 the manifestations of the heart-mind's energy-breath" in NY226.

93 故天下可附。
Allowed the world to depend on them;
94 暴王之惡天下,
The violent kings' hatred of all under Heaven
95 故天下可離。
Caused the world to abandon them.
96 故貨之不足以為愛,
Thus, rewards are not enough to demonstrate love,
97 刑之不足以為惡。
And punishments are not enough to demonstrate fierceness.[187]
98 貨者愛之末也。
For this love will end with the rewards,
99 刑者惡之末也。
And this fierceness will end with the punishments.

When the clouds part, the sun is sure to shine through. Refreshing and cultivating Virtue within, it is sure to shine forth in our intentions. Clarifying the heart-mind naturally purifies our intentions and allows this Virtue to bring its warmth to our environment.

Lines 80-99 provide a rich example of the proto-Daoists' esteem for warm-heartedness. With a "golden heart," one is even protected from external harm, and may forgo rewards and punishments. Such sentiments are also echoed in DDJ50:

> I have heard that those who are good at absorbing life
> Travel the land without encountering rhinoceros or tigers

---

[187] XSX80–97 correspond to NY216-230, while XSX92-95 and 98-99 do not appear in the *Nei Ye*. Note the difference between XSX96-97 and NY229–230, where the *Nei Ye* replaces "以為愛 be considered love" with "以勸善 encourage goodness," and "以為惡 be considered fierceness" with "以懲過 discourage misbehaviour." This greater specificity in the *Nei Ye* may further suggest that it was a later redaction.

They walk into groups of soldiers
Without requiring armour or soldiers for protection
The rhinoceros has no place to thrust its horn
The tiger has no place to grab with its claw
And the soldier has nowhere to place his weapon

Most of *Xin Shu Xia* lines 80-99 appear in lines 216-230 of the *Nei Ye*, though with some significant differences. Line 80's "a golden heart within" appears in the *Nei Ye* as "the heart-mind remains within (全心在中)," exchanging "金 golden" for "全 maintaining (remaining)" by omitting two strokes from the character. "Golden heart (金心)" is repeated in line 89 of the *Xin Shu Xia*, thereby fitting the imagery in line 90: "The manifestations of a golden heart (89) illuminate like the sun and moon (90)". The *Nei Ye*'s terminology, however, reads instead "the manifestations of the heart-mind's *energy-breath* illuminate like the sun and moon (心氣之形, 明於日月)." This alteration might suggest that the *Nei Ye* developed from a corrupted copy of the *Xin Shu Xia*, where "金 golden" was written as "全 maintaining" in line 89, forcing the editor to make sense of this mistaken terminology and so explain it in *Nei Ye*'s line 226 as "energy-breath of the heart-mind."

Lines 80-99 also tie in to XSX109-119 which speak of intention preceding words, explaining in part why *"unspoken words are heard like drums of thunder, while the golden heart illuminates like the sun and moon."* Similarly, lines 92-95 tie into lines 109-112. Cultivating positive intention would thus appear to be part of the reason behind the proceeding lines (100-108) which advocate music, courtesy, respect, and internal quiet as ways to alleviate emotions that lead to distress and a deterioration or depletion of life energy. This deterioration can also pollute one's intent.

Lines 92-96 do not appear in the *Nei Ye*, though one could perceive a parallel sentiment in lines 231-234. XSX lines 96-97 bear a resemblance to *Nei Ye* lines 229-230, while XSX lines 98-99 do not appear in the *Nei Ye*. Following this section in the *Nei Ye* are verses which echo the XSX, lines 28-36.

100 凡民之生也,
Invariably, people's lives
101 必以正平,
Require alignment and balance.
102 所以失之者,
What causes them to lose this, however,
103 必以喜樂哀怒。
Is certainly euphoria, pleasure, sorrow, and anger.
104 節怒莫若樂,
To moderate anger, nothing compares to music;
105 節樂莫若禮,
To moderate music, nothing compares to courtesy;
106 守禮莫若敬。
To preserve courtesy, nothing compares to respect.
107 外敬而內靜者,
Externally respectful, and internally quiet,
108 必反其性。
One is sure to return to their pure nature (xīng).

Under our emotions, desires, thoughts, and beliefs, is the undivided unity of spirit surveying our body, mind, energy, and life, like an eagle watching the world from above, all-knowing yet unaffected.

The XSX's comment that euphoria, pleasure, sorrow, and anger endanger one's cultivation of pure nature, is analogous to DDJ50, especially in light of Heshang Gong's commentary:

> *"To depart from life is to enter death"*
> When emotions and desires leave the five internal organs, the hun-spirit (in the liver, governing anger) becomes calm, and the po-spirit (in the lungs, governing sorrow) becomes settled. Vitality then flourishes.

When emotions and desires go deep into the consciousness of the heart (胸臆), vital essence is over-exerted, and the spirit becomes confused. This causes death.

"The companions of life are thirteen, The companions of death are thirteen"
Lao Tzu is saying that (the path to) life and death are both governed by thirteen things: the nine bodily apertures and four closures.[188] To nourish life, the eyes should not observe frantically, the ears should not listen frantically, the nose should not smell frantically, the mouth should not speak or taste frantically, the hands should not grasp frantically, the feet should not walk frantically, and the vital spirits should not be frantically engrossed. For death, it is the opposite of this.
"In their way of living, people are ensnared by way of (these) thirteen"
People know to seek life; however, in doing so, they instead bring about death by these thirteen things.
"Why is this so?"
Asking why death arrives this way.
"Because they seek a life of excess"
Those who die by seeking life try to make a living in order to support an excessive lifestyle. Defying Dao and disobeying Heaven, their frantic behaviour causes them to lose the true path.

While Heshang Gong speaks to the ways by which people are ensnared, ie. by over-indulgence in, and reliance on, the senses, the *Xin Shu Xia* speaks to the next stages of this ensnarement, specifically the pleasure and joy, or sorrow and anger determined by whether or not the desires of the senses are fulfilled. Thus, Lao Zi and Heshang Gong caution against over-stimulation, while the *Xin Shu Xia* also offers methods to ease the symptoms of this over-stimulation, cultivate positive intention and regain the stability that allows a return to *xìng* – true-nature.

Lines 100-108 resemble lines 85-95 of the *Nei Ye*, with the exceptions that:

---

[188] The nine apertures are the eyes (2), ears (2), nose (2), mouth, anus, and urethra. The four closures refer to the feet and hands.

1. In the *Nei Ye*, "euphoria, pleasure, sorrow, and anger" are replaced with "euphoria, anger, sadness, and worry." The *Nei Ye* also makes a similar statement in line 27, but lists "sorrow, pleasure, euphoria, anger, desire, and avarice."
2. In the *Nei Ye*, poetry (rather than music) is prescribed for anger, while music is prescribed for sadness.
3. The *Nei Ye* adds the line "to maintain respect, nothing compares to silence"
4. The *Nei Ye* also adds a final line "pure nature will then be firmly established."

109 豈無利事哉？
When is there no benefit from my affairs?
110 我無利心，
When there is no benefit in my heart-mind.
111 豈無安處哉？
When is there no peace where I reside?
112 我無安心，
When there is no peace in my heart-mind.
113 心之中又有心：
At the center of the heart-mind, there is again another heart-mind.[189]
114 意以先言，
Intention precedes words;
115 意然後刑，
From intention follows decision;
116 形然後思，
From this formulation follows thought;
117 思然後知，
From thought follows knowledge.

---

[189] XSX109–123 correspond to NY160-180, while XSX114–119 also correspond to NY97-104

118 凡心之刑,
   Invariably, the heart-mind's decisions
119 過知失生。
   Will supersede knowledge,
   even at the expense of one's life[190].

120 是故內聚以為泉原,
   Therefore, all that is collected internally
   (should be) regarded as a wellspring.
121 泉之不竭,表裡遂通。
   When this source is not exhausted,
   internally and externally, it circulates freely;[191]
122 泉之不涸,四支堅固。
   When the source is not dried up,
   the four limbs will become firm and solid,
123 能令用之,被服四固。
   Enabling command of their functions,
   and keeping them fit and strong[192],[193]
124 是故聖人一言解之。
   Therefore, the Sage uses a single saying to unravel this:
125 上察於天,
   "For what is above, study the Heavens;
126 下察於地。
   For what is below, study the Earth."[194]

---

[190] Some credit is due to Graziani's translation of this line. It is usually translated in the *Nei Ye* to the effect of "when thoughts cross into knowledge, one loses vitality." Graziani's (French) translation reads (in English) "In general, the mind is disposed in such a way that it will lose its life to think in excess."

[191] See DDJ5 on not speaking but guarding balance within.

[192] Reminiscent of Taiji Chuan where one allows the internal qi to command the movements, creating greater responsiveness and inner-outer connection.

[193] "被服 Bedding" in this case means to keep things in good shape, like one's clothes.

Feelings, thoughts, and emotion rise up into decisions that may not be fully connected to the wisdom found in the absence of these urgings. Remaining alert and responsive while not allowing thoughts and decisions to distract from the underlying source of intention, we do not get stuck, like mud, but rather move freely through any course, adapting and penetrating like water, without the restrictions and limitations of mental debris.

Lines 109-126 speak to the essential role of intention in cultivating life energy. Purifying intention is both an aim and effect of becoming internally peaceful and practicing the "art of the heart-mind." As the Guigu Zi[195] states:

> Genuine intention must begin with the heart-mind technique (xin shu). Seek, through non-doing, stable tranquility of the five internal organs, and harmony throughout the six bowels. When the vital-essence, spirit (shen), yang-spirits (hun), and yin-spirits (po) are steadfastly guarded and unmoving, you can internalize your gaze and return your listening; settle your will and contemplation on cosmic emptiness, and attend to the spirit's leaving and returning.

With genuine intention, one's energy becomes more positive and life nourishing, allowing the eyes to sparkle and the demeanour to reflect peace, patience, and kindness. Emotional turmoil and overpowering desires suffocate this effect, making the breathing short and the mind narrow. Thus, cultivating energy is not simply filling up the body with fuel, but opening up the windows to the soul and letting fresh positive energy into your spirit. As said in lines 80-82:

> A golden heart within cannot be hidden.

---

[194] NY155-184 appears almost as a commentary on this section of the XSX109-124, though this section of NY has additional content and begins with the saying at the end of XSX124-126.

XSX109-112 could be compared to NY159-163, though is quite different; XSX113-124 also correspond to NY164-182; XSX124-126 corresponds to NY 154-156.

[195] See introduction, "Guan Zi's influence on the Guigu Zi."

Externally, it is observed in the physical form
And can be recognized in the appearance of the face.

Lines 109-112 confirm that self-cultivation occurs, not only in seclusion, but should be ongoing in daily affairs. Further guidance for practicing 'the art of the heart-mind' in daily affairs can be found in DDJ8, which describes how to become an embodiment of water in all instances.

> The highest excellence is like water
> The excellence of water benefits all things
> And does not fight against them
> It dwells in the places that people detest
> How close it is to Dao!
> Such excellence in dwelling can be found in the Earth
> Such excellence in the heart can be found in its depths
> Such excellence in giving can be found in benevolence
> Such excellence in speech can be found in sincerity
> Such excellence in alignment can be found in order
> Such excellence in professionalism can be found in competence
> Such excellence in action can be found in appropriate timing
> Simply because it does not fight
> (Water) has no enemy

By giving awareness to internal energy, thoughts about the past and future are outshined by the power of the present. Lines 113-123 describe a process of spontaneous energy cultivation that takes place upon reaching the inner stillness and silence of the heart-mind (see especially lines 120-123). Without specifically referring to this internal energy work, DDJ15 has often been interpreted as describing the same process:

> Who, by the power of their stillness
> Can make clouded water slowly become clear?
> Who, by the power of their serenity
> Can sustain this progress until life slowly arises?

As with the *Bai Xin*'s line 204 ("Without soaring (into the sky), without spilling over, the destined life-force (ming) will be extended"), Lao Zi cautions moderation and balance in this work, by continuing:

> Those who maintain this Dao do not desire fullness
> It is because they are not full that they can remain covered
> And not let what is new come to an end

When this 'stillness-qigong' becomes internally active, energy circulates and nourishes where there is lacking. As the *Nei Ye* states in lines 208-215:

> Invariably, Dao
> Is sure to enclose, sure to condense
> Sure to expand, sure to open
> Sure to strengthen, sure to solidify
> It preserves excellence (yet) does not dwell
> It removes excess and nourishes where there is weakness
> Having known the furthest limits
> Return to Dao and Virtue

Heshang Gong also describes the nourishing power of inner harmony in his comments on DDJ55:

> "*When the mind is attuned to the breath, this is called 'powerful'*"
> When the mind unifies in harmony and softness, spirit-energy flourishes within. The body then becomes pliant. Reverting to frantic actions, the harmonized energy-breath abandons equilibrium, and the body gradually becomes unyielding.

The depiction in XSX109-126, of a clear mind allowing for a reservoir of energy to develop and nourish the body, provides a backdrop by which to read DDJ5 and DDJ6 as a single stream of thought.

> ... The gate of Heaven and Earth
> Is it not like a bellows?
> Empty yet not finished

It moves, and again more is pushed forth
To speak countless words is worthless
This is not as good as guarding balance within

(Chapter Six)
The valley with a spirit does not die
This is called the Fathomlessness of the Female
The gate to the Fathomlessess of the Female
Is called The Root of Heaven and Earth
Soft and gentle
This is her way of existence
To engage her is not laborious

The *Xin Shu Xia* ends by emphasizing the importance of learning from the natural world. The saying "For what is above, study the Heavens; for what is below, study the Earth," sums up the statements in lines 109-123 (please review these lines again), and indicates the still-point in the Heavens which also exists in the heart-mind. From this still-point of the Heavens emanates the vital essence of life, much as from the still-point of the heart-mind emanates the thoughts and their subsequent phenomena. It thus appears significant that the first matter addressed in the *Nei Ye* is this primordial Heavenly essence and its manifestations.

Of this inner center, Heshang Gong says the following in his commentary on DDJ1:

"(This) mystery, ever more mystifying"
Returning to the center of Heaven, there is another Heaven. It dispenses energy-breaths which can be potent or weak. Obtaining harmonious fertile fluid (和滋液) from its center, this gives birth to the worthy and wise; If one receives polluted, chaotic, and aberrant (energies), this gives birth to greed and licentiousness.
"(Is a) multitude of gates, all leading to the subtlety within"
Heaven can return to the Heaven within itself, and dispense energy-breaths which are either potent or weak. Eliminating strong emotions, abandoning desires, and guarding balance and harmony within: this is called "knowing the gate-key to the door of Dao."

Heaven, therefore, nourishes life on earth as the heart-mind and spirit naturally promote essence in the lower body. According to Daoist alchemical theory, the body is supplied with energy that is stored in the 'lower dantien', located just below the navel, and generates vital essence in the kidneys and sexual organs. Following the analogy of Heaven and Earth, the primordial essence nourishes the physical essence of the body. When this primordial essence is distilled through stillness and silence, it generates wisdom, virtue, and longevity. Heshang Gong explains this process in his commentary on DDJ6:

> Heaven feeds people with the five energy-breaths. They go in through the nose, and are stored in the heart-mind. The five energy-breaths are refined to make the vital essence, shen-spirit, intelligence, clear vision (enlightenment), vocal expression, and the five intrinsic natures.

The transformation of this primordial essence proceeds to create virtue in an individual by means of the five intrinsic natures. The five intrinsic natures both support and rely on the health of the internal organs which, according to Daoist theory, correspond to these intrinsic natures as follows: humanity (仁 ren) in the liver; propriety (礼 li) in the heart; sincerity (信 xin) in the spleen; loyalty (義 yi) in the lungs; and wisdom (智 zhi) in the kidneys. This correspondence between virtue and physicality accounts for the opening lines of the *Nei Ye* in which its author(s) states that it is essence stored in the breast (also the house of the mind and spirit according to the ancient Chinese) that makes a Sage. The breast contains the 'middle dantien (energy center)' – an area of development in Daoist internal cultivation usually given focus after the lower dantien has been firmly established.

Given the role of Heaven (the heart-mind), and its nourishing effect on Earth (the body), the *Xin Shu Xia* shows the role of Earth (the body) in the process of refining essence, as it is the body which cherishes energy absorbed from the "center of the heart-mind."

> Therefore, all that is collected internally (should be) regarded as a wellspring.

When this source is not exhausted, internally and externally, it circulates freely.
When the source is not dried up, the four limbs will become firm and solid,
Enabling command of their functions, and keeping them fit and strong.
(*Xin Shu Xia*, lines 120-123)

These lines should not be mistaken to suggest an inert lifestyle, but simply one that is not over-taxing. Exercise that over-strains the body has a deleterious effect in later years. By contrast, relaxed movement, utilizing the body's natural structure and alignment, as is the case in Daoist exercises and martial arts, extends the body's longevity. Such movement also allows relaxation of the mind and disengagement of the emotions in the midst of physical activity. While Daoist martial arts (Taiji, Baguazhang, Xing Yi) and Qigong also develop agility, stamina, strength, and martial skill, the "stillness in movement" cultivated through repeated foundational movements is their not-so-hidden treasure.

By the statement "When this source is not exhausted, internally and externally, it circulates freely," the *Xin Shu Xia* also refers to mental and emotional exhaustion, teaching moderation in the heart and mind's indulgences, much as the *Nei Ye* speaks on eating habits.[196] Daoist self cultivation requires that one consider if maybe that extra serving won't be missed; maybe thoughts latching onto every phenomena are unnecessary; maybe anger, fear, and disappointment can also be forgone. Making such choices is an important step in not exhausting the essence on which self cultivation relies, and rather developing an internal environment conducive to this essence. By reflecting and accepting the great emptiness and clarity of the universe, in its total void of ego and independence from conceptual knowledge, we "nourish life" and allow Dao to work unhindered in creating a mind like Heaven and body like Earth.

---

[196] See *Nei Ye*, lines 297-316

內 業
Internal Cultivation
Nei Ye

1 凡物之精,
  It is invariably the essence of things
2 此則為生。
  That gives them life
3 下生五穀,
  Below, it gives birth to the five grains;
4 上為列星。
  Above, it aligns the stars.
5 流於天地之間,
  Circulating between Heaven and Earth,
6 謂之鬼神。
  We call it ghosts and spirits;
7 藏於胸中,
  Collected within the bosom,
8 謂之聖人。
  We call them sages

9 是故民氣,
  As a result (of essence), the energy-breath of common people (becomes)[197]:

---

[197] The word min, 民 "the people," is usually suppressed in translations of this line

10 杲乎如登於天。
Bright! As though rising up to the Heavens;

11 杳乎如入於淵。
Dark! As though entering the depths;

12 淖乎如在於海,
Spacious! As though within an ocean;

13 卒乎如在於己。
Enclosed! As though entirely self-contained.

14 是故此氣也,
As a result, this energy-breath

15 不可止以力,
Cannot be stopped with effort,

16 而可安以德。
Yet can be made peaceful through virtue;

17 不可呼以聲,
Cannot be called over with a shout,

18 而可迎以音。
Yet can be welcomed with a harmonious tone (intention).[198]

19 敬守勿失,
Honour it and guard it within. Do not neglect it.

---

as it appears to read "the qi of the common people is: bright!.." By reading 是故 with its literal meaning of "as a result" rather than simply "therefore," the following lines appear to describe a transformation of the people's qi. The conclusion of this passage, "When virtue has ripened, wisdom comes forth, and the myriad things attain fruition," appears to support such a reading. Further statements such as "when the people attain it, they become fruitful" also suggest an interest in a transformation of "the common people."

[198] "音 Tone" is generally replaced here with yi, "意 intention." I have retained the received wording, where "tone" contrasts with "noise; shout." The *Nei Ye* later states that "to dispel sadness, nothing compares to music," and the *Xin Shu Xia* states that "to moderate anger, nothing compares to music." In "The Ten Faults" chapter of the Hanfei Zi (another important Legalist text), great weight is put on the importance of a ruler listening only to consonant music, stating that only rulers with a highly developed virtue can listen to melancholic and dissonant modes without falling into misfortune. "Healing sound qigong" uses vocal sounds to heal the internal organs, though its date of origin is uncertain. There is, therefore, reason to believe that 音 yin was intentional, if not just to contrast tranquility (harmonious tone) with anger (shouting). See also, *Nei Ye* line 167.

20 是謂成德。
This is called ripening virtue.[199]
21 德成而智出,
When virtue has ripened, wisdom comes forth,
22 萬物果得。
And the myriad things attain fruition.

Primordial essence cannot be forced, impressed, or convinced. It cannot be controlled or subjugated. Like the heavens, it cannot be contained, or reserved only for those with worldly influence. It responds to virtue, to deep inner silence, and harmonious intention.

Just as the *Dao De Jing* may be a compilation, representing the oral and written teachings of many Daoist sages, perhaps inspired by Li Er's (Lao Zi's) early lectures, the *Nei Ye* may be a compendium of earlier written and oral teachings focused on Daoist internal cultivation.[200] In its title, "內業 *Nèi Yè*," *nèi* means "inner, internal," and *yè* means "profession, vocation; work, endeavour." Thus, the *Nei Ye* describes the internal work of the Sage, perhaps in contrast to his or her external work of fostering balance and harmony throughout "all under heaven." 'Nei ye' carries essentially the same meaning as the more modern term 'nei *gong* (internal work)', translated as 'internal cultivation' and referring, as well, to the practice of life-energy transmutation. While the *Dao De Jing* provides guidance on leadership, politics, cosmogony, nature, and self-cultivation, the *Nei Ye* is a more concise and direct self-training manual for those requiring the illumination demanded of an advisor to world-altering decision makers.

Daoist internal cultivation relies especially on "three treasures." These three are essence (jing), energy-breath (qi), and spirit (shen). The process of transformation in this cultivation consists of transmuting jing into qi, qi into shen, and then shen into emptiness. In the

---

[199] The term "virtue" in lines 16, 20, and 21, may carry overtones of its synonym "attainment," as explained in *Xin Shu Shang* line 116.
[200] This inference, as explained in the introduction of *Thread of Dao*, is based on the *Nei Ye*'s similarities to other self-contained books found in the *Guan Zi*.

pursuit of physical, energetic, and spiritual immortality, this path of transformation continues further still.

As the proto-Daoist texts in the *Guan Zi* show, the practice of energetic transmutation through stillness was already taking shape in the 4th century BC. The *Nei Ye* begins with an explanation of such transformations, while appearing to differ slightly from later explanations by suggesting that jing-essence transforms qi, rather than transforms *into* qi (see lines 9-18). The difference here relies on the fact that the beginning of the *Nei Ye* refers to the *original* essence (yuan jing) of creation, rather than the essence of bodily substance. This original essence provides every living thing with its character, or DNA if you will. As original essence is 'unpacked', it gives rise to the earthly jing, said to reside in the kidneys and internal reproductive organs, as well as to qi and shen (spirit).[201] As the *Nei Ye* shows, yuan jing naturally expresses itself when the mind and body are not obstructed and obscured by emotions. Generally as a result of desire and its consequential emotions, the mind cannot give free expression to yuan jing and so yuan jing's full realization as qi, spirit, nature (xing) and destiny (ming) is limited. As one practices the art of the heart-mind, the process of internal cultivation clears away the limitations to a full expression of our heavenly endowments, and frees up spiritual resources needed to embrace our heaven-endowed potential.[202]

The *Huang Di Nei Jing, Su Wen (The Yellow Emperor's Canon of Internal Medicine, Plain Questions)*, which shows a deep connection to these early traditions, speaks to this natural potential in its first chapter where we find a depiction of the simplicity that allows people to enjoy these natural benefits:

> When the sages of high antiquity taught those below, they all told them of the evil that seeks out depletion, of the thieving winds (that cause it), of what to avoid in particular seasons, and that the spacious emptiness of calm cheerfulness (恬惔) is filled

---

[201] Jarrett, LS, (III): The returned spirit (gui ling) of traditional Chinese medicine, Traditional Acupuncture Society Journal, England, No. 12, Oct,'92, p.19-31

[202] For an extensive work on the role of destiny in Chinese theory, see: Jarrett, Lonny. *Nourishing Destiny: The Inner Tradition of Chinese Medicine*. Stockbridge: Spirit Path Press, 2000

with genuine qi.[203] With spiritual vitality protected within, what illness approaches? Thereby, the will is firmly established and desires are few; the heart-mind is peaceful and without fear. Though the body works hard, it is not fatigued, and the qi is compliant. Each person follows their wishes, and everyone achieves their goal.[204] Thus, they enjoy their food, have the clothes they need, take pleasure in customs, and neither those of high or low station have longings. The people were therefore called natural (pu). Cravings and desires did not strain their eyes, excess and wickedness did not confuse their hearts and minds. They were not afraid of being considered foolish, wise, competent, or incompetent. Thus, they were as one with Dao. Thereby they could all live to one hundred years and neither their movements nor their activities would decline. Their virtue remained intact, and so they were not at risk.[205]

Zhuang Zi illustrates this naturalness in his chapter "Fixed Ideas":

Thus it is said: If the body is over-worked and does not rest, it becomes worn out; if the spirit is employed without pause, it becomes over-worked; and when over-worked, it becomes exhausted. It is the nature of water that when free from other substances, it is clear, and when it is calm, it is level; but if it is collected, obstructed, and not allowed to flow, it cannot maintain its clarity. It is a reflection of Heaven's virtue.

Thus it is said: To be pure, genuine, and uncontaminated; to be calm, unified, and stable; to be content and not impositioning; to move according to the phases of Heaven: this is the way to nourish the spirit.

Now, if one has a sword from Gan or Yue, he hides it in a protective case and does not dare use it, for he considers it a most valuable treasure. But the spiritual vitality travels in all directions, flowing this way and that without limit. Above, it reaches the Heavens; below, it circles the Earth. It transforms

---

[203] Qi Bo explains in chapter 75 of the *Ling Shu Jing* that genuine qi (zhen qi) comes from Heaven and the grains, which both combine to fill the body.
[204] Having few desires, their goals and their happiness are easily attained.
[205] From *Huang Di Nei Jing, Su Wen*, chapter one. Translated by Dan G. Reid.

and nourishes all things, and cannot be equated with any image. Its name is "One with Divinity." The Dao of pure naturalness is the only way the correctly protect the spirit. Protected as such, it will not be lost, for the spirit will become unified. Unified, (yuan) jing will rejoin in symbiosis with Heaven. There is a saying in the hinterlands which states that "the multitudes concern themselves with profit; noble scholars concern themselves with reputation; aristocrats increase their ambitions; sages treasure essence." Thus, to be natural is to be uncontaminated; to be pure is to not diminish the spirit. One who can encapsulate naturalness and purity is called a Genuine Person (Zhen Ren).[206]

The concept of a "Genuine Person" is analogous to the common understanding of a "real man," though with some more specific qualifications. While the terms Genuine Person (also translated as "True Man") and 'real man' both suggest courage and confidence, the Genuine Person is courageous without being violent, courageously themselves yet respectful of others, self-expressive but peaceful, self-assured yet humble, natural and spontaneous but not inappropriate. It is because they hold to the level and smooth path of Dao that they can move in any direction without going off course.[207] It also goes without saying that the Genuine Person need not be male, but simply genuine.

To fully understand the implications of the terms Genuine Person and Sage, we may look again to the *Huang Di Nei Jing, Su Wen*, chapter one:

> Huang Di said: I have heard that in high antiquity there were Genuine Persons who would hold onto the leading hand of Heaven and Earth, and the hand of yin and yang, exhale and inhale qi essence, stand for themselves and guard their spirit. Their muscles and flesh were as one. Thereby, they could enjoy a lifespan undetermined by Heaven and Earth for they had no specific time to come to an end. This was their way of living in the Dao.

---

[206] From *Zhuang Zi*, chapter 15. Translated by Dan G. Reid.
[207] See *Huainan Zi*, chapter one, in my opening comments on the Xin Shu Xia.

In middle antiquity were the Perfected Persons, who by their natural Virtue could accord fully with Dao... They can also be counted as Genuine Persons.

Next were the Sages who dwelled in the harmony of Heaven and Earth and accorded with the principles of the eight winds. Their cravings and desires were suited to the era and local customs, and they had no hatred or anger in their hearts. In their activities they had no desire to avoid the world. In their dress and manner, they had no desire to be elevated and admired by popular people. Externally, they did not over-exert their bodies with endeavours; internally, they did not worry and speculate in their thoughts. They considered enjoying tranquility to be the highest application of oneself, and self-realization to be achievement. Physically, they did not deteriorate, and their spiritual vitality did not dissipate. (As with the Genuine Persons), they too could live for 100 years.[208]

These early discourses on health preservation indicate that the key to not only preventing illness, but realizing our human spiritual potential, is found in protecting our spiritual vitality from the contamination of contrivances to our essential nature. This free expression enlivens our vitality, as evidenced by the preceding context of Huang Di's description of Genuine Persons, which was an inquiry into how a man of advanced years can continue to be fertile. This background of preserving naturalness and spontaneity helps to bring out the underlying thread of such guidance as it weaves throughout the practices found in the *Nei Ye*.

Lines 1-22 of the *Nei Ye* contain a slightly different description of the beginnings of life than in the *Huang Di Nei Jing, Ling Shu Jing (The Yellow Emperor's Canon of Internal Medicine, Classic of the Spiritual Hinge)*, likely written or compiled a century or two after the *Nei Ye*. The early development of these ideas in the *Nei Ye* are nonetheless faintly detectable in chapter eight of the *Ling Shu Jing*:

---

[208] From *Huang Di Nei Jing, Ling Shu Jing*, chapter one. Translated by Dan G. Reid.

Qi Bo replied:

That which Heaven gives an individual is De (intrinsic virtue). That which Earth gives an individual is qi (energy-breath). When De and qi intermingle, there is life. From life, what then comes into existence is called jing (essence). When the two jing (of Heaven and Earth) combine and grasp each other, we have what is called shen (spirit). What follows the departures and arrivals of shen is called hun (yang spirits). What stays with the departures and arrivals of jing is called po (yin spirits). That which relies on things is called the heart-mind (xin). What the heart-mind recalls is called intention (yi, focus, idea). When the intention remains in a particular place, this is called will (zhi). What comes from the will as it processes and transforms is called thought (si). When thought travels a great distance (as though in search of its) beloved, this is called contemplation (lu). When contemplation arrives at its location, this is called wisdom (zhi).

Thus, wisdom nurtures life, for one must submit to the four seasons, make alterations according to cold and heat, harmonize euphoria and anger so that they abide peacefully, and moderate yin and yang to balance hard and soft. In this way, excessive imbalances will not arrive, and an extensive lifespan will be continually observed.[209]

In their commentary on chapter eight of the *Ling Shu Jing*, Claude Larre and Elisabeth Rochat de la Vallée point out that, like chapter 50 of the *Dao De Jing*, the *Ling Shu Jing* also delineates 13 facets of life which develop in the process of forming a human life, the same facets which degenerate in the process of death.[210] Lao Zi states in chapter 50,

> To depart from life is to enter death
> The companions of life are thirteen
> The companions of death are thirteen

---

[209] From *Huang Di Nei Jing, Ling Shu Jing*, chapter eight. Translated by Dan G. Reid.
[210] Larre, Claude and Rochat de la Vallee, Elizabeth. *Rooted in Spirit: The Heart of Chinese Medicine*. New York: Station Hill Press, 1992. p. 152

In their way of living, people approach death-traps
By way of (these) thirteen
Why is this so?
Because they seek a life of excess

These 13 facets in the *Ling Shu Jing* are: Virtue (from Heaven), qi (from Earth), life (生), jing (essence), shen (spirit), hun, po, the heart-mind, intention, will, thought, contemplation, and wisdom (competence, 智).

A shared tradition behind DDJ50 and LSJ8 may be evidenced by the fact that DDJ50 is followed by DDJ51's description of De, a description which supports the *Ling Shu Jing*'s role for De in the creation of life. Chapter 51 of the *Dao De Jing* states:

Dao actuates them
Virtue takes care of them
Power completes them (勢成之)
...
Dao actuates them
Virtue takes care of them, extends their lifespans
Teaches them, completes them
Tests them, raises them
And brings them back (to their pure natures)
Actuates them but does not possess them
Sets them in motion but does not expect of them
Extends their lives without ruling and controlling
This is called Fathomless Virtue

As Heshang Gong comments on DDJ51, De equates to Oneness, which may be understood as the aligning and balancing power of Dao[211] described in chapters 22 and 39 of the *Dao De Jing*:

(DDJ22)
That which is flexible is preserved
That which is bent is straightened

---

[211] More on this connection can be found in:
Reid, Dan G. *The Heshang Gong Commentary on Lao Zi's Dao De Jing.* Montreal: Center Ring Publications, 2015.

That which is empty is filled
That which is broken is repaired
That which is lacking acquires
That which is excessive becomes confused
Therefore, the Sage embraces Oneness
So as to bring the world into alignment

(DDJ39)
In the beginning was the attainment of Oneness

Heaven attained Oneness and became clear
Earth attained Oneness and became serene
Gods attained Oneness and became spiritually powerful
Valleys attained Oneness and became full
The myriad things attained Oneness and were born
Lords and kings attained Oneness and all under Heaven became loyal

A full picture of jing-qi-shen transformation in the *Guan Zi* texts could be drawn by combining the descriptions of jing and qi transformation in NY1-20 with the description of jing to shen transformation in XSS90-97:

What people occupy themselves with today is jing-essence.
Getting rid of desires should be the priority.
From this follows quiet stillness;
Quiet stillness brings about jing-essence;
From jing essence, singularity is established.
Singularity brings about illumination;
Illumination brings about spirit;
As for spirit, this is reaching the treasure.

Chapter 21 of the *Dao De Jing* offers additional perspective on the jing-essence referred to in the beginning of the *Nei Ye* – that of a universal essence which, similar to the earthly jing-essence in the body, is described as the most basic nourishment of life energy. Refining this basic nourishment into its more pure original substance is at the foundation of Daoist internal alchemy (Nei Dan). As shown in

the *Guan Zi* texts, and in the *Dao De Jing*, this transformation takes place through what might be called a distillation of the heart-mind. This distillation purifies worldly contrivances in the heart-mind and brings about the "pure essence."
DDJ21:

> Openness is Virtue's form
> With your attention on Dao alone
> This will arrive
>
> Dao acts on all things spontaneously and suddenly
> Sudden! Spontaneous! Within, there is image
> Spontaneous! Sudden! Within, there is being
> Obscure! Dark! Within, there is essence
> This essence of utmost reality
> Within it is sincerity
>
> It is ancient and it is modern
> Its attributes do not leave
> By it, we can examine how the multitudes began
> How am I able to know that the multitudes
> Began according to this nature of beginnings?
> By this

23 凡心之刑,
   Invariably, the heart-mind's decisions[212]
24 自充自盈,
   Naturally occupy it, naturally fill it.

---

[212] "Xing 刑 punishment/decision" is often replaced here with "xing 形 forms" in accordance with line 103 of the *Nei Ye*, believing 刑 to be the typo. However, 刑 appears more consistently in related lines of the *Nei Ye* and *Xin Shu Xia*. See also, line 115-120 of the *Xin Shu Xia*. It could be further argued that NY103 should be changed to "xing 刑 decision" in light of this consistency and the Legalist environment in which these texts appear, where it would seem natural to impute the concept of regulations when discussing mental faculties. See Introduction: Will, Intention and Thought.

25 自生自成。
They spontaneously arise, and spontaneously ripen.
26 其所以失之,
They can become wayward
27 必以憂樂喜怒欲利。
As a result of sorrow, pleasure, euphoria,[213] anger, desire, and avarice.
28 能去憂樂喜怒欲利,
If you can abandon sorrow, pleasure, euphoria, anger, desire, and avarice,
29 心乃反濟。
The heart will return back to the shore (of calm and stability)[214]

30 彼心之情,
It is the nature of the heart and mind
31 利安以寧,
To benefit from tranquility and relaxation.
32 勿煩勿亂,
Do not agitate it, do not disturb it,
33 和乃自成。
And harmony will naturally perfect it.
34 折折乎如在於側,
At rest! [215] As though right at your side;

---

[213] I have translated xi (喜) as euphoria, following the lead of Elisa Rossi in "Shen: Psycho-Emotional Aspects of Chinese Medicine (2002)." I have also translated le (樂) as pleasure based on Rossi's suggestion that the "joy" of this character is a harmonious and peaceful one related to rituals and ceremonies (the same character also means *music*).

[214] "濟 aid; ferry across" is often replaced with "齊 evenness" by removing the radical for water

[215] Zhe Zhe 折折 (at rest) is usually replaced here with zhe zhe 晢晢, meaning "bright." The meaning of 折折, and thereby also the subsequent line (where 忽忽 fleeting/quick is usually translated as "vague," also meaning "overlooked," to contrast with "bright"), is revealed when 折折 is understood as "leisurely" through the

35 忽忽乎如將不得,
Fleeting! Trying to snatch it, it is not obtained;
36 渺渺乎如窮無極。
Vast and Distant! It is void of all limits.
37 此稽不遠,
This investigation does not take place far off
38 日用其德。
But in the daily application of this Virtue.

We cannot chase Virtue, but only invite it. If your mind is like a quivering branch, the spirit will not alight.

Lines 23-38, above, may be well illustrated by a popular Zen parable:

> A learned scholar named Huike approached Boddhidharma and said, "My mind is disturbed, please pacify it for me." Boddhidharma responded, "Bring me your mind and I will pacify it for you." Upon reflection, Huike responded "Having sought it, I can no longer find it," to which Boddhidharma said "There you go then, I have pacified it."

In mindfulness practice, students learn to observe inner and outer reality without judgement, grasping, or expectation. This alone can calm the mind as influences, such as emotions and thoughts, when observed, often dissolve like snowflakes caught in the hand.

NY23-25 provide an important ancient Chinese psychological insight, which is that the mind works spontaneously. Thoughts do not arise out of effort, but *responsively*. This is why when Huike sought for his mind he could no longer find it. Concentration and study may give rise to thoughts and ideas, but those thoughts arise "of themselves."[216]

---

following example in the Liji, Tan Gong I: 吉事，欲其折折爾... 吉事雖止，不怠... 鼎鼎爾則小人 "It is desirable that festive affairs be carried out in a leisurely way... Though festive affairs may be delayed, they should not be transacted negligently... too much ease shows a small man" (trans. Legge).

[216] This is not to say that one couldn't intentionally think a particular word or sentence, but this is not how thinking normally takes place.

The mind does not construct these thoughts, but simply follows them along their respective paths as they rise up and garner the attention of the mind. Thus, clearing the mind does not consist of actively clearing the mind of thoughts, but of learning to stop following them along their journey. To do this, one must first become aware of the thoughts that carry them along, and eventually learn to just observe them. Simply observing them and letting them dissipate, one eventually finds they are no longer in the company of so many thoughts, and can thus relax in the openness that appears in their absence.

Lines 23-38 also help to clarify DDJ47 when contrasted with its images of seeking externally what can only be attained within oneself:

> Without going out the door
> Know all under Heaven
> Without glancing out the window
> See Heaven's Way
>
> The further out one goes
> The less they know
>
> Therefore, the Sage does not move
> Yet he knows
> He describes and names (things)
> Without seeing (them)
> He brings about perfection
> Without acting

39　夫道者所以充形也,
　　It is Dao which fills the body,
40　而人不能固。
　　Yet people are unable to secure it.
41　其往不復,
　　It leaves without returning;
42　其來不舍。
　　It arrives without remaining;

43 謀乎莫聞其音,
Strategic! No one hears its voice;
44 卒乎乃在於心,
Suddden! Right away it is within your heart-mind;
45 冥冥乎不見其形,
Dark and obscured! Its form cannot be seen;
46 淫淫乎與我俱生。
Immense and overflowing! It rises within all of us.
47 不見其形,
We do not see its form
48 不聞其聲,
We do not hear its voice
49 而序其成,
Yet its sequence of development
50 謂之道。
We call "Dao"

Like the sentiments of peace, wellbeing, and contentment, Dao is found in all living things.

Dao might be interpreted as the state of balance and harmony. Just as one is rarely aware of health until they lose it, or rarely aware of their emotional balance until they become perturbed, Dao's presence may actually make us less aware of it, while we can only but imagine it when it is absent.

Perhaps the most revealing word in lines 39-50 is also one of the most often edited in translations of the *Nei Ye*. Line 43, "*Strategic! No one hears its voice*" is usually found, today, with "mou 謀, strategic," replaced with "mo 漠, desert; indifferent," and translated as "silent." However, 謀 strategic also fits here in the sense that strategy implies something undisclosed and deceptive. As DDJ36 states in describing the effectiveness of unforeseen strategies: "The state's sharp instruments should not be revealed."

NY86-87 also use "謀 strategies" in the sense of something hidden and underlying: "Euphoria, anger, obtaining, and giving are the underlying motivations (謀) of humanity."

The description of Dao as strategic in line 43 compliments lines 49-50, "*Yet its sequence of development, we call 'Dao'*" – a statement supported by Heshang Gong's commentary on DDJ21:

> *"How am I able to know that the multitudes began according to this nature of beginnings?"*
> (In other words) "How can I know that the myriad things followed Dao to be infused with energy-breath?"
> *"By this"*
> "This" refers to "the present." In this very moment, the myriad things all receive the Dao's vital energy-breath in order to live, to move, to stand up, and to rise to their places. If not by a Path (Dao), this could not have happened.

Without giving undue weight to this line, it could be noted that, whereas the *Dao De Jing* can be read as concealing a great deal of subtle government strategy, the *Nei Ye* can be read as concealing a similar portion of subtle martial strategy. In either case, many insights into Dao and the heart–mind of human beings appear to have come from contemplating the path towards a peaceful society.

51 凡道無所,
At all times, the Dao is without a single location.
52 善心安愛,
(Yet) in a heart of goodness, where tranquility is cherished,[217]
53 心靜氣理,
In a peaceful heart, where the energy-breath is balanced,
54 道乃可止。

---

[217] In most translations, "愛 love, cherish, ai" is replaced here with "處 dwell, chu" to say "it dwells in a good heart."

Dao may linger.
55 彼道不遠，
For Dao is not far away.
56 民得以產。
When the people attain it, they are fruitful;
57 彼道不離，
When Dao does not leave,
58 民因以知。
The people become knowledgeable.

59 是故卒乎其如可與索。
Thus, it is sudden! As though capturing;
60 眇眇乎其如窮無所。
Minute! As though devoid of any location.
61 被道之情，
The nature of Dao
62 惡音與聲。
Is averse to clamorous noise.
63 脩心靜音，
By bringing the heart to a tranquil resonance (intention),[218]
64 道乃可得。
Dao may be obtained.

Sitting in stillness, the knowledge of the mind and body intersect, and what is known in the spirit finds its way to the surface.

Lines 51-54 show how Dao may be attained, and maintained, even by people who have never heard of Dao. Holding onto a natural simplicity and tranquility becomes a rather obvious priority for anyone trying to recover their health. The proto-Daoists, however, taught that doing so was not just a matter of health, but also of success, luck, and destiny (lines 55-58, and 69-73). In the same way that this

---

[218] "音 tone" is usually replaced here again with "意 intent."

inner harmony nourishes and repairs the body,[219] bringing the organs and circulations to an ideal balance, it will also bring an individual into balance with their exterior world, even effecting a harmonious, organic, relationship between external elements as well as and between those elements and the individual.[220] This theory underlies NY55-58 (above), NY69-73 (below), and most notably DDJ37:

> The Dao is always effortless yet without inaction
> When lords and kings can guard this within
> The myriad things eventually transform themselves
> Transforming, yet desiring to do so intentionally
> I pacify this desire with the simplicity of namelessness
> The simplicity of the nameless removes all desires
> When the tranquility of desirelessness is established
> The world stabilizes itself

As the *Nei Ye* also shows, this harmony cannot be attained impatiently, or fabricated with ingenuity. This is not to say that early Daoists dissuaded people from working consistently towards a goal, however. The Duke of Zhou's comment on the first line of the first hexagram (Heaven) in the Yi Jing (I Ching) states "Heaven moves with vitality. The junzi therefore sturdies himself to ceaseless activity."[221] The Daoist approach is simply a matter of progressing forward while maintaining an inner tranquility and harmony. As Heshang Gong comments on DDJ23:

> Men should conduct affairs like the Dao, in peace and stillness. They should not conduct affairs like gusting winds and violent rainstorms.

---

[219] Please see closing comments on the *Xin Shu Xia* for more on this.
[220] These relationships underlie much of Feng Shui theory.
[221] 天行健，君子以自強不息

65 道也者,
　　As for Dao,
66 口之所不能言也,
　　It is that which the mouth cannot speak of;
67 目之所不能視也,
　　It is that which the eyes cannot see;
68 耳之所不能聽也,
　　It is that which the ears cannot hear;
69 所以脩心而正形也。
　　It is that by which the heart-mind is enhanced,[222] and the body is aligned;
70 人之所失以死,
　　It is that which, when people lose it, they die;
71 所得以生也。
　　It is that which, when they obtain it, they live;
72 事之所失以敗,
　　It is that which, when endeavours lose it, they fail;
73 所得以成也。
　　It is that which, when they obtain it, they succeed.
74 凡道: 無根無莖,
　　Invariably, Dao is without root[223] and without stem;
75 無葉無榮,
　　Without leaves and without flowers.
76 萬物以生,
　　The myriad things are given life by it;
77 萬物以成,
　　The myriad things are completed by it.
78 命之曰道。
　　On account of this, it is called "The Path"

---

[222] "脩 dried meat used to pay teachers" is a variant of "修 study; cultivate"
[223] Dao is without root because Dao *is* the root. Please see DDJ4, "It is older than the primordial ruler (God)."

Dao is known to all, but does not try to compete with the senses. It is, thus, often obscured by what the senses "know," and so overlooked in favour of a narrower perspective.

Lines 65-78 venture to describe the indescribable, Dao, while at the same time acknowledging the ineffable and intangible qualities that make it "unnameable" in the Daoist sense of being indistinguishable from reality as a whole. Though the *Dao De Jing* makes constant reference to the influence of Dao throughout Heaven, Earth, and Humanity, as with the *Nei Ye*, it ultimately heeds the opening statement of chapter one: "The dao which can be told is not the eternal Dao. The name which can be named is not the eternal name."

More similarities can be seen here in regards to DDJ21. Line 74, "Dao is without root and without stem; without leaves and without flowers" is comparable to DDJ21's: "It is ancient and it is modern. Its attributes (names) do not leave." Lines 76-78 reflect the closing lines of DDJ21, and Heshang Gong's commentary on them, which suggests that Dao is called "the Path" because it is the path by which all things come into fruition.[224] Comparing DDJ21[225] and NY51-64, one may find still further resemblances.

79 天主正,
    Heaven is ruled by alignment;
80 地主平,
    Earth is ruled by balance;
81 人主安靜。
    People are ruled by peaceful[226] silence.
82 春秋冬夏,
    Spring, autumn, winter, and summer
83 天之時也;
    Are the seasons of Heaven;

---

[224] See my comment on *Nei Ye*, lines 49-50, for this excerpt.
[225] See my comments on *Nei Ye*, lines 1-22, for a translation of DDJ21
[226] "安 Stability; calm; comfort" is usually suppressed in translations of this line.

84 山陵川谷,
   Mountains, hills, streams, and valleys
85 地之枝也;
   Are the extensions of Earth;
86 喜怒取予,
   Euphoria, anger, taking, and giving
87 人之謀也。
   Are the underlying motivations of humanity.

88 是故聖人
   Therefore, sages
89 與時變而不化,
   Follow the times of change, yet are not transformed.
90 從物而不移。
   They adapt to things, yet are not displaced.

The nature of the Earth is to be level, and the nature of the heart-mind is to be tranquil. Emotions, like rivers, valleys, mountains, and streams, are exceptions to the norm. Just as the Sage does not curse the mountain for having to climb it, or deny that she can't walk on water, the Sage accepts that, at times, she must work through her emotions, and those of others, knowing that they may be a temporary obstacle, or otherwise a dire necessity.[227]

The "seasons of Heaven" change, yet are constant in their cycles. The "extensions (lit. "branches," see line 85) of Earth" transform, yet are constant in their types. Therefore, sages move and adapt as necessary, but are constant in their inner alignment and stillness. The ability to outwardly adapt while remaining inwardly stable is of great importance in proto-Daoist texts, which show that, by guarding inner

---

[227] While, in Chinese medicine, tranquility is considered most beneficial to one's health, the suppression or complete lack of any feeling is considered unhealthy and even dangerous. Though level ground is an ideal place to build one's house, the abundant variety of nature is to be appreciated, without losing contentment with the basis – with one's own.

balance while being outwardly flexible, dangerous straits in life can be successfully navigated

In a comment, attributed to Confucius, on the Yi Jing's water hexagram (Kan), we find:

> Two water trigrams indicate repeated dangerous passes. Water circulates rather than over-filling. It travels through a dangerous pass without losing its integrity. (King Wen's comment on this hexagram) "guarding the mind brings progress" refers to the strong line in the center (of the water trigram, which consists of two broken lines with a sold line between them).

Also, in DDJ8:

> The highest excellence is like water
> The excellence of water benefits all things
> And does not fight against them
> It dwells in the places that people detest
> How close it is to Dao!
> ...
> Simply because it does not fight
> (Water) has no enemy

91　能正能靜,
　　If you can be aligned, you can be silent.
92　然後能定。
　　Then you can be settled.
93　定心在中,
　　When the heart-mind settles in its very center,
94　耳目聰明,
　　The ears and eyes become acute and perceptive,
95　四枝堅固,

And the four limbs become solid and stable.[228]
96 可以為精舍。
You can thereby house the pure and vital essence.

97 精也者,
This pure essence
98 氣之精者也。
Is the pure essence of energy-breath.
99 氣道乃生,
The way of energy-breath is to flourish.

100 生乃思,
Flourishing, it becomes thoughts;
101 思乃知,
Thoughts become knowledge;
102 知乃止矣。
After knowledge, it stops.
103 凡心之形,
Invariably, mental formulations[229]
104 過知失生。
Will supersede knowledge even at the expense of one's life.

105 一物能化, 謂之神;
With Oneness, things can be transformed. We call this spirit.
106 一事能變, 謂之智。
With Oneness, situations can be changed. We call this wisdom.
107 化不易氣,
Transforming (things) without altering breath,
108 變不易智,
Changing (situations) without altering wisdom:

---

[228] See also the *Xin Shu Xia*, lines 122-123, "When the source is not dried up, the four limbs will become firm and solid, enabling command of their functions and keeping them fit and strong"
[229] See footnote for line 23 of the *Nei Ye*

109 惟執一之君子能為此乎。
　　Only the junzi who maintains Oneness can do this.
110 執一不失,
　　Holding Oneness and not losing it
111 能君萬物。
　　They can preside over the myriad things.
112 君子使物,
　　The junzi then conducts things,
113 不為物使,
　　And is not conducted by things,
114 得一之理。
　　(Having) attained the principle of Oneness.[230]

As silence is the pure nature of the heart-mind, one only need be still to attain it. Aligning the body to its natural shape, with a straight spine, square hips, relaxed shoulders, bent knees, and feet pointing straight ahead, the natural alignment of the body opens the heart and mind to inner tranquility and harmony, reflecting the mutual support and constant regeneration that occurs between Heaven and Earth.

The *Huang Di Nei Jing, Su Wen,* again reflects the *Nei Ye* here when the *Nei Ye* states in lines 97-104:

> This pure essence
> Is the pure essence of energy-breath.
> The way of energy-breath is to flourish.
> Flourishing, it becomes thoughts;
> Thoughts become knowledge;
> After knowledge, it stops.
> Invariably, mental formulations
> Will supersede knowledge even at the expense of one's life.

---

[230] See the excerpt from *Guigu Zi*, in the Introduction, for further elucidation of lines 91-114

The Su Wen, chapter 39, explains this phenomenon with further details:

> The hundred diseases are generated by qi.
> When one is angry, their qi rises
> When euphoric, their qi relaxes
> When sad, their qi dissipates
> When fearful, their qi descends
> When cold, their qi collects
> When over-heated, their qi leaks out
> When startled, their qi is chaotic
> When exhausted, their qi is wasted
> When pensive, their qi is knotted
> …
> When one is pensive, the heart-mind occupies a location
> And the shen-spirit keeps returning to a location
> The aligned qi is halted and does not circulate
> Thus, qi is knotted[231]

We find the method to untangle these knots in the *Nei Ye*, which suggests to detach ourselves from the mind's frantic chasing and return to inner unity. By following the guidance in lines 91-92, ("If you can be aligned, you can be silent. Then you can be settled.") one can experience what Lao Zi speaks of in *Dao De Jing*, chapter 56:

> Those who know, do not speak
> Those who speak, do not know
> Close your ports
> Shut your gates
> Dull your points
> Separate your tangles
> Soften your glare
> Be like ashes
> This is to say
> "Be one with the sacred"…

---

[231] From Huang Di Nei Jing, Su Wen, chapter 39. Translated by Dan G. Reid.

While Oneness carries a number of metaphysical connotations, lines 91-114 speak to its more immediate application in being of a unified and undivided consciousness. By keeping the heart-mind settled, focus is not easily agitated and dissipated, allowing the energy-breath and heart-mind to remain centered and reach the destination of their focus.

As Heshang Gong comments on DDJ10:

> *"Gather together the energy-breath and become soft"*
> Gather and embrace the vital energy-breath within. Then it will not be chaotic and the body will become soft and pliant.
> *"This is the power of an infant"*
> Have the power of an infant. Be, internally, without a thought or worry, and externally, without official duties. Then the vital spirits will not leave.
> *"Looking deeply, purify and eliminate"*
> One should wash the heart-mind until it is clean and pure. The heart-mind lives in the fathomless depths of emptiness. Investigate. Know its myriad engagements. This is called "investigating the fathomless."

Like NY105-114, Heshang Gong explains in DDJ14 that by holding Oneness we are able to become the active, rather than reactive, party in our own lives.

> *"Hold to the ancient Dao and ride it until you possess the present"*
> Sages hold and embrace the ancient Dao which gave birth to Oneness and allowed them to commandeer things. Understand the present by holding onto Oneness.

The *Xin Shu Xia* lines 114-119 carry a similar passage to NY100-106, but follow with the statement "Therefore, all that is collected internally (should be) regarded as a wellspring. When this source is not exhausted, internally and externally, it circulates freely."[232] Further, *Xin Shu Xia*, lines 37-38, read:

---

[232] *Xin Shu Xia* lines 120-121

一氣能變曰精。
Unified energy-breath can bring transformation. This is called "essence."
一事能變曰智。
Unified endeavours can bring transformation. This is called "wisdom."

rather than, in *Nei Ye*, line 105:

一物能化, 謂之神;
With Oneness, things can be transformed. We call this spirit.
一事能變, 謂之智。
With Oneness, situations can be changed. We call this wisdom

These differences suggest, not simply a suppression of thoughts, but a transmutation of the energy that becomes thoughts (see NY99-104). By aligning the posture[233] and remaining internally still and clear, this energy, normally occupied by wandering thoughts, can be returned to the resonance of intention, awareness (意 yi), associated in Daoist medical theory with the unifying earth element of the spleen.

Following the closing statement of the *Xin Shu Xia* "For what is above, study the Heavens; for what is below, study the Earth," this method could be described as "by the power of stillness, making clouded water slowly clarify / By the power of serenity, making life slowly arise" (DDJ15). Further, by clearing clouds (thoughts) from the sky (heart-mind), the light of the sun (spirit) can nourish the earth (body).

Lines 107-109 illustrate how those adept at the heart-mind method (xin shu/xin fa) can bring about change without losing their inner Oneness and spirit. This is described further in the proceeding lines (below), especially 129-150 which speak of spiritual intelligence. This spiritual intelligence is maintained by following the directions in the *Nei Ye* of not being swayed by emotions and fears, but rather, staying balanced in both breath and wisdom. This ability is cultivated in the practice of Tai Ji (Tai Chi), which teaches a continuous flow of breath and movement, and thereby a calm rhythm of breathing while

---

[233] See NY122-123 on the importance of posture.

transforming the obstacles (opponents) in front of oneself. Doing so allows the free flow of intuitive response in the application of learned skills. Thus, neither the power of one's breath, nor their ability, is diminished by adapting to unwieldy circumstances.

115 治心在於中,
   When the orderliness of the heart-mind reaches to the very center,
116 治言出於口,
   Orderly words leave the mouth
117 治事加於人,
   And orderly affairs increase amongst the people.
118 然則天下治矣。
   As such, all under Heaven will be orderly!
119 一言得而天下服,
   When one word is grasped, all under heaven fits together;
120 一言定而天下聽,
   When one word settles (in the heart),
   all under Heaven cooperates.
121 公之謂也。
   This is the meaning of 'serving the greater good.' [234]
122 形不正,
   When the bodily form is not aligned,
123 德不來。
   Virtue does not approach;
124 中不靜,
   When the center is not tranquil,
125 心不治。
   The heart-mind is not orderly.

---

[234] NY lines 105-121 are compared above with XSX, lines 43-64. As noted in my commentary on these lines in XSX, "one word" refers to Dao. It may also imply minimizing instructions on Confucian virtues, and instead simply following Dao.

126 正形攝德,
When the bodily form is aligned, it absorbs Virtue.
127 天仁地義,
Heaven's benevolent generosity and Earth's balancing righteousness
128 則淫然而自至。
Then naturally arrive in abundance.

When the body, heart and mind are one, the resonance of one's words speaks deeper than the words themselves, while ones' words are assuredly correct. Such oneness can unify with the environment and people around it, not disturbed by self-seeking, fear, greed, lust, or other emotions that exist only in the opposition of self and other.

By holding to oneness, all is brought to a beneficial order. By first bringing the heart-mind, the metaphorical "throne of the ruler,"[235] to a state of peace and order, peace and order then spreads throughout the rest of one's being. The proto-Daoists taught that a ruler who achieves peace and order within will effortlessly spread this peace and order throughout their kingdom. The *Nei Ye* uses to the word "公 gong, serving the greater good," to describe this process. Gong refers to the public, versus private, interest – to the individual serving the whole. Gong, often translated as impartial, is said in DDJ16 to be a reflection of Dao in humanity.[236]

NY127 ("Heaven's benevolent generosity…") seems to contradict chapter five of the *Dao De Jing*, which states that "Heaven (Nature) is not benevolent;" however, this saying in the *Dao De Jing* is believed to be in reference to learned benevolence, rather than to a natural inclination, as would be exhibited by Heaven.

To say that Earth is righteous (line 127) may be supported by line 80, above, which states that "地主平 Earth is ruled by balance." 平 Ping means peaceful, balance, and evenness. This balancing of Earth suggests righteousness, resulting from Earth being regulated by the Way (Dao) of Heaven, illustrated in DDJ77:

---

[235] See lines 1-2 of the *Xin Shu Shang*
[236] See comments on XSX48-64 for more on "gong," and comparable verses.

The Way of Heaven
Is it not like the stretching of a bow?
What is high, it causes to be pulled low
What is low, it causes to be uplifted
What has excess, it causes to be diminished
What is insufficient it causes to be restored

Lines 122-126 of the *Nei Ye*, as with the corresponding opening lines of the *Xin Shu Xia*, are historically significant in their emphasis on posture for cultivating the heart-mind. While these lines may not explicitly recommend extended periods of sitting, the *Bai Xin* does suggest something more akin to sitting meditation or Daoist "zuo wang / sitting and forgetting," in lines 27-29:

Therefore, the Sage's method of government
Is to still the body and wait (靜身以待之).
Things then arrive at their names, (showing what they are,) and naturally fall into place.

129 神明之極,
    The ultimate spiritual intelligence –
130 照乎知萬物,
    Luminous! It understands the myriad things
131 中義守不忒。
    When, in the center, righteousness is guarded without err,
132 不以物亂官,
    And things do not disturb the senses,
133 不以官亂心,
    Nor do the senses disturb the heart,
134 是謂中得。
    This is called inner attainment.

135 有神自在身。
    There is a spirit that alights in the body;
136 一往一來,

One moment it leaves, and one moment it arrives.
137 莫之能思。
No one can comprehend it.
138 失之必亂,
Losing it assures disorder;
139 得之必治。
Obtaining it assures order.
140 敬除其舍,
Respectfully purify its dwelling place
141 精將自來。
And the pure and vital essence will naturally return.
142 精想思之,
If planning and thinking about vital essence,
143 寧念治之。
Calm any thoughts about governing it.
144 嚴容畏敬,
Straightening your form, revere and honour it.
145 精將至定,
Essence will then become settled.
146 得之而勿捨,
Obtaining it, do not give up.
147 耳目不淫,
Do not indulge the ears and eyes.
148 心無他圖。
Keeping the heart and mind without any other designs,
149 正心在中,
And an aligned heart-mind within,
150 萬物得度。
The myriad things will (then) fall into accord.[237]

---

[237] *Nei Ye*, lines 129-150, bear many similarities to ideas in *Xin Shu Shang* about centering the mind and "purifying the spirit's dwelling place." See XSS 22-23, and 38-42.

As the saying goes, "when the student is ready, the teacher appears." Shen ming, the spiritual intelligence, is the inner sage of all people. To invite the shen ming, one must first order their house, the inner nation of body and heart-mind. On doing so, one will find the shen ming's counsel, wordless as it may be, speaking to them from within.

When the *Nei Ye* speaks of 'order,' this should not be understood as a fixed, rigid, and stultifying order, but a natural one in which things find comfort in their true elements.

As such, Lao Zi's method of government can be seen as developing directly from an early tradition of attaining inner power through non-interference and stillness. As he states in DDJ48:

> The pursuit of learning requires daily accumulation
> The pursuit of Dao requires daily reduction
> Reducing and reducing
> Until arriving at effortlessness
> Effortless, yet without inaction
>
> Conquering all under Heaven
> Is best done without the endeavour to do so
> Perpetually, this endeavour will continue without satisfaction
> Even when all under Heaven has been conquered

And in DDJ29:

> The wish to possess all under Heaven, and control it
> I see this has no end
> The world is an instrument of the gods
> It cannot be controlled
> Those who try, spoil it
> Those who grasp, lose

Chinese traditions of cultivating inner peace may very well have developed out of purification rituals meant to prepare a supplicant for making offerings to deities and spirits. These rituals date back well beyond the time of Confucius, who makes many references to obtaining the favour of shen ming, a term sharing the name for spiritual intelligence, but instead meaning 'spiritual lights'. The description above of power and stability, preserved by the residence of an inner spirit (see line 135), coincides closely with Heshang Gong's references to the shen ming and the protection they provide to those who follow the way of natural simplicity. See, for example, his following comments on DDJ7:

> All people love (sages) like their own mothers and fathers. The spiritual lights (shen ming)[238] protect them like a newborn child. Thus, they always remain.
> ...
> Sages act with love towards people, and are protected by the spiritual lights. Is this not because they are fair, upright, and without selfishness?

On the other hand, as the *Nei Ye* appears to be doing here, Heshang Gong more commonly uses the term shen ming to refer to something cultivated; for example, in his comments on DDJ12:

> *"Thus, sages are guided by their stomachs"*
> By guarding the five intrinsic natures, abandoning the six emotions,[239] and uniting the qi of concentration,[240] spiritual intelligence (shen ming) is fostered.

This idea of cultivating shen ming may not be entirely disconnected from the concept of these spiritual entities, however, as evidenced

---

[238] The shen ming are also mentioned in the Tai Yi Sheng Shui, and texts by Chuang Tzu, Confucius, and Mo Tzu. They are considered as emissaries of Heaven which determine fortune and misfortune according to the purity of one's virtue. Shen ming can also mean spiritual intelligence, or "brilliance of the spirit."

[239] See footnote in chapter six for an explanation of the five intrinsic natures and the six emotions.

[240] 志 Zhi, will, resolve, consciousness.
There are also "five wills, 五志 (wuzhi)." These are emotional states associated with the five organs, which can exist in balance, but cause the six emotions when imbalanced.
The five wills and their correspondences are: vigor/anger 怒(nu) in the liver, love/euphoria 喜(xi) in the heart, contemplation/worry 思(si) in the spleen, nostalgia/sorrow 悲(bei) in the lungs, and awe/fear 恐(kong) in the kidneys.

in Heshang Gong's comments in DDJ16:

> *"The way of impartiality shows the way of a king"*
> Impartial, honourable, and unselfish, one can become king of all under Heaven. By governing and aligning the body, form is unified. Countless spiritual lights then assemble in the body.
> *"The way of a king shows the way of Heaven"*
> Being a king, here, means that Virtue will gather spiritual lights and take you through the Heavens.

It appears that the author (or authors) of the *Nei Ye* was likely aware of this understanding of shen ming, and its relevance to one's own spirit and cultivation (see line 135). Heshang Gong, and the author(s) of the *Nei Ye*, do not so much advocate communion with the shen ming, as authors of Confucian texts did, but rather advocate embodying their power within oneself. This can be seen in NY1-8 and 235-253 (below). Perhaps one of the reasons for this departure is the proto-Daoists' tendency towards co-existent self-reliance, in contrast to the interdependence more characteristic of Confucian mores.

What the *Nei Ye* more directly refers to here is 'spiritual intelligence', the ultimate state of spiritual and mental clarity, unimpaired by imbalances that may result from psycho-physical tensions, emotions, and the ultimate cause of emotions: craving. The anger of not getting what we feel we deserve, the euphoria of getting it, and the sorrow of losing it can be transcended through the art of the heart-mind. By eradicating cravings, expectations, driving emotions, mental constructs, and limited cognitive knowledge of time and space, one can allow the illumination of the spirit to enter the emptiness of the heart-mind. This is further elucidated in chapter one of the Huainan Zi, which complements the instructions of the *Nei Ye* quite helpfully when compared with the discussion of order and alignment in NY115-128, and then the refinements needed to bring forth spiritual illumination discussed in NY129-150:

> Now, those who use their ears and eyes to hear and observe strain their bodies to understand correctly. Those who use knowledge and deliberation to govern correctly abuse the mind and achieve nothing. Therefore, sages use a single measurement,

complying with what has been well established. They do not alter its acceptability; they do not change its regularity. Thus, they can determine what accords to the level, knowing what is crooked by what is just.

Euphoria and anger are deviations from Dao;
Anguish and sorrow are losses of Intrinsic Virtue.
Likes and dislikes overtax the mind;
Cravings and desires disturb Pure Nature.

Intense anger ruins the yin;
Intense euphoria collapses the yang.
Weakened qi renders one mute;
Fear and terror causes insanity.
If one is anxious, sorrowful, and frequently angry,
Sickness will accumulate.
If likes and dislikes grow numerous,
Misfortunes will also follow.

Thus, when the mind is neither anxious nor jubilant, Intrinsic Virtue is refined.
When the mind is far reaching yet unchanging, tranquility is refined.
When cravings and desires do not burden the mind, emptiness is refined.
When the mind is without likes and dislikes, equanimity is refined.
When the mind is not scattered about on things, purity is refined.

If the mind can succeed in these five (refinements), it will break through to spiritual intelligence. To break through to spiritual intelligence is to attain what lies within.

Therefore, using the internal to control the external,
Your many endeavours will not fail.
If, internally, you can attain it,
Externally, you can harvest it.[241]

---

[241] From the *Huainan Zi* (edited by Liu An, 139 BC), chapter one. Translated by

151 道滿天下。
　　Dao fills the world.
152 普在民所,
　　It is widespread amongst the people,
153 民不能知也。
　　Yet the people cannot understand it.
154 一言之解,
　　One saying unravels it:
155 上察於天,
　　For what is above, study the Heavens;
156 下極於地,
　　For what is below, exhaust the limits of the Earth –
157 蟠滿九州。
　　Circling throughout the nine regions[242,243]
158 何謂解之,
　　So what does this saying reveal?
159 在於心安。
　　It is found in the peaceful heart.
160 我心治, 官乃治。
　　When my heart is orderly, my senses are orderly;
161 我心安, 官乃安。
　　When my heart is peaceful, my senses are peaceful.
162 治之者心也,
　　What sets them in order is the heart-mind;
163 安之者心也。
　　What makes them peaceful is the heart-mind.
164 心以藏心,
　　The heart-mind conceals another heart-mind.
165 心之中又有心焉。

Dan G. Reid. Please see my comments on XSS1-20 for more of this excerpt.
[242] See also, XSX 124-126
[243] "The nine regions" is an early term referring to regional divisions of China, independent of changing state or kingdom borders.

Within the center of the heart-mind, there is another heart-mind.

166 彼心之心,

In this heart of the heart-mind,

167 音以先言,

There is a resonance (intention) which precedes words.[244]

168 音然後形,

Resonance is followed by forms;

169 形然後言。

Forms are followed by words;

170 言然後使,

Words are followed by directives;[245]

171 使然後治。

Directives are followed by order.

172 不治必亂,

When there is disorder, there is sure to be confusion.

173 亂乃死。

Confusion leads to death.[246]

---

[244] "音 sound/tone," appearing in the 'received text', is usually replaced in translations of lines 167-168 with "意 notion, intention, awareness." See *Nei Ye* line 224 which speaks of "wordless tone." That line also appears in XSX line 88 as "unspoken words." "音 Tone," therefore, may have had a significance regarding unspoken "sentiments," as in a "resonance" or feeling in the heart-mind that induces thought.

[245] The word "使 directives" in line 170 means, literally, to send messages and instructions. This suggests a more perfect mental process than in chapter eight of the *Ling Shu Jing* which frames the more basic junctures that may or may not lead to a pathology. Regardless, there seems to be a common thread of metaphors between "envoy, messenger, directive (使)" in NY170 and the *Ling Shu Jing*'s "When thought travels a great distance (as though in search of it's) beloved, this is called contemplation (lu). When contemplation arrives at its location, this is called wisdom (zhi)." More of this excerpt from the *Ling Shu Jing* can be read in my commentary on lines 1-22 of the *Nei Ye*.

[246] See XSX48-64 in comparison to NY159-173

The Heaven's adjust to change without hesitation, while the Earth is always solid and stable. To follow Dao is to also follow Earth, as Earth follows the seasons of Heaven, Heaven follows the order of Dao, and Dao follows its own spontaneous nature. Earth transforms according to the seasons, but does not change its nature. Holding to pure nature in the heart–mind, we can adapt and transform according to external changes without losing this pure nature (xing).

Lines 151-173 ask the reader to consider the seeds of emotion, thoughts, and action, created by the heart–mind. A peaceful heart–mind sprouts peaceful emotions, thoughts and actions. An agitated heart–mind sprouts agitated emotions, thoughts and actions. Thus, the state of our environment is shaped by our heart–mind, and the seeds of emotion, thought, and action that it creates.

Lines 160–163 of the *Nei Ye* resemble lines 109–112 of the *Xin Shu Xia*, which illustrate this point somewhat more directly, in saying:

> When is there no benefit from my affairs?
> When there is no benefit in my heart-mind.
> When is there no peace where I reside?
> When there is no peace in my heart-mind

While the NY and XSX reflect the opening lines of the *Xin Shu Shang* with sentiments of the heart-mind as ruler, they are somewhat more methodical in their techniques, and so go on to provide directions for looking deeply into the "heart of the heart–mind" where one can delve into the soil of intention (yi), uproot the weeds of agitation and rumination, and thereby foster seeds of inner and outer harmony. This technique begins in lines 122-128 of the *Nei Ye*, which approximate to the opening lines of the *Xin Shu Xia*, providing a physical complement to the art of the heart-mind:

> When the bodily form is not aligned,
> Virtue does not approach;
> When the center is not tranquil,
> The heart-mind is not orderly.
> When the bodily form is aligned, it absorbs Virtue.
> Heaven's benevolent generosity and Earth's balancing righteousness

Then naturally arrive in abundance.
(NY122-128)

Lao Zi expands on the process of cleansing the heart–mind in *Dao De Jing*, chapter three:

Therefore, the Sage's government
Empties the mind and enriches the stomach
Softens the will and strengthens the bones
People then remain uncontrived and without desires
While the scheming do not dare to act
Act by not acting
And everything will fall into place

In Daoist meditation, focus is put on the lower energy reservoir under the naval (lower dantien), while the heart and mind release the constraints of thinking and emotion. The meditator does not try to control the course of nature (ie., softens the will), but allows an inner alignment to naturally come about. This reverses the effects of stress-response and helps the body and mind to return to balance, allowing nutrients to be properly absorbed and circulated (strengthens the bones). Heshang Gong comments on the line "strengthens the bones": "He cherishes his vital essence and takes seriously what was bestowed upon him. Thus, his bone marrow is full, and his bones are strong."

When the mind and breath have naturally settled and become peaceful, and the energy of thoughts is about to arise, one can become aware of the subtle resonance of thought that is about to arise and gently direct it to the lower dantien, or to the bone marrow. This allows the mind to remain silent and undistracted, and the intent to direct energy back into the body's reservoirs, described in the proceeding lines (NY174-184). If the mind becomes distracted and clouded by thoughts, the intent is deferred, allowing thoughts to become chaotic, which in turn causes the intent to be directed by limited patterns of the mind. Emotion, stress, and confusion may then disturb the harmonious balance (order) of the heart-mind and deplete vital energy. Therefore, to preserve this harmonious balance, it is best to stay unified in awareness, and "without (doubt or) division."

Rumination is understood in Chinese medicine as a superficial, or pathological, expression of the spleen's earth energy. On observation, one may find that their thoughts are an instinctual attempt to reconnect to the grounded earth energy of the spleen, which is actually found in the *yi*, intention (also associated with the spleen). As the *Nei Ye* shows, by returning to the original open awareness that lies underneath the thoughts, one can restore balance, clear away the clouds of thought, and thereby uncover the heart of the heart-mind.

174 精存自生,
    When pure and vital essence remains,
    life-energy spontaneously emerges.
175 其外安榮,
    One is then externally peaceful and radiant,
176 內藏以為泉原。
    (Allowing them to) conceal this surging wellspring within.
177 浩然和平,
    As a flood of harmony and peacefulness,
178 以為氣淵。
    It becomes an abyss of energy-breath.
179 淵之不涸,
    If this abyss does not dry up,
180 四體乃固,
    The four limbs solidify;
181 泉之不竭,
    If this wellspring is not exhausted,
182 九竅遂通,
    The nine bodily orifices are free and unblocked.
183 乃能窮天地,
    One can then absorb all of Heaven and Earth,
184 被四海。
    Covering the four seas.
185 中無惑意,

Within, one's intention is not vacillating;
186 外無邪菑,
Externally, they are without affliction and calamity.
187 心全於中,
Their heart-mind is maintained, within,
188 形全於外,
And their body is maintained, externally.
189 不逢天菑,
They do not meet upon calamity,
190 不遇人害,
Nor do they encounter hostile people.
191 謂之聖人。
We call them "sages."

Observing the Earth where springs run under the surface, the ground is fertile, solid, and healthy. As all beings are a microcosmic reflection of Heaven and Earth, we can see how this image relates to our own being. Where Heaven and Earth (mind and body) are in harmony, the soil is radiant with life energy.

The "abyss of energy-breath," "wellspring" and "flood of harmony and peacefulness" in lines 174-178 may indicate a shared oral tradition with Meng Zi's (Mencius') teaching on "flooding qi":

> (Meng Zi replied), 'It is difficult to describe it. This is qi: It is exceedingly great, and exceedingly strong. Being nourished by rectitude, and sustaining no injury, it fills up all between heaven and earth. This is qi: It is the mate and assistant of righteousness and reason. Without it, man is in a state of starvation. It is produced by the accumulation of righteous deeds; it is not to be obtained by incidental acts of righteousness. If the mind does not feel (satisfied with one's) conduct, the nature becomes starved. I therefore said, "Gao has never understood righteousness, because he makes it something external." There must be the constant practice of this righteousness, but without the

object of thereby nourishing the qi. Let not the mind forget its work, but let there be no assisting the growth of that nature. Let us not be like the man of Song. There was a man of Song, who was grieved that his growing corn was not longer, and so he pulled it up. Having done this, he returned home, looking very stupid, and said to his people, "I am tired today. I have been helping the corn to grow long." His son ran to look at it, and found the corn all withered. There are few in the world who do not deal with their qi as if they were assisting the corn to grow long. Some indeed consider it of no benefit to them, and let it alone – they do not weed their corn. They who assist it to grow long, pull out their corn. What they do is not only of no benefit to the nature, but it also injures it.'[247]

Though Meng Zi has a moral cultivation as the base of his qi cultivation, the influence of Daoist cultivation practices are evident in his advocacy for allowing to nature what nature does best.

Such descriptions of "abyss," "wellspring" and "flood" in *Nei Ye* lines 74–191 are also reminiscent of the valley (谷) in *Dao De Jing*, chapters six[248] and 28.

DDJ28:
    Knowing the male, guard the female
    And be a valley under Heaven
    Be a valley under Heaven
    And Virtue will never flee
    But will return to her infant son

    Knowing the white, guard the black
    And be a guide for the world
    Be a guide for the world
    And Virtue will remain without wavering
    Return to Wuji, Supreme Nothingness

---

[247] Legge, James, translator. *The Life and Works of Mencius: With Essays and Notes.* London. Trubner and Co. 1875. pp. 165-6.
I have edited Legge's term "passion nature" to restore the Chinese word "qi."
[248] See XSX lines 109-126 for more on the valley in DDJ6.

Knowing glory, hold fast to humiliation
And be a valley under Heaven
Being a valley under Heaven, Virtue will always fulfill you
Return to your unaltered substance
Unaltered wood is shaped into vessels
Sages make use of this model
When acting in positions of leadership
Thus, the greatest establishment is undivided

Seeing similarities in the teachings of DDJ28 and the *Nei Ye*, the metaphor of 'the state as the self' can be seen in Lao Zi's words "the greatest establishment is undivided" with reference to the same types of unification prescribed in the *Nei Ye*.

From a Chinese medical perspective, lines 174-191 also follow the creation cycle of the five elemental phases. This begins with the notion that life energy is rooted in the jing (vital essence) of the kidneys:

When pure and vital essence remains, life-energy spontaneously emerges.
One is then externally peaceful and radiant,
(Allowing them to) conceal this surging wellspring within.
As a flood of harmony and peacefulness,
It becomes an abyss of energy-breath. (NY174-178)

The water phase of kidney-jing gives rise to the wood phase of the liver, expressed in the muscles and the forward yang-energy of growth and determination.

If this abyss does not dry up,
The four limbs solidify; (NY179-180)

The wood phase gives rise to the fire phase of the heart-mind, which may be associated with the "nine orifices" in line 182. Though the ears, eyes, nostrils, mouth, urethra and anus are associated with various particular phases, the "free and unblocked" state of the head's orifices suggests consciousness, and the heart-mind. This connection is also made evident in the opening lines of the Xin Shu Shang: "The heart-mind holds the throne of the ruler. The nine apertures hold offices of various public servants. When the heart-mind remains with Dao, the nine apertures act reasonably."

> If this wellspring is not exhausted,
> The nine bodily orifices are free and unblocked.
> One can then absorb[249] all of Heaven and Earth,
> Covering the four seas. (NY181-184)

The fire phase gives rise to the earth phase, associated with the spleen, the absorption of the stomach, and intention.

> Within, one's intention is not vacillating;
> Externally, they are without affliction and calamity.
> Their heart-mind is maintained, within,
> And their body is maintained, externally. (NY185-188)

This shows the progressive transformations that take place as life-energy reaches through one's being. The only phase not yet touched on in these lines is the metal-phase, associated with the lungs and skin. Suffice it to say, when one's intention is not vacillating, their breath becomes more natural, deep, and full. This strengthens the lung phase and thereby the skin, mentioned in lines 192-193, below, which refer to the healthy glow of the skin that follows the practice of aligning and quieting oneself, also mentioned earlier in lines 91-114.

192 人能正靜,
   When people can align and quiet themselves,[250]
193 皮膚裕寬,
   Their skin's surface is rich and full;

---

[249] The word translated here as "absorb" means more literally to make empty or exhaust (窮 qiong), and was used to rhyme with and allude to orifices (竅 qiao). Both characters take their meaning from the shared radical for cave (穴) that sits above them.

[250] Lines 192-204 of the *Nei Ye* reflect lines 70-79 of the *Xin Shu Xia*

194 耳目聰明,
    Their ears and eyes are acute and perceptive;
195 筋信而骨強,
    Their muscles and tendons are strong and flexible;
    their bones are strong and firm.
196 乃能戴大圜,
    They can wear the great circle (Heaven) as their head covering,
197 而履大方。
    And the great square (Earth) as their shoes.
198 鑒於大清,
    In the great clarity, they are reflected;
199 視於大明。
    With the great illumination, they observe.
200   敬慎無忒,
    Being respectful and careful, they are without error;
201 日新其德;
    Daily refreshing their virtue,
202 偏知天下,
    They know every place under Heaven.
203 窮於四極,
    Wherever there is deficiency in the four directions,
204 敬發其充,
    They reverently supply.
205 是謂內得。
    This is called "internal attainment."
206 然而不反,
    From this, they do not depart,
207 此生之忒。
    For doing so would give rise to error.

Balance and harmony starts from within, generating an atmosphere that cannot help but align with the beauty and power of stability and balance.

We see here, again, how the heart of the mind must be tended to so as to ensure beneficial emotions, thoughts, and actions. This benefit spans the body, the senses, perceptiveness, and social relationships, ensuring that none of these impinge on the circumstances of the others. With this vitality, perception, and peacefulness, sages bring everything around them closer to harmony. Line 205 might also be translated as "attaining from within," following an explanation of the same phenomena in the Huainan Zi, chapter one:

> To break through to spiritual intelligence is to attain what lies within. (得其內者也)
> Therefore, using the internal to control the external,
> Your many endeavours will not fail.
> If, internally, you can attain it,
> Externally, you can harvest it.
> With this inner attainment (中之得則),
> The five major organs will be peaceful;
> Thoughts and worries will be stabilized.
> The tendons will be strong, and your strength will be powerful;
> Your ears and eyes will be acute and clear…[251]

NY192-207 also describe an ability to reflect Heaven and Earth in mind and body – returning the muscles and tendons to their "信 true state" of youthful flexibility, and having the clarity of the sky beyond the clouds with the mental brightness of the sun and moon (see lines 196-199).[252] This is returning the body and mind to an original, unaltered, state of harmonious balance, referred to by Daoist Alchemists as "pre-heaven."

---

[251] For more of this excerpt, please see my comments on lines 1-20 of the *Xin Shu Xia*.
[252] The character for 明 illumination / enlightenment is composed of the radicals for sun and moon, also meaning "clear vision."

Internal Cultivation

208 凡道
   Invariably, Dao
209 必周必密,
   Is sure to enclose, sure to condense,
210 必寬必舒,
   Sure to expand, sure to open,
211 必堅必固。
   Sure to strengthen, sure to solidify.
212 守善勿舍,
   It preserves excellence (yet) does not dwell.
213 逐淫澤薄。
   It removes excess and nourishes[253] where there is weakness.
214 既知其極,
   Having known the furthest limits,
215 反於道德。
   Return to Dao and Virtue.

In the words of Dao De Jing, chapter 22:

   That which is flexible is preserved
   That which is bent is straightened
   That which is empty is filled
   That which is broken is repaired
   That which is lacking acquires
   That which is excessive becomes confused
   Therefore, the sage embraces Oneness
   So as to bring the world into alignment...

NY208-215 could be read alongside DDJ77 for further reflection:

   The Way of Heaven
   Is it not like the stretching of a bow?
   What is high, it causes to be pulled low
   What is low, it causes to be uplifted

---

[253] "澤 Swamp, fertilize" is usually replaced here with "釋 release"

What has excess, it causes to be diminished
What is insufficient it causes to be restored

Heaven's Way diminishes what has excess
And restores what lacks sufficiency
The way of man, however, is not this way
Diminishing what suffers lack
And assisting where there is excess
Who can have in excess, and care for all under Heaven?
Only those who have Dao
Therefore, sages act but do not expect anything in return
They achieve their ends without lingering
And have no desire to exhibit inner worth

216 全心在中,
    Though the heart-mind remains within,[254]
217 不可蔽匿。
    It cannot be concealed;
218 和[255]於形容,
    The harmony of the body reveals it.
219 見於膚色。
    It is seen in the skin's colour.

220 善氣迎人,
    Welcoming others with an energy-breath of goodness
221 親於弟兄。
    Is like embracing them with the affection of brothers and sisters;
222 惡氣迎人,
    Welcoming others with an energy-breath of wickedness

---

[254] See lines 80-99 of the *Xin Shu Xia* for comparison with lines 216-230 of the *Nei Ye*

[255] "和 harmony" is usually replaced here with "知 knowledge, known by," as it appears in *Xin Shu Xia* line 82.

223 害於戎兵。
　　Is like injuring them with a soldier's spear.
224 不言之聲,
　　Its wordless tone[256]
225 疾於雷鼓。
　　Strikes like thunder.
226 心氣之形,
　　The manifestations of the heart-mind's energy-breath
227 明於日月,
　　Illuminate like the sun and moon,
228 察於父母。
　　And are perceived as though by one's own mother and father.
229 賞不足以勸善,
　　Rewards are not enough to encourage goodness;
230 刑不足以懲過。
　　Punishments are not enough to discourage misbehaviour.
231 氣意得
　　When (the unity of) energy-breath and intention is attained,[257]
232 而天下服。
　　All under Heaven coordinates;
233 心意定
　　When the heart-mind and intention become settled,
234 而天下聽。
　　All under Heaven cooperates.

---

[256] In a similar passage of the XSX, line 87 reads "不言之言 unspoken words." That the *Nei Ye* refers again to "tone," this time with a character bearing no resemblance to intent (using 聲 rather than 音), suggests that resonance and tone were not typos but rather used to refer to something less formed than thoughts, such as "sentiment." It may be that intent (意) was still being defined at this point, and so notions of inner tone and resonance were used to describe it.

[257] Reading line 231 as such follows the many references to inner unification throughout the text. The term "energy of intent (意氣)" can be found in line 12 of *Xin Shu Xia*, where the syntax suggests it.

One's true feelings, like essence, will shine through in their demeanor, tone, and energy. We must cultivate good intentions, like we must cultivate harmonious essence, so that we can offer sweet and not poison fruit.

NY216-234 provide an early clarification of the Daoist's approach to social harmony, and may support their rejection of the perceived[258] Confucian focus on cultivating external conduct: If one's energy is not balanced and harmonious, it cannot be hidden by external conduct.[259] Thus, it is deemed more beneficial to cultivate "internal virtue,"[260] thereby reclaiming essence and original nature, rather than external behaviours and actions. These lines also profess the superiority of Daoist methods over Legalist methods of government (see especially lines 229-230).

The approach to successful governing found in NY229-234 is central to Daoist advice given to rulers, and helps to contextualize DDJ13:

> ... What does it mean to say "Appreciate the great worrying
> That (favour and disgrace) cause to your person?"
> The reason I have great worries is because I have a self
> If I did not have a self, what worries would I have?
>
> Therefore, those who (govern) the self as the world
> And cherish it as such
> On them the world can rely
> Those who (govern) the self as the world
> And love it as such
> To them the world can be entrusted

DDJ13 can be read as advising that a ruler ought not rely on others' opinions of them, but simply care for and cultivate oneself and the

---

[258] Confucian teachings also stressed the importance of rectifying oneself internally, and not just in behaviour; however, Confucian formality was sometimes gratuitous, according to Daoists like Zhuang Zi.

[259] Please note that NY216-217 appear in XSX80 as "A golden heart within cannot be hidden."

[260] See NY205

world as though they were one and the same thing. Thereby, they will not be seduced by pursuits for glory and fame at the expense of both the nation and their own body. Similarly, the *Nei Ye* counsels that cultivating internal harmony and vitality should be the first priority of a ruler.

Zhuang Zi also advises this approach in his chapter "Retiring to Non-attachment (chapter 11)":

> I have heard of retiring to non-attachment; I have not heard of ruling all under Heaven. As for retiring, it is for fear of corrupting the pure nature of all under Heaven. As for non-attachment, it is for fear that the intrinsic virtue of all under Heaven will shift. When all under Heaven does not corrupt their pure nature, nor shift their intrinsic virtue, then order has been attained!
>
> [...] Thus, even the greatness of all under heaven would not suffice for rewards and punishments. Since the time of the three dynasties, there has been nothing but clamour over the business of rewards and punishments. What leisure have they had to find peace in the reality of their pure nature and destiny? Their enjoyment of clear vision? Just debauching in lust. Their enjoyment of hearing? Just debauching in sounds. Their enjoyment of benevolence? Just throwing their intrinsic virtue into disorder. Their enjoyment of righteousness? Just opposing common sense. Their enjoyment of ceremonies? Simply an exhibition of skills. Their enjoyment of music? Simply exhibitions of lewdness. Their enjoyment of wisdom? Simply an exhibition of craft. Their enjoyment of knowledge? Just expositions of fault.
>
> If all under Heaven were to find peace in the reality of their pure natures and destinies, it would make no difference if these eight things existed or disappeared. When all under heaven does not find peace in the reality of their pure natures and destinies, these eight things begin to warp and swell, throwing all under Heaven into chaos. When all under Heaven begins to revere and insist on them, how extensively are all under Heaven mislead! Then they do not simply partake and move on, but will fast before speaking of them, they will kneel when presenting them, they will sing praises of them and dance about. What can I do once it has gone this far?

Therefore if the junzi cannot resist engaging in administration of the world, there is nothing better than to do nothing. Doing nothing, he can then find peace in the reality of his nature and destiny. Therefore, valuing his body as he values the world, to him the world can be entrusted. Having love for his body as he has love for the world, on him, the world can rely. Therefore, if the junzi can contain and not indulge his five senses, nor bring out his intelligence and perception, he will be still as a corpse yet displaying a dragon, quiet as an abyss yet with a voice like thunder. His spirit's movements will be entrained with Heaven. Though at ease and without action, myriads of things will accumulate around him. (Following this, he will ask) "What leisure do I have to govern the world?"[261]

As Lao Zi says in DDJ33 "Those who overpower others are strong. Those who overpower themselves are powerful."

235 搏氣如神,
By consolidating[262] energy-breath (and becoming) spirit-like,[263]
236 萬物備存。
The myriad things perfect their existence.
237 能搏乎？能一乎？
Can you consolidate it? Can you unify it?[264]
238 能無卜筮
Can you, without divining by yarrow stalks,
239 而知吉凶乎？

---

[261] Translated by Dan G. Reid
[262] Literally, "roll up into a ball" like dough or clay, often translated as "concentrate."
[263] Lines 235-253 can be further understood by studying the three chapters from *Guigu Zi*, provided in the introduction.
[264] Similar to chapter 10 of the *Dao De Jing*, "Guarding the fortress of your bodily spirits, embrace Oneness. Can you do this without letting it flee? Gather together the energy-breath and become soft. This is the power of an infant."

Know what is fortunate and what is perilous?
240 能止乎？能已乎？
Can you stop (peril from arriving)? Can you make it cease?
241 能勿求諸人
Can you not seek this from others
242 而得之己乎？
But attain it in yourself?
243 思之思之，
If you think about it and think about it,
244 又重思之；
And then go back and think about it some more,
245 思之而不通，
Your thinking about it will not reach (comprehension).
246 鬼神將通之：
Ghosts and spirits move forward and reach this (comprehension of altering fortune),
247 非鬼神之力也，
Not because of the ghost's and spirit's efforts (in thinking about it),
248 精氣之極也。
(But because of) the extent of their vital essence and energy-breath.
249 四體既正，
When the four limbs are aligned,
250 血氣既靜，
The blood and energy-breath are tranquil
251 一意摶心，
When unifying intention and consolidating the heart,
252 耳目不淫，
The ears and eyes do not indulge,
253 雖遠若近。
Yet what is far off is as though near.

One must be acquainted with their internal energy. Consolidating attention and aligning the body, one can observe their energy from a state of calm objectivity, allowing it to move and change until it eventually settles and consolidates, uniting with the will, the breath, and the heart-mind.

To understand the implications of consolidating qi and becoming "spirit-like," it helps to understand *ling* and *ling qi*, the cultivation of which is the focus of lines 327-353, below. It is *ling*, spiritual potency, that spirits are said to consist of, and so to consolidate qi and become spirit like is to cultivate this ling qi. The above precautions concerning thought correlate to the following lines, 254-266, which show how thinking, a major source of stagnation due to knotted qi (Su Wen, chapter 39), can bring one out of the natural balance that fosters inner potency. Ling also carries the meaning of the efficacy of Dao. As Dao is sometimes referred to as a carpenter's level or chalkline, showing what is just and what is crooked,[265] to move away from Dao would bring the loss of this efficacy, and thereby misfortune (see line 240). To be careful of excessive thought is to remain close to this guiding line and avoid illnesses and calamities before they arrive (see 327-353). Remaining close to Dao in such a way, one does not "wait until thirsty to dig a well" as Qi Bo explains in *Nei Jing, Su Wen*, chapter two:

> As for Dao, the sages practice it; the foolish decorate themselves with it. To accord with yin and yang leads to life; to oppose them leads to death. To accord with yin and yang leads to order; to oppose them leads to chaos... Therefore, sages did not establish order to stop illness, they established order before illness arose. They did not establish order to stop chaos, they established order before chaos arose. To provide medicine after illness is already affixed, or instill order after chaos has already ensued, this is like digging a well after one is already thirsty, or fashioning weapons after war has already begun.[266]

---

[265] See Huainan Zi, chapter one.
[266] Translated by Dan G. Reid

Lines 235-253 may also help to show the early teachings behind DDJ10, especially as it pertains to inner consolidation and freeing the mind of inner dialogue.

DDJ10:
>Guard the fortress of your bodily spirits
>Embrace Oneness
>Can you do this without letting them flee?
>Gather together the energy-breath and become soft
>This is the power of an infant
>
>Looking deeply
>Purify and eliminate
>Can you be without flaw?
>Caring for the people and governing the nation
>Can you be without effort?
>Heaven's gate opens and closes
>Can you act the part of the female?
>With your awareness shining on every corner
>Can you be without knowledge?
>
>Giving them life and cultivating them
>Giving them life yet not possessing them
>Acting for them yet not expecting of them
>Leading them forward but not managing them
>This is called Fathomless Virtue

254 思索生知,
 Thinking and searching give rise to knowledge;
255 慢易生憂,
 Sluggishness and idleness give rise to anxiety;[267]
256 暴傲生怨,

---

[267] *You* (憂) appears elsewhere in the *Nei Ye* with the meaning "sorrow" in common groupings of emotions, but appears here with its meaning as "anxiety" as evidenced by the context.

Aggression and arrogance give rise to anger;
257 憂鬱生疾,
Anxiety and constraint gives rise to illness.
258 疾困乃死。
When illness overwhelms, there is death.[268]
259 思之而不捨,
By thinking about it, and not letting go,
260 內困外薄。
Internally, one is overwhelmed, and externally one is frail.
261 不蚤[269]為圖,
If one does not make premature determinations,
262 生將巽[270]舍。
The life-force will later re-establish itself.
263 食莫若無飽。
Eat, but not as though you cannot be filled.
264 思莫若勿致。
Think, but not as though there is no objective.
265 節適之齊,
Regulate these things accordingly,
266 彼將自至。
And they will eventually do so of themselves.

As the connection between body and spirit is integral to life, the mind is inseparable from the body's ecosystem. Regulating what goes into our internal ecosystem requires awareness of the food, water, air,

---

[268] This could be read as a cause and effect progression from over thinking through to death, and should be considered alongside the general Daoist attitude towards superfluous knowledge. Thus, "thinking and searching lead to knowledge" and a downward spiral, rather than aiding in fluid adaptation to change "without being displaced." It also leads to overwhelming the mind and body to a perilous degree, perhaps explaining how one predicts the future without divining (NY235-253). part of the course for "changing fortune" mentioned in the passage above.

[269] 蚤 means "early" in ancient texts

[270] 將 and 巽 both suggest "proceeding; later"

and ideation that we allow to pass through this physical and spiritual self.

NY254-258 could be read as a cause and effect progression from over thinking through to death, explaining the general Daoist attitude towards superfluous knowledge. Thus, "thinking and searching lead to knowledge," beginning this downward spiral. This descent may also be hinted at in NY238-240:

> Can you, without divining by yarrow stalks,
> Know what is fortunate and what is perilous?
> Can you stop (peril from arriving)? Can you make it cease?

Reading NY254-258, it can be understood that thinking and searching give rise to *knowledge* which leads to inaction, or "*sluggishness and idleness*" which give rise to *anxiety*. This anxiety then leads to fear-based *aggression and arrogance*, the consequences of which bring a great deal of *anger* into one's environment. This environment of conflict leads to deeper *anxiety, constrained qi,* and thus *illness*, which leads to *death*. How does one reverse this escalation of illness? "*If one does not make premature determinations, the life-force will later re-establish itself*" (lines 261-262). This caution is corroborated by Classical Chinese medical theories of knotted qi, brought about by over-thinking, and the constraint (yu, 鬱) of qi that this knotting will produce. Constrained qi, according to the famed Chinese physician Zhu Danxi (1281-1358), is the root of all pathological changes.[271] Such an understanding was also illustrated in Zhuang Zi, chapter 15:

> It is the nature of water that when free from other substances, it is clear, and when it is calm, it is level; but if it is collected (鬱), obstructed (閉), and not allowed to flow, it cannot maintain its clarity. It is a reflection of Heaven's virtue.
>
> Thus it is said: To be pure, genuine, and uncontaminated; to be calm, unified, and stable; to be content and not impositioning;

---

[271] Rossi, Elisa. *Shen: Psycho-Emotional Aspects of Chinese Medicine*. London: Churchill Livingstone Elsevier, 2002, p. 77

to move according to the phases of Heaven: this is the way to nourish the spirit.[272]

A helpful strategy to avoid over-thinking, and the consequent knotting and constraint of qi, can be found in the Tibetan Buddhist teaching, "Tilopa's Six Nails":

Don't recall. (Let go of what has passed.)
Don't imagine. (Let go of what may come.)
Don't think. (Let go of what is happening now.)
Don't examine. (Don't try to figure anything out.)
Don't control. (Don't try to make anything happen.)
Rest. (Relax, right now, and rest.)[273]

Though an over-reliance on thinking allows the mind, rather than the spirit, to control one's life, this divergence from the path can be corrected by bringing the heart-mind back into peaceful alignment, as shown in the *Nei Ye*'s proceeding lines. Doing so encourages the thoughts to yield to inner silence.

267 凡人之生也,
    In regards to the lives of all people:
268 天出其精,
    Heaven produces their pure and vital essence;
269 地出其形。
    Earth produces their form.
270 合此以為人;
    This combination (of essence and form) is used in the

---

[272] From *Zhuang Zi*, chapter 15. Translated by Dan G. Reid. See commentary on NY1-22 for more of this excerpt.

[273] Tilopa (988–1069). Translation, from Tibetan, by Ken McLeod (source publication unknown). On attempting my own translation with an online Tibetan dictionary, I see that McLeod's elaborate translation is faithful to the meaning of the original six imperative words (five with a negative prefix) that make up this entire list.

creation of human beings.
271 和乃生,
   When (form and essence) are in harmony, they create life;
272 不和不生。
   If they are not in harmony, they do not create life.
273 察和之道,
   Investigating the Dao of harmony.
274 其精不見,
   Its essence cannot be seen;
275 其徵不醜。
   Its evidence is indistinct.

276 平正擅匈,
   When balance and alignment claim the breast,[274]
277 論治在心,
   And inner debates and dialogue are brought to order,
278 此以長壽。
   This lengthens the lifespan.
279 忿怒之失度,
   If you lose your temper to fury[275] and anger,
280 乃為之圖。
   Enact the following plan:
281 節其五欲,

---

[274] In his article Psychology and Self-Cultivation in Early Taoistic Thought, Harold Roth suggests that "chest" in line 276 refers to the lungs, and thus evening out and aligning the breath.
Harvard Journal of Asiatic Studies
Vol. 51, No. 2 (Dec., 1991), p. 619

[275] "Fury" is usually changed here to "euphoria," in other translations, so as to reflect the fourth line down; however, "忿怒 fury and anger" often appear together in ancient texts as a compound word meaning "rage," and may have been intended. Anger was discussed in lines 254-258, above, as a turning point towards illness. The "strategy" mentioned here, to quell rage, is to forgo both anger and pleasure. Though it seems common sense to quell rage through pleasure, rage is often the result of not attaining what one wants; so by forgoing the desire, the anger and rage resulting from it are uprooted. Removing one to quell the other makes this a plan (see line 280).

Seal the desires of the five senses,
282 去其二凶。
And banish the two calamities.[276]
283 不喜不怒,
(Accepting) neither euphoria, nor anger,
284 平正擅匈。
Balance and alignment will reclaim the breast.

While extremes of yin and yang are more obvious, the harmony that remains between them is more subtle. Seeking within ourselves, our emotions, our desires, this subtlety between opposing extremes, harmony and balance can be known. Seeking that harmony from either extreme, we are unable to hear it, taste it, or learn from it.

Lines 267-284 speak to the effect of inner balance and harmony in fostering life and health. Western medicine differentiates between physical health and mental and emotional health, prescribing various doctors for physiological or psychological issues. Chinese medicine, however, unifies the health of the body and the mind, both because of their mutual influence, and because they both determine any single individual's experience of health and vitality. Excessive anger, sadness, euphoria, fear, and worry can easily destabilize a person's life and deny them the basic enjoyment of life and vitality. Thus, a person's mental-emotional experience is treated as an important indicator of the overall balance of their system, much like imbalances may also be revealed through the skin, hair, or fingernails. According to Chinese medicine, emotional imbalances can signal potential imbalances in specific internal organs that those emotions affect or arise from. For example, excessive anger may indicate "fullness" of the liver, and excessive fear may indicate "emptiness" of the liver.[277] Though the intricacies of the mind-body system in Chinese medicine were likely developed somewhat later than the *Nei Ye*, the *Nei Ye* provides a glimpse into early discussions of the importance of emotional balance

---

[276] Euphoria and anger. See line 283.
[277] See Ling Shu Jing, chapter eight.

for guarding the vitality of mind, body, and spirit. We can see how understandings of the emotions' impact on health developed over about two hundred years by comparing the *Nei Ye*'s teachings on emotional balance with The Yellow Emperors Classic of Internal Medicine (Huang Di Nei Jing, Su Wen),[278] chapter five:

> Heaven has four seasons and five elemental phases. (The former) brings about birth, growth, gathering, and storing. (The later) brings about cold, heat, dryness, dampness, and wind. People have five storehouses (organs) which transform the five qi,[279] giving rise to euphoria, anger, thought (rumination),[280] sorrow, and fear. Thus, euphoria and anger harm the qi, while cold and heat harm the body. Violent anger harms the yin, while violent euphoria harms the yang. Weakened qi moves upwards; filling the vessels, it leaves the body. If euphoria and anger are unrestrained, and cold and heat are excessive, life lacks solidity.[281]

As the *Nei Ye* shows in lines 267-284, a harmonious balance of heavenly and earthly essences brings about life,[282] and the inner balance of emotions preserves it. The result is that one becomes peaceful and *zheng* (correctly aligned and balanced) in their breast. Referring to "the breast," the *Nei Ye* makes a number of indications, the breast being the place where (yuan) jing collects and develops a Sage (see NY 1-8), also the place of the heart which governs the inner kingdom, and the lungs which "hold the office of the grand tutor; they bring forth order and moderation."[283] As such, we could also

---

[278] Likely written after 200 BC, based on variances in medical theory found in the Mawangdui tombs that were sealed in 186 BC (Wikipedia).
[279] I would speculate that the five qi refer to the innate qi of the organs, or otherwise to cold, heat, dryness, dampness and wind.
[280] The Nei Jing's ensuing discussion on this statement shows that grief (悲) was a typo for thought (思). Perhaps grief was a substitution for *you* (憂), which can mean either sorrow or anxiety.
[281] Translated by Dan G. Reid.
[282] For comparison with the *Huang Di Nei Jing*, see *Ling Shu Jing*, chapter 8, in my commentary on *Nei Ye* lines 1-22.
[283] See excerpt from chapter eight of the *Nei Jing, Su Wen* in Introduction: *Xin Shu Shang* and *Xin Shu Xia*.

infer zheng qi – the properly aligned and balanced qi that prevents "thieving winds" from harming the body.

While NY267-284 teach the ancient Chinese art of the heart-mind, they also show how to reclaim what became known in the late 1990s as emotional intelligence (EQ). Emotional intelligence refers to one's capacity to recognize their own emotions and mitigate the negative effect of these emotions in their lives. Such negative effects might include limitations on impulse control, on one's ability to differentiate sense and reality, and on self-actualization. An interpersonal component of emotional intelligence also exists, which involves empathy and recognizing how and why others are experiencing emotions. Reference to the interpersonal and empathetic side of EQ can be found in NY192-207:

> When people can align and quiet themselves
> ...
> In the great clarity, they are reflected
> *With the great illumination, they observe*
> *Being respectful and careful, they are without error*
> Daily refreshing their virtue
> They know every place under Heaven
> Wherever there is deficiency in the four directions
> They reverently supply
> This is called "internal attainment."

For returning from a state of emotional turmoil, the *Nei Ye* counsels limiting sense stimulation and refraining from euphoria and anger until the emotions are again balanced and "upright (aligned)" (see lines 276–284). "Balanced and aligned" illustrates a state of peacefulness, presence, and awareness: a state of calm preparedness, uninfluenced by the erratic tendencies of anger and euphoria.

Correlations to EQ in the *Nei Ye* begin, especially, in lines 216-228, which demonstrate the effective consequences of not being aware of one's own emotions when interacting with other people.

> Though the heart-mind remains within
> It cannot be hidden and concealed
> The harmony of the body reveals it

It is seen in the skin's colour
Welcoming others with an energy-breath of goodness
Is like embracing them with the affection of brothers and sisters;
Welcoming others with an energy-breath of wickedness
Is like injuring them with a soldier's spear.
It's wordless tone
Strikes like thunder
The manifestations of the heart-mind's energy-breath
Illuminate like the sun and moon
And are perceived as though by one's own mother and father

In summary, knowing one's own emotions, and finding inner peace, one can develop empathy and not let their emotions get in the way of a harmonious inter–being.

285 凡人之生也,
    Invariably, people's lives
286 必以平正。
    Require balance and alignment.
287 所以失之,
    What causes them to lose this
288 必以喜怒憂患,
    Is certainly euphoria, anger, sadness, and worry.
289 是故止怒莫若詩,
    To put an end to anger, nothing compares to poetry;
290 去憂莫若樂,
    To dispel sadness, nothing compares to music;[284]
291 節樂莫若禮,
    To moderate music, nothing compares to courtesy;
292 守禮莫若敬,

---

[284] "Music" can also mean "happiness, and pleasure." The pairing of "music and courtesy," ie. "music and rites" along with "respect" suggests Confucian terminology, but the context suggests a broader usage.

> To maintain courtesy, nothing compares to respect;
> 293 守敬莫若靜。
> To maintain respect, nothing compares to silence.
> 294 內靜外敬,
> Internally silent, and externally respectful,
> 295 能反其性。
> One can return to their pure nature.
> 296 性將大定。
> Pure nature is thereby greatly established.

In the harmony of words, we have poetry; in the harmony of sounds, we have music; in the harmony of actions, we have courtesy; in the harmony between two people, we have respect. Seeing the improvements that harmony brings to speech, sound, and social relations, we can consider the potential availed to us in bringing harmony to ourselves through deep inner silence, and by expressing this harmony outwardly in respect towards other individuals.

Lines 285-296 carry what appears to be a Confucian influence; however, the practice and teaching of poetry, music, courtesy, and respect were long a part of the Zhou-influenced education that Confucius received prior to becoming a teacher, himself, and making such education vastly more accessible. The principles of music are known to have existed in China for centuries before Confucius' teachings, with one of the surviving bronze bells, played by ensembles to make harmony and melody, dating to approximately 900 BC.[285] As we can see in the *Book of Music* (*Yue Ji*), found in the *Book of Rites* (*Li Ji*), much of the early Chinese arts were developed to teach a sort of minimalism that allowed one to appreciate beauty, without stimulating desire in such a way that satisfaction would be elusive. This aesthetic is also highly evident in the traditional Chinese methods of tea ceremony (gong fu cha) where tea is brewed lightly and appreciated with cups

---

[285] Nivison, David S., and Shaughnessy, Edward L. *The Jin Hou Su Bells Inscription and its implications for the Chronology of Early China.* (Early China 25). 2000.
http://www.dartmouth.edu/~earlychina/publications/early_china_journal/early-china-25-2000.html

that hold only three savoured sips. Minimalist calligraphy scrolls, earthen teaware, and the spacious sounds of a guqin radiate a beauty that can only be found in the meeting of simplicity and harmony. Practicing the arts in this way, a balance of sense, emotion, and rectitude is preserved:

> ... In the ceremonies of the great sacrifices, the dark-coloured liquor took precedence, and on the stands were uncooked fish, while the grand soup had no condiments: there was much flavour left undeveloped. Thus we see that the ancient kings, in their institution of ceremonies and music, did not seek how fully they could satisfy the desires of the appetite and of the ears and eyes; but they intended to teach the people to regulate their likings and dislikings, and to bring them back to the normal course of humanity (反人道之正).
>
> It belongs to the nature of man, as from Heaven, to be still at his birth. His activity shows itself as he is acted on by external things, and develops the desires incident to his nature. Things come to him more and more, and his knowledge is increased. Then arise the manifestations of liking and disliking. When these are not regulated by anything within, and growing knowledge leads more astray without, he cannot come back to himself, and his Heavenly principle is extinguished.
>
> Now there is no end of the things by which man is affected; and when his likings and dislikings are not subject to regulation (from within), he is changed into the nature of things as they come before him; that is, he stifles the voice of Heavenly principle within, and gives the utmost indulgence to the desires by which men may be possessed. On this we have the rebellious and deceitful heart, with licentious and violent disorder. The strong press upon the weak; the many are cruel to the few; the knowing impose upon the dull; the bold make it bitter for the timid; the diseased are not nursed; the old and young, orphans and solitaries are neglected – such is the great disorder that ensues.

Therefore the ancient kings, when they instituted their ceremonies and music, regulated them by consideration of the requirements of humanity.[286]

From the Confucian point of view, music is a model of the necessary qualities of good character and the ideal art to bring them about. Participation in musical ensembles makes immediately apparent the necessity for courtesy and respect. If a member of the ensemble takes it upon themselves to indulge their whims and dismiss their role's subordination to the greater cause, the quality of music will quickly deteriorate and bring shame to all involved. Listening to and respecting the other musicians as equals, allowing them their space, and contributing the appropriate amount of one's own input, all determine the quality of music and potential for a cooperative group of people to benefit from their interaction. This practice also teaches the benefits of humility – as Lao Zi states in DDJ81: "having helped others, oneself gains more." Interacting with others through this collective harmony and cooperation is sure to enrich all involved, and help return them to the simplicity of their pure nature, as the *Nei Ye* points out in lines 292-296.

297 凡食之道,
    Invariably, the Dao of eating
298 大充
    Is that to over-fill
299 傷而形不臧。[287]
    Causes injury, and for the form to be misshaped.
300   大攝骨枯
    Being overly conservative in one's diet causes the bones to dry out

---

[286] *The Sacred Books of the East: The texts of Confucianism*. Translated by James Legge. Vol. 4. Clarendon Press, 1885. pp. 96-97
[287] 不臧 bu cang is often read here as "not storing," however it commonly appears in ancient texts to mean "wrong; not good."

301 而血冱。
  And the blood flow to weaken.
302 充攝之間,
  To be between filling and conserving
303 此謂和成。
  Is called "achieving harmony."
304 精之所舍,
  This is where vital essence resides,
305 而知之所生。
  And knowledge flourishes.
306 飢飽之失度,
  When hunger and fullness lose their proper balance,
307 乃為之圖。
  Enact the following plan:
308 飽則疾動,
  If you eat to capacity, expend effort;
309 飢則廣思,
  If you are hungry, broaden your thoughts (to think about something else).
310 老則長慮,
  If you are elderly, be even more careful in this.
311 飽不疾動,
  If you eat to capacity but do not expend effort,
312 氣不通於四末,
  Energy-breath will not circulate within your limbs.
313 飢不廣思,
  If, when hungry, you do not broaden your thoughts –
314 飽而不廢。
  You will satiate yourself without leaving a scrap.
315 老不長慮,
  If you are elderly and do not take extra care in these matters,
316 困乃邀竭。
  An onset of illness will exhaust you.

Vitality and essence resides between yin and yang. This essence can be substantiated through diet by keeping a balance and harmony between the substance consumed and the function that we apply it to. Increasing the substance (ingesting food) without applying it (using energy) will cause imbalance. Likewise, excessive function without replenishing substance will lead to imbalance. Balancing function (yang) and substance (yin), we increase our capacity to generate and transform jing and qi, leading to a vital body, mind, and spirit.

NY297-316 contradicts a common misconception about Daoism and proto-Daoism which purports that their philosophies prefer indulgence to limiting one's whims, believing that limiting whim is limiting nature. To the contrary, indulging in whims can easily become an extreme behaviour leading to imbalance and confusion.

As the proto-Daoist texts show, it is through balance and harmony that pure nature is realized. Thus, Daoist self-cultivation often employs strategies to avoid extremes; for example, training in the martial arts, or tempering the emotions with music and poetry as seen earlier in NY285-296. The *Bai Xin* recommends taking an upright posture to aid in inner stabilization, regarded in BX201-203 as a necessary technique for people who have unavoidably become caught up in the busyness of society. So, cultivating awareness and moderation of one's emotions, and taking command of impulses, should not be seen as an unnatural or un-Daoist thing to do. Of course, at a certain level, one might transcend these emotions and impulses, and thereby any need to moderate them. For those still seeking such a level of attainment, however, techniques may be relied upon as important components of self-cultivation.

Regardless, while techniques are sometimes necessary, it should not be forgotten that Daoists still cherish simplicity. As Heshang Gong comments on DDJ27, the best method is not complicated, and the work of seeking balance and harmony does not take place only in isolation:

> *"Excellent walking leaves no trail of footprints"*
> Those who are excellent at walking the Dao seek it in themselves, and do not go down to the hall or out of the gates. Thus, they leave no trail of footprints.

...
"Excellent counting does not use counting devices"
Those who are excellent at finding a strategy to attain Dao simply guard Oneness within and do not shift from it. Their strategies are not numerous, and so they do not use counting devices to know them all.
"Excellent closing requires no bolts yet the seal cannot be broken"
For excellence in the way of sealing off desires and strong emotions, guard the vital spirits within and do not be like gates and doors. Locked bolts can be opened.
"Excellent binding requires no rope to secure it, yet cannot be unbound"
Achieve excellence by tying Dao into your usual affairs. Then you can tie it to your heart. This is to not use ropes and cords, which can be untied.

The *Nei Ye*'s suggestion that "knowledge flourishes" when food intake is regulated, is supported by a November 2014 article in the Journal of Neuroscience, which states:

> Recent findings... provide a window into the molecular and cellular mechanisms by which exercise and IERs [intermittent energy restrictions/fasting] bolster brainpower, protect neurons against injury and neurodegenerative disorders, and improve systemic energy metabolism and function of the autonomic nervous system.[288]

317 大心而敢,[289]
　　Boldly expand the heart and mind;
318 寬氣而廣,
　　Broadly expand energy-breath.
319 其形安而不移。
　　With your body peaceful and unmoving,
320 能守一而棄萬苛,

---

[288] Journal of Neuroscience 12 November 2014, 34 (46) 15139-15149 http://www.jneurosci.org/content/34/46/15139
[289] "敢 bold; brave" is often replaced here with "敞 spacious; wide"

You can preserve unification,[290]
and reject 10,000 annoyances.

321 見利不誘,
Seeing profit, it will not seduce you;

322 見害不懼。
Seeing danger, it will not frighten you.

323 寬舒而仁,
(You will remain) spacious, comfortable,
yet attentive and considerate.

324 獨樂其身,
When in solitude, enjoying yourself:

325 是謂雲氣;
This is called "qi floating like clouds."

326 意行似天。
Your intent then functions like that of Heaven

As the body and mind become settled, breath naturally expands, nourishing and massaging the internal organs. Like the constancy of heavenly orbits, the body's systems begin again to self-regulate and return to their correct mutual alignments. A harmony of the body and spirit brings pleasant tones to resonate throughout and calls on the healing light to enter and illuminate "all under Heaven."

A similar teaching to NY317-326 is found in XSX9-20, which also suggests that a pleasant feeling of qi is greatly beneficial:

> Therefore it is said: "When things do not confuse the senses,
> And the senses do not confuse the heart-mind
> This is called 'inner Virtue'."
> Thereby, the energy of intention is settled;
> Having (settled), it returns to alignment.
> Energy-breath then fills the body,

---

[290] May refer to unification of the heart-mind (xin), intention (yi), and energy-breath (qi) as mentioned in lines 235-253.

And one's conduct is righteous and upright.
If this fullness (of energy-breath) is not pleasant, the heart-mind does not benefit.
If one's conduct is not upright, the people will not be provided for.
Therefore, sages resemble Heaven during such times. They are without thought of self when sitting above all.
They resemble Earth during such times. They are without thought of self when supporting all.
As for thought of self, it puts the world in chaos.

A similar expression can be found in DD20[291]

... The crowd is joyous and buoyant
As though having caught a massive beast
Or celebrating spring rites
I alone am like the clearness of still water
Alas, in this way, making no predictions
Nor making myself predictable
Like a newborn baby
Not yet able to make these distinctions
Roaming! As though having no home to return to

The people in the crowd all have more than they need
But I alone am as one who has lost everything...

On a later line of DDJ20, Heshang Gong comments:

"Drifting! As though without any place to stop"
I alone am drifting and floating about, as though high, spreading out, and without any place to stop. My will and intent are in the land of the gods.

---

[291] DDJ20 can be found in my comments on *Xin Shu Shang*, lines 49-59.

327 凡人之生也,
   The lives of all people
328 必以其歡。
   Must have happiness.
329 憂則失紀,
   When anxious, they lose their reason;
330 怒則失端。
   When angry, they lose their direction.
331 憂悲喜怒,
   (If people are hindered by) anxiety, grief, euphoria, and anger,
332 道乃無處。
   Dao is then without any (empty) place to abide.
333 愛慾靜之,
   Attachment and lust: quiet them;
334 遇[292]亂正之。
   Encountering confusion, correct it.
335 勿引勿推,
   Do not pull, do not push.
336 福將自歸。
   Then good fortune will approach and naturally return.
337 彼道自來
   This Dao of (allowing good fortune to) approach spontaneously
338 可藉與謀。
   Can be relied on by following this strategy:
339 靜則得之,
   If tranquil, you will attain it;
340 躁則失之。
   If agitated, you will lose it;

---

[292] "遇 meeting" is normally replaced here with its homonym "yu, 愚, stupidity." The proceeding line "do not pull, do not push" might suggest that "encountering" was intended here as a wu wei approach, given that the text earlier discouraged thinking too much and making "premature determinations."

341 靈氣在心,
   The magical energy-breath (ling qi)²⁹³ within the heart-mind:
342 一來一逝。
   For a moment it draws near, and the next it disperses.
343 其細無內,
   So thin, there is nothing inside of it;
344 其大無外。
   So wide, there is nothing outside of it.
345 所以失之,
   The reason you lose it,
346 以躁為害。
   Is because agitation obstructs it.
347 心能執靜,
   If the heart-mind can remain quiet,
348 道將自定。
   Dao will approach and (ling qi will) naturally affix itself.
349 得道之人,
   People who attain Dao
350 理丞 而屯泄,
   Are aided by its principles, which fill²⁹⁴ and flow through them.
351 匈中無敗。
   Within the breast, they are not defeated (by pleasure, anger, sadness, or worry).
352 節欲之道,

---

²⁹³ See also "shen ling" in technique #1 of *Guigu Zi*, found in the Introduction.
²⁹⁴ "Tun, 屯, village, station" is normally replaced with "mao, 毛, hair" to say "flows through to the tips of their hair." In *The Complete I Ching*, Alfred Huang comments on hexagram three, which is entitled "Tun, 屯": "The character for the name of the gua has two meanings and is pronounced in two different ways. In most cases, it is pronounced tun, carrying the meaning of gathering, assembling, and filling up with abundance. In ancient China, a warehouse was called tun. In the I Ching, and only in the I Ching, this character bears the meaning of beginning. In this case, it is pronounced zhun."

Applying the dao of restraining the desires (of the five senses),[295]

353 萬物不害。
The myriad things bring no harm.

Happiness, contentment, peace, wonder, creative inspiration, and love of life do not follow our commands. They can only be encouraged to grow by providing the conditions which foster their maturation, just as plants cannot be made to grow in dry or depleted soil. As in Meng Zi's parable of the impatient farmer who pulled at his crops, anxious thinking will also not help to invite peace and deep insight.

It should be understood, that the *Nei Ye* is not simply a manual for improving one's emotional state, cultivating better interpersonal relationships, and thereby improving one's overall sense of wellbeing. While it may have remained limited to these elements were it fully entrenched in Confucianism, the *Nei Ye* was born of the proto-Daoist culture found in the 4th century B.C., and so largely concerns the cultivation of humanity's Heaven–endowed life force (ming), pure nature (xing), jing, qi, shen, intrinsic virtue (De), inner and outer reflections of Heaven and Earth, and of course, aligning all of these things with their origin: Dao. Ancient China was a world of mysticism, spirits, ghosts, gods, divine power, rituals, and resonant spiritual influence that could predict and change the future. Though modern readers may leave these elements of the text behind, the *Nei Ye* should not be misrepresented as simply a manual for emotional regulation. In actuality, these facets are skilfull means towards the text's higher goals: Daoist internal cultivation, energy transmutation, and spiritual awakening.

---

[295] See above NY279-284:
乃為之圖　Enact this plan:
節其五欲　Restrain the desires of the five senses
去其二凶　And forgo the two calamities
不喜不怒　(Accepting) neither pleasure, nor anger
平正擅匈　Then peace and alignment will reclaim the breast

In speaking of attracting the spontaneous approach of good fortune, lines 327-353 reflect another concept that might be easily absorbed by modern terminology. What is is today called *"the law of attraction"* describes what was called *ganying*, 感應 "feeling response," (often translated as "resonance response") in ancient China. Ganying is the phenomenon of mutual attraction that exists between things of the same type, much as a ruler who is chaotic in his heart–mind will bring chaos to his realm, an ordered body brings an ordered mind, and internal organs of a particular elemental phase will attract essences from a herb of that same phase. This principle was notably observed while playing the imperial bells when all the bells of the same tonal frequency would mysteriously resonate after only one of them had been struck.[296]

The earliest explanation of this principle is found in the Wenyan (文言) commentary (from the "10 Wings") on the Yi Jing (I Ching), chapter one (Heaven/Qian), line five.

> What is the meaning of the words under the fifth yang line, "A dragon is flying through the sky – it will be advantageous to see a great man?" The Master said: "Identical notes resonate together; identical energies seek each other; water drifts towards what is wet; fire approaches what is dry; clouds follow the dragon; wind follows the tiger; the Sage comes forth and all things look to him; what originates in heaven is drawn towards what is above; what originates in the earth is drawn towards what is below. So does everything follow its kind."[297]

Heshang Gong helps to illustrate that DDJ23 speaks to the same principle as in the *Nei Ye* — that anger and frustration hinder good fortune. In doing so, he also illustrates that this occurrence comes about through the spontaneous attraction of identical types. Note that he also repeats much of the Wenyan commentary, above:

> *"Those who are one with Dao, Dao is also happy to have them"*

---

[296] Referred to as "sympathetic resonance" and "acoustic resonance," this is the ultimate predicament of acoustic engineers who must ensure that structures do not resonate with various tones. It is also the basis of ultra-sound therapy.
[297] Translated by Dan G. Reid

Those who encounter Dao, and are one with it, Dao is also happy to have them.
"Those who are one with Virtue, Virtue is also happy to have them"
Those who encounter Virtue, and are one with it, Virtue is also happy to have them.
"Those who are one with loss, loss is also happy to have them"
Those who encounter loss, and are one with it, loss is also happy to *lose* them.
"Where faith and trust is not satisfactory"
Rulers who do not sufficiently trust those below them are not trusted by those below them.
"There will be no faith and trust"
This explains that things which are of the same type return to each other. Identical notes resonate together; identical energies seek each other; clouds follow the dragon; wind follows the tiger; water drifts towards what is wet; fire approaches what it is dry. This is the spontaneous nature of types.

Heshang Gong's comment, "Those who encounter loss, and are one with it, loss is also happy to *lose* them," suggests that by not dwelling on loss in frustration, and thereby internalizing it, loss will eventually detach itself. The beginning lines of DDJ23 (see below) seem to refer to this dwelling on loss, and bringing it up again and again rather than letting it go. By, instead, watering the seeds of Dao and Virtue, Dao and Virtue can take root and reach throughout one's life. The closing lines of DDJ23 explain that one must have faith and trust in Dao and Virtue so that they can restore themselves in one's life.

DDJ23:
    To speak rarely is natural
    Gusting wind does not last in the early morning
    Sudden rainstorms do not last all day

    Who acts in this way? Heaven and Earth
    If Heaven and Earth cannot continue in such a way
    What then, should be the case for men?
    They should follow the method of Dao!

(To be a person of) Dao, be one with Dao
(To be a person of) Virtue, be one with Virtue
(To be a person of) loss, be one with loss

Those who are one with Dao
Dao is also happy to have them
Those who are one with Virtue
Virtue is also happy to have them
Those who are one with loss
Loss is also happy to have them

Where faith and trust is not satisfactory
There will be no faith and trust

So, this silent faith – that returning to tranquility will draw harmony into one's circumstances – is connected to the strategy in the *Nei Ye* for attracting good fortune (lines 337-353).

Lines 337-353 also illustrate an important concept, translated here as "magical qi": *ling qi*. Ling takes on a number of definitions including the efficacy of spirits and the potency of Dao. Attained in a similar way to the spiritual vitality (jing-shen[298]) and genuine qi (zhen qi) referred to in Zhuang Zi's chapter 15 and chapter one of the *Huang Di Nei Jing, Su Wen*,[299] ling qi "fills the spacious emptiness of calm cheerfulness"[300] and is nourished by "the Dao of pure naturalness."[301]

The *Nei Ye* recognizes a similar basis for accommodating these vital energies in speaking of a happiness (歡 *huan*) that is neither pleasure (樂 *le*), nor euphoria (喜 *xi*), but the sort of joy and happiness that accompanies the fulfillment and enjoyment of life. While

---

[298] In chapter 15 of his book *"Discourse on Chuang Tzu: Expounding on the Dream of a Butterfly,"* Hu Xuezhi, a Daoist adept and teacher of Daoist meditation on Wudang Mountain, explains jing-shen as the convergence of jing, qi, and shen into a unity, saying that jing-shen reverts to its original nature when thoughts remain in voidness, thereby building in brilliance and "unimpeded power." It may be that jing-shen is a dormant potential of ling.

[299] See my commentary on lines 1-22 of the *Nei Ye* for a translation of excerpts from these chapters.

[300] See chapter one of the Su Wen.

[301] See *Zhuang Zi*, chapter 15, quoted under NY lines 1-22.

pleasure, euphoria, lust, and attachment may simply result in sluggishness and idleness, leading to anxiety[302] and further emotional obstacles to a full expression of Dao, this is the happiness of self-expression and living out one's destiny (ming).

The place that the *Nei Ye* gives here to *huan* (歡 happiness), distinct from pleasure and euphoria, is later subsumed in Chinese medicine by *le* (樂 pleasure), which is translated as joy and differentiated from euphoria as a pleasant and harmonious happiness, like a thriving symphony of fulfillment and connectedness rather than the erratic, oblivious, impulsiveness of elation and euphoria.[303] This sense of fulfillment, and inner and outer harmony, as though part of a beautiful symphony between nature and destiny, Heaven, Earth, and Humanity, and all the many interweaving facets of life, is akin to the state of a nation that the great sages of antiquity sought to bring about and disappear within. It assures the smooth functioning of the nation's many facets, and makes the nation nearly impossible to attack, let alone defeat, for even opposing soldiers would come to its defence. As Lao Zi explains in chapter 67, by upholding kindness and moderation, and refraining from putting oneself ahead of all others, the nation remains secure in perpetuity. Following Lao Zi's course allows one to become part of the symphony of life, and not upset its harmony, while allowing selfish desires to close our ears ensnares us in a wasteland of self-gratification.

As the *Nei Ye* points out, the thriving energy of this perfect symphony brings about *ling qi* – the energy of spiritual potency. Ling qi, in turn, brings about health, and protects one from inner and outer afflictions,[304] whether by nourishing the mind and spiritual intelligence or though its symbiotic relationship with the Heavenly phases.[305] When ling qi enters "the spacious emptiness of calm cheerfulness" it restores and assures an internal balance[306] that is free of anxiety, sorrow, anger, euphoria, attachment, lust, and confusion (see

---

[302] See *Nei Ye*, line 255.
[303] Rochat, Elizabeth. *Elation and Joy*. http://www.elisabeth-rochat.com/docs/26_xi_le.pdf
[304] See *Nei Ye*, lines 327-340.
[305] See *Zhuang Zi*, chapter 15 in my comments on *Nei Ye* 1-22.
[306] See jing-shen in *Huang Di Nei Jing, Su Wen*, chapter one, in my comments on *Nei Ye* 1-22.

Nei Ye lines 327-340). It thereby further protects people from foolish, erratic, actions and the emotional turmoil that upsets the internal organs and their harmonious exchanges or "communications."[307]

The *Bai Xin*, *Xin Shu*, *Nei Ye*, and *Dao De Jing* are filled with guidance on returning to the state of inner calm and faith (xin), as are the Buddhist excerpts quoted in *The Thread of Dao*. Finding a quiet place to sit and practice the 'art of the heart-mind' is an accessible means to accomplish this goal, for most people at some point during their day. Once caught up in the frantic pace of modern life, however, it is important to remember that stress does not increase our effectiveness, and that focus and calm are more conducive to efficiency and competency. If we can't afford to slow down our bodies, we can at least slow down our breath and, thereby, our heart-rates, making them both peaceful and even until we can find a way to enjoy our place in life as we are living it in the given moment, stressful as it may seem at the time. This will assist in bringing about an inner stillness that improves our responses to whatever requires presence and attention. In doing so, we reclaim self-determination and further apply Lao Zi's words from DDJ47, "Without going out the door, know all under Heaven. Without glancing out the window, see Heaven's Way. The further out one goes, the less they know." Seeking peace and transformation in ourselves – cultivating ourselves and our world from within rather than seeking to change everyone and everything around us – our internal-cultivation expresses itself as *external*-cultivation, improving the way we relate and reciprocate with the essential social, biological, and other ecosystems in which we live.

> When is there no benefit from my affairs?
> When there is no benefit in my heart-mind.
> When is there no peace where I reside?
> When there is no peace in my heart-mind.
> *(Xin Shu Xia*, lines 109-112)

---

[307] See *Su Wen*, chapter eight, a translated excerpt of which appears in *The Thread of Dao*'s "Introduction: Internal Cultivation in the *Guan Zi*, *Xin Shu Shang* and *Xin Shu Xia*"

A Meditation, inspired by the material in *The Thread of Dao*

"Excellent binding requires no rope to secure it, yet cannot be unbound"
Achieve excellence by tying Dao into your usual affairs.
Then you can tie it to your heart.
This is to not use ropes and cords, which can be untied.
- *The Heshang Gong Commentary on Lao Zi's Dao De Jing*, chapter 27

Improvement in any art or skill requires practice. Like painting or playing a musical instrument, regular, if not daily, periods of time should be devoted to developing our new strengths, and in the process finding and working on our weaknesses. Cultivating the art of the heart-mind is, in some ways, very similar to musical training. At first, we may feel wholly uncoordinated and unsuited to the task. So long as we stick with our practice and don't push ourselves so far beyond comfort that we risk injury,[308] we will find that what was initially difficult is now a comfortable foundation. By patiently working on these layers of foundation, we eventually reach a level where practice is joyful, even blissful, and effortless. We can surely enjoy the fruits of our effort (or "non-effort" as it may be), but may also find that we soon feel like a beginner all over again. This is a good place to be. It means that we see the path ahead. Like climbing a mountain, the further up you get, the more you can see of what the world has to offer beyond the mountain itself.

In practicing the art of the heart-mind, it should be understood that injury is possible, and so one should be careful to heed the advice of Lao Zi's chapter nine:

---

[308] Please see the disclaimer at the beginning of this book.

To take hold and continue filling is not as good as coming to a stop
If you obsessively refine a spear, it will not be long enough to protect you

Excessive effort in practicing stillness can lead to various "qi deviations," the most common of which is excessive build up of qi in the head, leading to shen (spirit) disturbances. To avoid this, focus is put on the lower dantien ("elixer field") to ground qi at the body's "center of gravity." It is also possible for sitting in stillness to make a person too "yin," making them lethargic. To avoid this, placing the hands over the dantien, bring energy from the root chakra (at the base of the sacrum and "governing vessel" that runs up the spine according to Chinese medicine; this is also where sexual energy tends to collect if not transmuted into qi and shen) to the lower dantien. This will help to balance yin and yang energy in the "elixer field" below the navel. To further avoid excessive yin, be sure to straighten the spine by feeling a string drawing the crown of the head, along with the cervical spine (in the neck), towards the sky, stretching the spine while tilting the head slightly forward so that the crown[309] points to the sky. Lastly, tilt the pelvis slightly forward and line up the crown above the sacrum, thereby straightening the lower spine and mirroring the tilt of the pelvis with the tilt of the head, sending energy from below and above to the dantien. These adjustments allow the yang-floating energy of the head to merge at the lower dantien with the yin-sinking energy of the hips. At first, these adjustments can make abdominal breathing more difficult, but will ultimately cultivate a more stable bodily frame.

The following meditations offer several of many more possible ways the material in *The Thread of Dao* can be adapted for practice. They includes techniques that I have encountered on my own journey of Daoist and Buddhist teachings and practices, and are not meant to detract from or discredit the diversity of methods and systems in these traditions. If you have the good fortune of personal study with a

---

[309] The crown is called the "baihui" (hundred convergences) point. This is the topmost point of the head when the head is tipped forward, slightly tucking in the chin.

meditation instructor, I would advise continuing with their instructions, or otherwise, presenting them with the techniques and guidance below and asking what parts of it might help with what you are already learning.

If you are new to meditation, the first several sessions should be devoted to simply learning to sit, or even lie down, and do nothing without any simultaneous activities such as listening to music, reading, watching television, talking to someone, driking, eating, etc. This, in itself, is difficult for most people who are not experienced meditators, and so you must first find comfort in simply doing nothing for 10 minutes. When this is accomplished, in the next session do nothing for 15 minutes. Then the next time for 20 minutes, then 25 minutes, and then 30 minutes. Only when you are comfortable just "staring at the wall," or doing nothing, for 30 minutes, should you begin with the following techniques. For this preliminary meditation, you are free to ponder whatever you like. The goal is simply learning how to do nothing, comfortably.

The one activity, however, that can done during this stage of "doing nothing," which will help prepare you for meditation, is the following: put your right hand on your chest and your left hand on your stomach. As you breathe, breathe into your diaphragm so that only your left hand (stomach) moves up and down, with your chest relaxed and not moving. When this exercise can be done naturally and effortlessly (which may take minutes or weeks), allow your breath to subtly fill your entire torso, with your stomach having, by far, the most noticeable movement.

Please note that the "preparation" and "closing" sections of this meditation can be followed as though part of a guided meditation. The "techniques" section, however, is meant to be read and absorbed beforehand, and simply taken into consideration following the "preparation" stage.

Preparation

The following meditation can be done while sitting on a folded and rolled-up towel, or firm cushion, in cross-legged, half-lotus, or full-lotus position. It can also be done while sitting near the edge of a medium-height chair with your feet flat on the floor. Begin by placing your hands on your thighs, and finding your posture. Your back should be straight, yet relaxed — finding that position where the muscles, structural alignment, and circulations return to their effortless functions. Please also note the mirrored tilting of the head and pelvis mentioned above.

After sitting in this balance for a moment, thank the spirits of your current environment for allowing your practice to be fulfilling, by clasping your right fist in your left hand and giving a gesture of thanks, salutation, and respect in front of your bowed forehead. After bringing your hands down, circle them up to the sides and, using your intent, gather heaven-qi down in front of you, over and through your body, and into the earth. Bring down this heaven-qi three times.

Now, in a similar motion as when gathering heaven-qi, gather the qi to the lower dantien. Circle your arms from your sides to gather qi in front of you, and then place your hands over your lower dantien: place your right palm over the lower-dantien, about 2.5 inches below the navel, and place your left palm over your right hand, lining up the lao-gong points at the center of the palms with the dantien (left thumb and fingers can lightly grasp the right wrist).

Finally, lean your torso to one side and circle the torso from the waist in a clockwise or counter-clockwise direction, three times, and then in the opposite direction three more times. Next, gently bend the torso forward and then back to alignment three times. Lastly, take three deep breaths, beginning with an exhalation to clear the lungs of carbon-dioxide. Following the third inhalation, meditation begins.

As the saying goes, "it takes 20 minutes before water starts to boil." Do not expect immediate immersion. Allow the mind to sit, undisturbed. Let it relax and find balance, just as you did earlier with the body. Put your awareness to the centering oneness that resides behind your mind, and allow everything to settle until your will and intention becomes genuine. This, in itself, is enough to guide your entire meditation session; however, the following guidelines are also helpful to bring you back to this point.

Techniques

Quieting the mind

A common and helpful technique to calm the mind and abide in openness is to count your breaths from one to ten, counting on the exhale of each breath. When you get to 10, start again from one. By the second (or third) round, do not engage any thoughts between the numbers. The only word you should create in your mind is the number of the breath, and maybe an internal "ahhhh" or "mmmmm." To take the place of thoughts, you can also allow the mind to open up to the sounds of your environment, and to a general awareness of where you are at in the present moment, just being where you are while looking straight ahead at a chosen spot on the floor. Your central focus should not be disturbed by sounds, but simply aware of how sound-and-silence passes through your consciousness without any disturbance, like clouds passing through the sky: "Abiding nowhere, let the mind arise." As you go deeper into internal silence, all of this may disappear as well.

The big exception to this exercise, especially for those new to it, is as follows: Consider thoughts as nouns and verbs. Thoughts will spontaneously pass through your mind and occur to you – consider these as nouns. The trick is not to follow these thoughts and turn them into verbs – thinking. As the mind clears, like the sun shining through a clearing sky, things will occur to you; they will become apparent; you will have realizations. This is fine. Just let the realization pass through your mind, like you would watch a cloud pass through the sky, and then move back into the open clarity of not-thinking.

If you begin to add to, and expand on, this realization with additional thoughts, rather than moving back to open clarity, this is thinking. When you notice this happen, begin counting the breaths again from 1. If thoughts rise up in your mind but you then return to open clarity (not-thinking) before the next number, continue counting your breaths up to 10, and then begin from 1 again.

After some time, these spontaneous thoughts will stop rising up and you will simply abide in the present moment. Without thoughts, where else can you be but in the present, right there, staring at the floor, or gazing internally – pure awareness. Continuing to practice like this, as your mind occupies itself with experience rather than thoughts, you can eventually stop counting, like a space shuttle releasing its rocket boosters. When you realize your mind has gone off track again, simply begin again from 1, or focus on the breath as though every breath is the first breath and try to at least still your thoughts during the brief absorption of qi between inhalations and exhalations.

Body and self as the nation
Lao Zi says

> Those who (govern) the self as the world
> And cherish it as such
> On them the world can rely
> Those who (govern) the self as the world
> And love it as such
> To them the world can be entrusted.

To love oneself as all things and all things as oneself is to first cultivate oneself before trying to heal the world. Much as is seen in the *Bai Xin*, *Xin Shu*, and *Nei Ye*, Lao Zi teaches the way of governing the body according to the same principles by which the Sage governs the nation. This dual application is largely the focus of Heshang Gong's commentary.

The Sage's method of governing by non-doing and non-interference, and its evident application to self cultivation, is decidedly pronounced in chapter 37 of the *Dao De Jing*:

> The Dao is always effortless yet without inaction
> When lords and kings can guard this within
> The myriad things eventually transform themselves
> Transforming, yet desiring to do so intentionally
> I pacify this desire with the simplicity of the nameless

The *Xin Shu Shang* begins by stating: "In the body, the heart-mind is the throne of the emperor." From his throne, the emperor brings peace and harmonious stability (order) to the nation and its people, just as the heart-mind effortlessly brings harmonious order to the domain of the self and body, governing through "non-action." As stated in the *Xin Shu Xia* and *Nei Ye*, the stability of the heart-mind can be initiated by bringing peace and alignment to the body. As this peace and alignment of the body can initiate peace and alignment in the heart-mind, the heart-mind can initiate peace and alignment throughout one's entire being. Cultivate quiet stillness, both externally and internally, and effect order "without doing."

"For what is above, study the heavens. For what is below, study the earth."
Chinese sages taught that peace and harmony in the nation will influence the heavens to bestow natural abundance through harmonious weather and seasons. This is perhaps brought about by a realization of primordial jing-essence. As *Nei Ye* explains:

> It is invariably the essence of things that gives them life
> Below, it gives birth to the five grains
> Above, it aligns the stars
> Circulating between Heaven and Earth
> We call it ghosts and spirits
> Collected within the bosom
> We call them sages

Heshang Gong refers to this heavenly jing in his comments on Lao Zi's chapter one:

> Returning to the center of Heaven, there is another Heaven. It dispenses energy-breaths which can be potent or weak. Obtaining harmonious fertile fluid from its center, this gives birth to the worthy and wise.

When peace and harmony endure, the heavens bless the nation with jing – life energy. This operation is mirrored further in the mind and body:

> Who, by the power of their stillness
> Can make clouded water slowly become clear?
> Who, by the power of their serenity
> Can long sustain this progress, until life slowly arises? (DDJ15)

With a clear mind, the clouds of thought part, and the sun-energy (attention) of the mind and spirit can shine on the Earth (lower dantien), and nourish it. Just as the primordial jing is needed to fertilize the fields, it is also needed to develop the body and self. Thus, we can invite it by opening the heart-mind and intention to it.

Thoughts may rise up, like steam forming clouds. Allow the energy of these thick clouds to rain down into the Earth (dantien). Just forget everything, and let everything settle like earth and gravity. Eventually, clarity will return.

Wu Wei
Dao De Jing, chapter seven states:

> Heaven has longevity, Earth has continuity
> Heaven and Earth have the power of longevity and continuity
> because they do not live for themselves
> This is how they can live for so long
> Therefore, sages leave themselves behind
> And they end up in front
> They do not cater to themselves
> Yet they persist
> Is it not because they are without selfishness and wickedness
> That they are able to fulfill themselves?

Chapter seven of the *Dao De Jing* is one of the best, yet least understood, descriptions of wu wei. Wei (為) can be translated as effort, and so wu wei as "effortless." In Daoism, this effort is meant in contrast to "zi ran" – the spontaneity of nature.

Heshang Gong comments on DDJ1,

> "The path that can be told is not the Eternal Path":
> It is not the Path of natural spontaneity (zi ran) and long life. The Eternal Path nourishes the spirit with effortlessness (wu wei). Taking no initiative, it brings peace to the people.

As can be understood from DDJ7, wei is action issued forth from the ego, rather than the action of Dao. To cultivate wu wei ("without wei") in oneself, then, entails a suspension of egoic interference in what Dao is better able to accomplish. This is why Daoist texts warn against emotions such as euphoria, anger, pleasure, sorrow, and fear – because these emotions make it almost impossible to act from Dao rather than from ego. Training in Daoist meditation teaches the cultivation of Dao's natural power, and presents a way to handle worldly obstructions just as we do our own emotional obstructions – without wei. Daoist cultivation is therefore also intrinsically a cultivation of effortless virtue, teaching us how to act from Dao, the greater principle, rather than from the limitations of our own desires. By removing the egoic impulses that cloud our inter-being with the world, cultivating wu wei may even seem, from the outside, an effort to cultivate morality. This is not the case, however, as the resulting "morality" is as natural to wu wei as wetness is to water. DDJ65 speaks to this simultaneously internal and external cultivation:

> The ancient masters who aligned society with Dao
> Did not do so by enlightening the people
> But rather, fostered their (own) simplicity
>
> Difficulty in governing people
> Comes from (the ruler's) wealth of wisdom
> Hence, when knowledge is used to govern the nation
> This results in thievery from the nation
> Not using knowledge to govern the nation
> Blesses the nation
>
> Understand the broader application of these two principles
> There is an infinite understanding
> Which can be found in these principles
> This is called Fathomless Virtue
> Fathomless Virtue, profound and far-reaching
> Following it, things return back to their nature
> Arriving at great submission

The Bai Xin also speaks to this in saying:

> Knowing oneself is called "investigating" (jī);
> Knowing others is called "crossing the river" (jī).

> By knowing what is frivolous and what is necessary, one can bring the world into unison.
> Internally, solidifying oneself into a unified whole, one may lengthen their lifespan.
> Discussing the application of this principle reveals the way to rule all under Heaven.
> (BX163-167)

This principle can also be found DDJ48:

> The pursuit of learning requires daily accumulation
> The pursuit of Dao requires daily reduction
> Reducing and reducing
> Until arriving at effortlessness
> Effortless, yet without inaction (無為而無不為)

"Reduce excessive taxes"
Consider the Daoist governmental practice of eliminating excessive taxes. Do not ask of the body but leave it be so as to allow its necessary absorption of jing.

"Do not rely on rewards and punishments"
Not thinking also relates to Daoist warnings against relying on rewards and punishments: Do not think about the potential benefits (rewards) and losses (punishments) of sitting practice but allow the natural process to unfold.

"When achievement is attained, the Sage withdraws"
When all is well, the Sage does nothing; when the body is enriched, thoughts may cease to arise. These thoughts no longer need to direct the ruler – the heart-mind – though an occasional thought here and there may help in steering the kingdom back to self-sustaining harmony. On returning to this state, allow *Dao* – allow nature to flow along undisturbed.

Thoughts often rise up like dreams during sleep if we enter a state of deep relaxation and our awareness and intent become lax. As you reach the "heart of the heart-mind," you may find that this inner chamber of the heart-mind also needs to be quieted. One method to rectify this is the Zen practice of looking at the floor to stay present in the immediate and not travel through the mind.

Unity and Oneness

Unify the will by eliminating the distractions of desire. This unity contains no thought — no division of the mind-will-consciousness by following distractions — yet still contains flexibility. Like the solid yang line surrounded by two yin lines in the water trigram, allow flexibility so that the one yang may develop. Though force should not be used, maintaining this unity tests and conditions our will and resolve.

The *Bai Xin* states:

> Without soaring (into the sky), without spilling over, the destined life-force (ming) will be extended.
> Harmonize by returning to the center, and both body and pure nature (xing) will be preserved.
> Be unified and without (doubt or) division. This is called "knowing Dao."
> Wishing to be enveloped by it, you must unify to the furthest extent, and solidify that which is protected within.
> (BX 204-207)

When thoughts stop, oneness with the present comes to visit. The mind is not scattered, and thoughts of future and past return to present awareness. "Ming/enlightenment" most often refers to "clear sightedness" — a clear awareness of the present in relation to the future and past. Oneness in awareness brings comfort and balance, or having a place in given circumstances rather than resisting them. Oneness in the self becomes oneness in, and with, a person's environment and circumstances, both internally and externally. Our troubles and our joys are "not two." This is that and that is this. The *Nei Ye* states "your thinking about it will not reach comprehension."

"Those who know others are wise, those who know themselves are clear sighted."

Bai Xin, lines 198-200 state:

> By rejecting what is close and chasing after what is far, how can

one but squander their power?
Thus it is said: "Desiring to take care of myself, I must first know my true inner state.
By observing the universe, I investigate my own body."
As such, comprehending this image, one thereby understands the tendencies of their true inner state.
Knowing the tendencies of their true inner state, they will know how to nourish life.

We can cultivate a deeper awareness of both ourselves and our environment using the same technique: "abiding nowhere, let the mind arise." Close your eyes and, without any attachment to what is there, notice the sounds and silence. As the Buddha taught, note their 4 stages of existence in the mind: 1) *arising:* the sound arrives; 2) *abiding:* the sound remains; 3) *declining:* the sound is passing; 4) *ceasing:* the sound has ceased. Note these sounds without attaching any judgements of good or bad to them. Just passively observe them without straying from the basis – from your balance in the center within. As the *Xin Shu Shang* (commentary) states in lines 203-221:

> *"He responds, but does not initiate; moves but does not possess."*
> This is called "the basis."
> The basis is to reside in one's own, while according with other things.
> (The junzi) responds to feelings, yet does not initiate them.
> Following the principle, he moves (things), but does not possess (them).
> *"If one is excessively headstrong, they will err when adapting to changes."*
> If headstrong, one cannot be empty.
> If not empty, one becomes the same as other "things."
> With change and transformation, there is growth. With growth, there is bound to be confusion.
> Thus, the treasure of Dao is the basis (of responding and not initiating; moving yet not possessing). On this basis rests ability. This is called usefulness.[310]

---

[310] DDJ11 states: "But it is where there is nothing that the room is used. So, substance is gained, and emptiness is used."

> The junzi remains in the state *"of not knowing."*
> This is called "arriving at emptiness."
> *"Responding to things as though by coincidence."*
> This is called "adapting to the season" –
> Like a shadow taking the shape of a form,
> Or an echo responding to a sound.
> Thus, when things reach them, (the junzi) responds.
> When these things move on, (the junzi) remains in place.
> This means (the junzi) reverts back to emptiness.

After practicing this outer observation, and being able to do so passively and without disturbance, put the mind to your feelings and thoughts. Note their 4 four stages of existence in the same way as you observed the sounds – without any attachment to what is there, and without any judgements of good or bad. Note 1) *arising*: a feeling is arising; 2) *abiding*: a feeling is present and abiding; 3) *declining*: the feeling is diminishing and ceasing; 4) *ceasing*: the feeling is no longer present in any way whatsoever. Now, apply this same practice of observance to your thoughts, noticing when a thought arises, when thinking is present, when your thinking is wrapping up, and when those thoughts have disappeared. When they have disappeared, abide in that space of openness and emptiness. Lao Zi speaks of this silence in chapter 16 of the *Dao De Jing*:

> Arrive at supreme emptiness
> Embrace deep silence
> Myriad creatures arise together
> I thereby observe them return
> So many things blossoming
> And each returns back to its roots
>
> Returning to the roots is called silence
> This is called returning to eternal life

Continue abiding in silence until you feel the session of sitting has reached its saturation point, remembering *Dao De Jing*, chapter 15:

> Who, by the power of their stillness

Can make clouded water slowly become clear?
Who, by the power of their serenity
Can long sustain this progress, until life slowly arises?

Closing

When you feel the saturation point of the session has been reached, gently open your eyes (if they were closed) and place your palms on your thighs. Now again, "abiding nowhere, let the mind arise." The mind, like an empty cup, can also be identified by what is inside of it. Without actively listening or being drawn toward any sounds, allow them to pass in and out of your awareness. Do not hold onto them, do not seek or grasp them, but let them pass through the clear awareness of your mind. Notice that you can be aware of far more things, and that your awareness can stretch much further, when it is not seeking to be aware of anything in particular. "Abiding nowhere, let the mind arise."

Now, in the same way, see what is in your environment. Do not get stuck looking at anything, but allow things to passively come into your visual awareness. Allow your visual awareness to awaken to the things and movements in your environment. These two exercises, of auditory and visual awareness, need not last more than 15-30 seconds each, as they are only preparing you to be more centered and receptive as you go about your day and to transition you from internal awareness to both internal and external awareness. By the same token, there is no reason they can't be practiced in silence for several minutes or more.

Lastly, thank the teachers that have helped to guide, support, and protect you in life. Clasping your left hand over your right fist at the level of your brow, making the same gesture as earlier, thank your teachers on the earthly plane. Beginning again to make a second gesture slightly higher than the first, thank your teachers on the spiritual plane (for example, guardian angels, Lao Zi, the Buddha, etc). Making a third gesture, somewhat higher than the second, thank the universe, the Dao. After bringing your hands down, circle them up to the sides and bring heaven-qi down through your body and into the earth. Bring down this heaven-qi three times. After the third time, bring your hands around the front and gather qi as you place your right hand over the dantien and cover your right hand with your left hand. Hold the qi like this for a brief moment.

If concluding a standing meditation, following the final holding of qi in the dantien, gather qi through your dantien and down toward your legs into the earth three times, beginning your step into the world at the end of the third motion.

Bibliography

Blofeld, John & Reid, Daniel P. (translator). *My Journey Through Mystic China: Old Pu's Travel Diaries*. Rochester: Inner Traditions, 2008

Broschat, Michael Robert. *Guiguzi: A Textual Study and Translation*. University of Washington Ph.D. Thesis, 1985

Chan, Wing-Tsit, translator. *A Source Book in Chinese Philosophy*. New Jersey: Princeton University Press, 1963.

Chang, Leo S and Yu, Feng, translators. *The Yellow Emperor's Four Canons*. Hunan: Yuelu Publishing House, 2005.

Cleary, Thomas, , translator, editor. *Vitality, Energy, Spirit: A Taoist Sourcebook*. Boston: Shambhala, 1991.

Cleary, Thomas, translator, editor. *The Book of Balance and Harmony: A Taoist Handbook*. Boston: Shambhala, 2003.

Cleary, Thomas, translator. *Thunder in the Sky: On the Acquisition and Exercise of Power*. Boston: Shambhala, 1993.

Cohen, Kenneth. *The Way of Qigong*. New York: Random House, 1999.

Crane, George. *Bones of the Master: A Journey to Secret Mongolia*. New York: Bantam Books, 2000.

Ctext.org

Goddard, Dwight, editor. *A Buddhist Bible*. Boston: Beacon Press, 1938.

Graziani, Romain, translator. *Écrits de Maître Guan: Les Quatre Traités de l'Art de l'esprit*. Paris: Les Belles Lettres, 2011.

Hu Xuezhi, translation, annotation and commentary. *Discourse on Chuang Tzu: Expounding on the Dream of a Butterfly, Volumes I & II*. Calgary: ChuangChou Classics Press, 2016.

Bibliography

Hu Xuezhi. *Resonance and Transcendence with Great Nature: A Guide for Understanding the Mind, Reality, and Enlightenment*. Calgary: ChuangChou Classics Press, 2016.

Jarrett, Lonny. *Nourishing Destiny: The Inner Tradition of Chinese Medicine*. Stockbridge: Spirit Path Press, 2000

Jarrett, Lonny. The returned spirit (gui ling) of traditional Chinese medicine, Traditional Acupuncture Society Journal, England, No. 12, Oct,'92, p.19-31

Jin Yunting, Ling Guiqing, John Groschwitz (trans). *The Xingyi Boxing Manual*. Berkley: Blue Snake Books, 2015. p. 29

Larre, Claude and Rochat de la Vallee, Elizabeth. *Rooted in Spirit: The Heart of Chinese Medicine*. New York: Station Hill Press, 1992.

Legge, James, translator. *The Sacred Books of the East: The texts of Confucianism*. Vol. 4. Oxford: Clarendon Press, 1885.

Legge, James. *I Ching: Book of Changes*. New York: Bantam Books, 1994.

Legge, James, translator. *The Chinese Classics Vol. III: The Shoo King or The Book of Historical Documents*. London. Trubner and Co. 1865.

Legge, James, translator. *The Life and Works of Mencius: With Essays and Notes*. London. Trubner and Co. 1875.

Norbu, Namkai. *The Mirror: Advice on the Presence of Awareness*. New York: Barrytown, Ltd., 1983.

Nqa.org

Price, A.F. and Wong, Mou-Lam, translators. The *Diamond Sutra & The Sutra of Hui-Neng*. Boston: Shambhala Publications, Inc., 1990

Red Pine, translator. *Lao-Tzu's Tao Te Ching: With Selected Commentaries from the Past 2000 years*. Port Townsend: Copper Canyon Press, 2009.

Reid, Dan G., translator. *The Heshang Gong Commentary on Lao Zi's Dao De Jing*. Montreal: Center Ring Publishing, 2015.

Rickett, Alynn, translator. *Guanzi: Political, Economic, and Philosophical Essays from Early China, Volume I and II*. New Jersey: Princeton University Press, 1998.

Rinaldini, Michael. *A Daoist Practice Journal: Come Laugh With Me*. Sebastpool: (Independent) 2013.

Rinaldini, Michael. *A Daoist Practice Journal, Book 2: Circle walking, Qigong & Daoist Cultivation*. Sebastpool: (Independent) 2016.

Rossi, Elisa. *Shen: Psycho-Emotional Aspects of Chinese Medicine*. London: Churchill Livingstone Elsevier, 2002.

Roth, Harold, translator. *Original Tao: Inward Training (Nei-yeh) and the Foundations of Taoist Mysticism*. New York: Columbia University Press, 1999.

Sha, Zhi Gang. *Power Healing*. San Francisco: Harper Collins, 2003.

The Rise and Fall of the State of Chu, CCTV-9 Documentary, 2016

Wang Li Ping. *Ling Bao Tong Zhi Neng Nei Gong Shu*. (Independent), 2012.

Watson, Burton, translator. *Han Fei Tzu: Basic writings*. New York: Columbia University Press, 1964.

Wikipedia.org

Wu Jyh Cherng. *Daoist Meditation*. Philadelphia: Singing Dragon, 2015.

P. Van Der Loon. "On the Transmission of Kuan-tzŭ." *T'oung Pao*, Second Series, 41, no. 4/5 (1952): 357-93. http://www.jstor.org/stable/4527337

Index

Dao De Jing chapters index:

"GD" indicates that parts of this chapter appear in the Guodian copy of the *Dao De Jing* (c. 299 BC)

Please note that the chapters left empty, below, may also have corresponding ideas, but were not referred to in *Thread of Dao*.

1. pp. 21, 29, 74-5, 81, 100, 104-5, 124, 222, 288, 289
2. GD, pp. 7, 29, 62, 73, 93, 95, 133, 163
3. pp. 8, 54-5, 80, 82, 86, 115, 241
4. pp. 8, 105, 221
5. GD, pp. 5, 19, 29, 76-7, 79, 124, 160, 196, 199-200, 231
6. pp. 6, 172, 199-201, 224, 244
7. pp. 10, 95, 174, 235, 289-90
8. pp. 10, 198, 224
9. GD, pp. 11, 29, 48-9, 82, 84, 107, 117, 160, 282, 86
10. pp. 65, 124, 139, 142, 160, 175, 179, 228, 254, 257
11. pp. 115, 139, 142, 160, 168, 294
12. pp. 135, 159, 235
13. GD, pp. 96-7, 174, 252
14. pp. 100-1, 139, 228, 150
15. GD, pp. 123, 198, 229, 288-9, 295
16. GD, pp. 43-4, 110, 115, 124-5, 186, 231, 236
17. GD
18. GD, pp. 163
19. GD, pp. 116, 145, 147-8
20. GD, pp. 154-5, 273
21. pp. 212-3, 218, 222
22. pp. 64, 211, 249
23. pp. 130, 220, 277-8
24.
25. GD, pp. 184
26.
27. pp. 115, 141, 224-5, 270-1, 282
28. pp. 183, 244-5

29. pp. 86, 234
30. GD, pp. 19, 85-6, 186-7
31. GD, pp. 18-20
32. GD
33. pp. 134, 174-5, 254
34. p. 168
35. GD, pp. 75-6, 188
36. pp. 217, 237
37. GD, pp. 88-9, 133, 220, 287
38. pp. 88, 115, 159, 163, 180-1
39. pp. 48-9, 64-5, 211-2
40. GD
41. GD, pp. 126, 139
42.
43.
44. GD
45. GD
46. GD p. 86
47. pp. 31, 111, 119-20, 141, 150, 216, 281
48. pp. 234, 93-4, 147, 234, 291
49.
50. pp. 210, 191-4, 210-1
51. pp. 63-4, 66, 87, 112, 211
52. GD
53.
54. GD, p. 87-8
55. GD, p. 199
56. GD, p. 227
57. GD, pp. 106, 108
58.
59. GD
60.
61.
62.
63. GD
64. GD
65. pp. 111-2, 290
66. GD

67. pp. 72, 84, 280
68.
69. p. 84
70. p. 119
71. p. 119
72. pp. 72, 119
73. p. 86
74. p. 86
75. pp. 151-2
76. p. 20
77. pp. 72, 93, 231-2, 249-50
78.
79.
80.
81. pp. 97, 109, 159, 268

Paragraphs (zhang) in the *Nei Ye* according to Harold Roth's translation, with corresponding lines from *The Thread of Dao*:

1) 1-8	10) 115-121	19) 235-253
2) 9-14	11) 122-128	20) 254-266
3) 15-33	12) 129-134	21) 267-284
4) 34-50	13) 135-150	22) 285-296
5) 51-64	14) 151-173	23) 297-316
6) 65-78	15) 174-191	24) 317-326
7) 79-90	16) 192-207	25) 327-340
8) 91-104	17) 208-215	26) 341-353
9) 105-114	18) 216-234	

Adapt: 165-70, 184, 243
Analects (Confucian): 12
Bakunin: 144-5
Body/health: 206-7, 211, 218, 242-3, 261-2, 266-7, 289
Book of Balance and Harmony: 91
Book of Music (Confucius): 2, 4, 266-7
Buddhism: 43, 45, 56, 59-62, 91-2, 101, 105, 116, 121, 134-5, 139, 152-3, 161, 166, 174, 260, 283, 293, 295
Chu State: 12-22, 28, 113

Confucius: 1-3, 12-3, 18, 20, 23-5, 27-8, 60, 92, 115, 152-3, 168, 224, 234-5, 236, 252, 265-8, 276
Dantien: 55, 123, 201, 241, 283, 285, 289, 296
Dao: 1, 8-9, 19, 26, 29, 30, 32, 38-9, 46-7, 53, 59, 62-66, 72-81, 85-90, 93. 101-4, 115-6, 118, 120, 122-131, 132-4, 139-43, 148-154, 157-162, 166, 168, 174-5, 180-1, 184-88, 194, 198-9, 207-9, 211, 213, 216-22, 228, 231, 234, 237, 238, 240-1, 246, 249-50, 256, 261, 268, 270-81, 287, 290, 292-3, 295
De (Virtue): 2-6, 24-5, 30, 36-42, 46-8, 58, 63-4, 66, 77, 83, 87-9, 111-2, 114, 123, 129-31, 140-2, 149, 160-1, 170-9, 189, 201, 204-11, 215, 230-1, 236-7, 244-5, 247, 249, 253, 257, 259, 272, 278-9, 290
Dharma: 35, 120, 135, 161
Diet: 268, 270
Divination: 1, 3, 5, 87-8, 180, 276-7
Duke Huan of Qi: 12-4, 17
Duke of Zhou: 3-4, 112, 220
Ego: 10-1, 45, 82, 94, 96, 104, 122, 146-7, 289-90
Einstein, Albert: 98
Emotions: 120-1, 124, 134, 142, 167, 175-6, 185, 192-5, 197, 200, 202, 206, 223, 240-1, 262-5, 270-6, 290
Emotional intelligence (EQ): 39, 264
Emptiness: 6, 10, 44, 53-5, 59, 64, 79, 90, 120, 133, 138-9, 141-2, 146-7, 153, 158-60, 164, 166-9, 176, 180, 206, 212, 228, 237, 241, 280, 293-5
Enlightenment: 43, 70, 125-6, 292
Five phases/elements: 4-6, 201, 229, 245, 263, 277
Flow state: 147, 241
Ganying: 277
Governing: 1, 8, 22-3, 25, 27-9, 37, 44, 53, 66, 70, 78, 80-1, 90, 96-7, 103, 106-8, 111, 133, 139, 142, 175, 185, 218, 234, 236, 252, 254, 257, 287, 290-1
Guan Zhong: 12-15, 17, 21-3
Guigu Zi: 45-54, 58, 63, 197, 226, 254, 275
Guodian: 11, 16, 21, 65, 82, 107
Heaven & Earth: 1-2, 4-5, 9-11, 26-7, 37-8, 41-4, 47-9, 53, 60, 65-6, 70-84, 92-100, 111-9, 124-6, 128-30, 140-2, 146-9, 153, 160, 164, 168, 172-4, 179, 182-4, 186, 189, 196, 199, 200-12, 220, 222-3, 229, 231-2, 235-6, 238, 240, 242-50, 254, 259, 260, 263, 267, 272-3, 276-8, 280-1

Heshang Gong: 2132, 36, 44, 63-6, 70, 73, 75, 77, 79-80, 82, 86, 94, 104-5, 124, 135, 139, 141-2, 149, 163, 179, 193-4, 199, 200-1, 211, 218, 220, 228, 235-6, 241, 273, 277-8, 282, 287-9
Huainan Zi: 4, 12, 21-3, 175-77, 236-7, 245, 256
Huang Di Nei Jing (Classic of Internal Medicine): 34-6, 45, 55, 57, 120-1, 206-7, 209-11, 226-7, 256, 263, 279, 280
Huang Di Si Jing (Four Canons of the Yellow Emperor): 14, 16
Humility: 84-5, 143
Intent/Yi: 38, 41-3, 50-9, 63, 92, 153, 171, 178-9, 183, 192, 194-7, 204-5, 210-1, 213, 219, 229, 239-43, 246, 251-2, 255, 272-3
Jing (essence): 6, 36, 40-2, 44, 53, 57, 112-5, 142, 158, 160, 181, 184, 194, 197, 200-3, 205-6, 208-13, 225-6, 233, 241, 242, 245, 252, 255, 260-1, 263, 269-70, 288
Ji Zi: 3-5
Karma: 105
King Wen: 1, 3-4, 243
King Zhuang: 17-20, 28
Law: 12-4, 19, 22, 24-7, 35, 76, 78-9, 89, 100, 106, 108, 110, 143, 161-2
Legalism: 13-7, 20-1, 23-7, 213, 252
Ling qi: 49, 212, 256, 275, 279-80
Liu Xiang: 21-3, 37-9, 173
Mencius (Meng Zi): 12, 14, 16, 243-4, 276
Mindfulness: 31, 119-20, 133-4, 139, 141, 215
Martial Arts: 58-9, 131, 202, 218
Mysterious Pass: 91-2, 161
Name/Ming: 65, 74-5, 78-82, 88-91, 100, 102-4, 116, 119-20, 124, 133, 148-50, 165-6, 177-9, 208, 216, 220, 222, 232
Nei Dan: 39, 91, 126-8, 161, 170, 212, 279
Oneness: 46, 49, 53 ,60-6, 115, 124, 142, 149, 179, 182, 211-2, 225-9, 231, 249, 254, 257, 271, 285, 292
Qi (energy-breath): 34, 38, 40-3, 45, 55, 57-9, 63, 35, 80, 113, 120-1, 140, 142, 149, 160, 170-1, 173, 176, 179, 181, 183, 190-2, 196, 199-204-7, 210-2, 218, 225-7, 228-9, 235, 237, 242-5, 250-7, 259-60, 263-5, 269-76, 279-80, 283, 285, 287, 295-6
Qigong: 153, 199, 202, 204
Shen (spirit): 9, 33, 35, 40, 42, 46, 48, 51-3, 55, 65, 113-4, 133, 138-9, 142, 158, 171-2, 193, 200-1, 205-9, 212, 227, 229, 260, 270, 272, 283,

289

Shen Ming/Spiritual Intelligence: 33-4, 37, 39-41, 44, 47, 51-3, 75, 105, 110, 121, 134-7, 146-7, 175-6, 229, 232-7, 248, 280

Spirits of the body (hun, po, etc.): 92, 105, 149, 172, 176, 179, 193-4, 197, 210-1, 271

Spirits (supernatural): 1-2, 5, 29-30, 41, 43, 44, 104-5, 197, 199, 203, 254-6, 276, 279-80

Sitting Meditation: 6, 28, 30-1, 37, 63, 80, 114, 122-3, 139, 184, 132, 241, 279, 282-96

Speak/not speak: 9, 45, 59, 62, 88, 95, 123, 125, 130, 146-8, 163, 194, 196, 221, 227, 239

Sun and Moon: 43, 74, 77, 79, 94, 107, 182, 182-4, 190-2, 248, 251,

Tai Yi Sheng Shui: 65-6, 80, 235

TCM: 56, 242, 262, 280

Tesla, Nikola: 98

Thoughts (calming thoughts): 40, 48, 50-1, 54-8, 90-1, 107, 113-4, 120, 123, 132, 160, 176, 179-80, 182-3, 195-7, 198, 200, 209-11, 215-6, 225-6, 228-9, 233, 239, 240-2, 248, 251, 256, 260, 263, 269, 273, 286-7, 289, 291-4

Valley: 9-11, 49, 126, 172, 183, 200, 212, 223, 244-5

Wang Bi: 36, 76

Water: 4-11, 25, 34, 65-6, 74, 82, 98, 104, 107, 123, 129, 154, 188, 198, 207, 224, 229, 245, 259, 277-8, 292, 295

Wu Wei: 4-11, 38, 129, 130, 274, 289

Xin Xin Ming: 61-2

Xing and Ming: 30, 32, 64, 122, 124, 128, 170, 175, 193-4, 206, 211, 237, 240, 253, 266, 270, 276, 292

Xun Zi: 12, 14, 36, 52, 135-6

Yi Jing: 1, 3, 92, 103, 220, 224, 277

Yin & Yang: 4, 14, 43, 53, 54-5, 65-6, 86, 92, 123, 127, 157, 176, 183, 208, 210, 237, 245, 256, 263, 270, 277, 283, 292

Zhuang Zi: 4, 12, 16, 32, 59-60, 122, 138, 145, 147, 152-3, 207-8, 253, 259-60, 279, 280,

Zuo Yan: 5

ABOUT THE AUTHOR

Dan G. Reid taught himself how to read Classical Chinese with the help of textbooks, online tools, and internet forums. His self-published work has been acclaimed by notable translators and scholars such as Red Pine, Dr. Michael Saso, Daniel P. Reid (no relation), Daoist Abbot Michael Rinaldini, and Wudang Daoist meditation teacher Hu Xuezhi. Dan practices traditional Chinese sports medicine as a Tuina massage therapist in Montreal, Quebec, including herbalism, and a variety of traditional Chinese therapeutic modalities. He also studies and practices sitting meditation, Qigong, internal martial arts (Xingyi, Baguazhang, Taji Chuan), and is a multi-instrumentalist including guqin, guitar, and percussion.

Bibliography:

Reid, Dan G., translation and commentary. *The Heshang Gong Commentary on Lao Z's Dao De Jing*. Montreal: Center Ring Publishing, 2015, 2019.

Reid, Dan G., translation and commentary. *The Thread of Dao: Unraveling Early Daoist Oral Traditions in Guan Zi's Purifying the Heart-Mind (Bai Xin), Art of the Heart-Mind (Xin Shu), and Internal Cultivation (Nei Ye)*. Montreal: Center Ring Publications, 2017, 2019.

(co-editor)
Hu Xuezhi, translation, annotation and commentary. *Discourse on Chuang Tzu: Expounding on the Dream of a Butterfly, Volumes I & II*. Calgary: ChuangChou Classics Press, 2016.

www.ingramcontent.com/pod-product-compliance
Lightning Source LLC
Chambersburg PA
CBHW020417010526
44118CB00010B/287